G.W.F. Hegel

MODERNITY AND POLITICAL THOUGHT

Series Editor: Morton Schoolman
State University of New York at Albany

This unique collection of original studies of the great figures in the history of political and social thought critically examines their contributions to our understanding of modernity, its constitution, and the promise and problems latent within it. These works are written by some of the finest theorists of our time for scholars and students of the social sciences and humanities.

*The following titles are available as New Editions from
Rowman & Littlefield Publishers, Inc.*

The Augustinian Imperative: A Reflection on the Politics of Morality
by William E. Connolly

Emerson and Self-Reliance
by George Kateb

Edmund Burke: Modernity, Politics, and Aesthetics
by Stephen K. White

Jean-Jacques Rousseau: The Politics of the Ordinary
by Tracy B. Strong

Michel Foucault and the Politics of Freedom
by Thomas L. Dumm

Reading "Adam Smith": Desire, History, and Value
by Michael J. Shapiro

Thomas Hobbes: Skepticism, Individuality, and Chastened Politics
by Richard E. Flathman

Thoreau's Nature: Ethics, Politics, and the Wild
by Jane Bennett

G.W.F. Hegel: Modernity and Politics
by Fred R. Dallmayr

The Reluctant Modernism of Hannah Arendt
by Seyla Benhabib

G.W.F. Hegel

Modernity and Politics

New Edition

FRED R. DALLMAYR

Modernity and Political Thought Series

ROWMAN & LITTLEFIELD PUBLISHERS, INC.
Lanham • Boulder • New York • Oxford

ROWMAN & LITTLEFIELD PUBLISHERS, INC.

Published in the United States of America
by Rowman & Littlefield Publishers, Inc.
A Member of the Rowman & Littlefield Publishing Group
4720 Boston Way, Lanham, Maryland 20706
www.rowmanlittlefield.com

PO Box 317
Oxford
OX2 9RU, UK

Originally published in 1993 by Sage Publications, Inc.
New Preface and Introduction Copyright © 2002 by
Rowman & Littlefield Publishers, Inc.

British Library Cataloguing in Publication Information Available

Library of Congress Cataloging-in-Publication Data

Dallmayr, Fred R. (Fred Reinhard), 1928–
    G.W.F. Hegel : modernity and politics / Fred R. Dallmayr.
        p. cm. — (Modernity and political thought)
    Originally published: Newbury Park, Calif. : Sage Publications, c1993. With new
frontmatter.
    Includes bibliographical references and index.
    ISBN 0-7425-2136-2 (cloth : alk. paper) — ISBN 0-7425-2137-0 (pbk. : alk. paper)
    1. Hegel, Georg Wilhelm Friedrich, 1770–1831—Contributions in political science.
I. Title. II. Series.

JC233.H46 D35 2002
320'.01—dc21   2002015224

Printed in the United States of America

♾™ The paper used in this publication meets the minimum requirements of American
National Standard for Information Sciences—Permanence of Paper for Printed Library
Materials, ANSI/NISO Z39.48-1992.

For Ilse: wife, companion, friend

A good wife who can find?
She is more precious than jewels.

PROVERBS (31.10)

Contents

Series Editor's Introduction

Fred Dallmayr's *G.W.F. Hegel: Modernity and Politics* is the ninth volume in the Rowman & Littlefield series **Modernity and Political Thought** to be published in a second edition. It follows publication of the new editions of William E. Connolly's *The Augustinian Imperative: A Reflection on the Politics of Morality*; Richard E. Flathman's *Thomas Hobbes: Skepticism, Individuality, and Chastened Politics*; Michael Shapiro's *Reading "Adam Smith": Desire, History, and Value*; Tracy B. Strong's *Jean-Jacques Rousseau: The Politics of the Ordinary*; George Kateb's *Emerson and Self-Reliance*; Jane Bennett's *Thoreau's Nature: Ethics, Politics, and the Wild*; Thomas Dumm's *Michel Foucault and the Politics of Freedom*; and Stephen White's *Edmund Burke: Modernity, Politics, and Aesthetics*.[1] Seyla Benhabib's *The Reluctant Modernism of Hannah Arendt*, the tenth and final volume originally belonging to **Modernity and Political Thought,** is also scheduled to appear in a second edition in 2003.[2] In addition, new works for **Modernity and Political Thought** are under way, and among others will focus on such diverse thinkers as Plato, Aristotle, Thomas Aquinas, Thomas More, Niccolo Machiavelli, John Locke, Karl Marx, Friedrich Nietzsche, John Stuart Mill, William James, and Sigmund

Freud, as well as on a selection of contemporary political thinkers. As those who are familiar with the previous works of series authors would expect, taken together their studies adopt a variety of approaches and pose significantly different questions. As contributors to **Modernity and Political Thought,** however, their efforts also are commonly devoted to effecting critical examinations of major political theorists who have shaped our understanding of modernity—its constitution, and the problems, promises, and dangers that are latent within it.

Fred Dallmayr is uniquely qualified to author the series study on Hegel. He is a scholar distinguished by a comprehensive understanding of modern political and social theory, and its contemporary trends and intellectual and historical roots. Much of his work has focused on traditional schools of philosophical thought and their intimate ties to the development of modernity, and on theoretical developments that reject the assumptions of these schools and argue for the emergence of a postmodern order. It is clear from the critical and interpretive sensitivity that Dallmayr brings to these discussions that Hegel cannot be comfortably situated in either of these two camps. According to the terms of Dallmayr's earlier writings, Hegel is neither to be construed as an unequivocal proponent of traditional metaphysics and the philosophical foundations it provides for modernity, nor simply as an opponent of postmodernism and post-metaphysics. Dallmayr's past forays into Hegel's thought reveal a philosophy and political theory that supports both sides while offering insights, understandings, and arguments that promise to transcend the framework within which the modernity-postmodernity debate unfolds. This is evident especially in Dallmayr's *Twilight of Subjectivity: Contributions to a Post-Individualist Theory of Politics* and *Critical Encounters: Between Philosophy and Politics* in which, among other concerns, he reconstructs the history of Hegel's philosophy as an axis around which many, frequently opposing systems of thought were conceived and developed.[3]

In Dallmayr's *Between Freiburg and Frankfurt: Toward a Critical Ontology*, a novel argument anticipates one of the central themes of the present study.[4] Drawing support from a range of scholarship undertaken by contemporary thinkers, Dallmayr explains that in Western philosophy the idea of "reconciliation" is not uncommon, even outside the confines of medieval philosophical theology. Traces can be discovered in Plato's notion of *eros*, Aristotle's ontological conception of *dynamis*, and even in socialist utopias from Thomas More through Karl Marx. Yet, with his focus on dialectical "mediations" and their consummation in the "absolute spirit," Hegel is the most prominent spokesman for reconciliation in the modern context.

This is evident, Dallmayr argues, when we remember that the fundamental experience initiating the entire labor of Hegel's philosophical system is the experience of division or, more technically, "diremption," and that the task that Hegel pursues is the reconciliation of all forms of divisiveness. After having undergone multiple forms of alienation and estrangement throughout its history, human spirit ultimately comes to blend with the absolute spirit, which for Hegel heals and overcomes divisions and furnishes a warrant for reconciliation. Dallmayr emphasizes, though, that the premise of the redemptive power of absolute spirit, upon which the dialectics of reconciliation is predicated, is to be correctly understood as a synonym for the divine spirit. With this affirmed, Dallmayr recalls the analogy, suggested by Hans-Georg Gadamer, between the theological legacy of the absolute spirit and the "speculative" quality of language, that is, its quality as a divine disclosure or manifestation (exemplified in the act of creation as the "word" of God). Most importantly, though, in the mystery of incarnation, in the suffering of the redemptive act performed by Christ, and in the suffering of the world at large, "urgent pleas" are contained for reconciliation and for the healing of brokenness and divisiveness, pleas which, until the "second coming," will be the heart of all human speech and action. Dallmayr finds this view of language instructive for its resonances with the Hegelian themes of diremption (as suffering) and reconciliation (as healing).

The thematic focus of Dallmayr's argument in *Between Freiburg and Frankfurt* foregrounds the approach to Hegel's thought that he adopts in *G. W. F Hegel*. This is particularly apparent when diremption and reconciliation become the twin poles around which many of the most important arguments of this new study are constructed. First and foremost, Dallmayr stresses in this work, it is as a theorist of division that Hegel possesses a profound understanding of modern culture and modern consciousness. Hegel's thought is intensely sensitive to the essentially divisive character of human existence, to those of its features that impel conflict and opposition, contradiction and differentiation. Throughout history existence is replete with such ineliminable turmoil, but it is modernity's emancipation of the individual from tradition and other forms of conventional authority that converts diremption into a qualitatively new phenomenon and modernity's distinguishing feature. Hegel's concept of modernity thus corresponds to our own historical experience, for when we think of modernity societies rent with economic, political, and cultural divisions come to mind.

At the same time, the emancipation of the individual from traditional forms of authority, which Hegel believed to be the paramount achievement of modernity, brought in its wake only apparently irresolvable conflicts between the individual and the possibility for community, the private and public spheres, man and nature, and between opposing forms of thought articulating these and related interests. The gain in individual freedom at the expense of traditions that orient individuals toward a common good need not threaten to tear modern society apart. For Hegel diremption is an instrument of progress, unavoidably painful, though a particularly promising one in its modern formations. In *G.W.F. Hegel*, Dallmayr directs our attention to Hegel's turn toward Greek thought, a turn made not out of nostalgia for antiquity, but for insight into whether there could be a form of life able to resolve the conflicts rooted in the possibly exclusive prerogatives of individual freedom and those of shared ethical beliefs and values. Insofar as it finally subordinated individual autonomy to the needs of the community, the Greek experience failed to show how this singular achievement of modernity might be preserved. Yet, in its ideal of an individuality nurtured with regard to shared ethical norms, the *polis* offered Hegel a model for the task of political theorizing which, in Dallmayr's words, "was precisely to seek the integration and transcendence of the respective merits of antiquity and modernity through the conceptual formulation of a modern *polis*."

In Dallmayr's estimation it is this "integrative move" that distinguishes Hegel as an outstanding theorist of modernity. In light of it, we come to see Hegel as a thinker who is more for our time, that of late modernity, because our modern self-understanding of freedom recognizes, however darkly, that it necessarily entails conflicts the resolution of which may require an abandonment of private self-centeredness and the transformation and reconstitution of autonomy from the standpoint of a shared ethical life. Hegel's modern *polis* embodies a critique of our present form of existence, but not as a reminder that individual freedoms can be pursued only at the cost of common goods, that our alternatives can lie only at one of either extreme, and that we must choose between the ancient and the moderns.

Rather, Hegel's concept invites consideration of an ethical life in which individual and community undergo reconciliation, a transfiguration that preserves the interest and realizes the potential of each of us only by incorporating the aspirations of every other.

With the modern *polis* Hegel takes a decisive step on the "high road of modernity," as Dallmayr puts it in this book. This high road does not merely celebrate Hegel's ideas and aspirations as he refuses to collapse modernity into its divisions and to sustain its diremptions, it also articulates Hegel's conception of the possibilities for ethical life actually inherent in modernity. Winding, often torturously, toward the reconciliation of the modern world's deepest and most disruptive divisions, the high road leads eventually far beyond the conflict-ridden horizon of the technologically developed world to the reconciliation of its differences with the nations of the industrially developing world, differences over the nature of freedom, the claims on that freedom of public needs and values, differences over the limits to growth and the socially responsible role of scientific and technological progress—in short, differences over what is moral, rational, and true. And the same critical movement toward reconciliation characterizing the evolution of the developed world can take root in the developing world, as well, healing its internal divisions, assimilating the values of modern cultures without compromising the integrity of its own, pressing it toward the resolution of its normative conflicts with differently developed worlds. The "high road" is the direction taken by reason as it questions its commitments, tempers if not retreats from its imperialist drive toward mastery. For Dallmayr, Hegel proves to be the architect of a "dialectic of enlightenment" radically different from that in which he is alleged to be implicated by his critics.[5] Hegel is sympathetic to the reservations of anti-Enlightenment thinkers, who have equated Enlightenment reason with domination. For Hegel, this equation is an expression of reason. Yet, it is also only one stage in the development of modernity, one stop on modernity's "high road." Through Dallmayr's work, Hegel thus speaks against the Enlightenment in the name of the Enlightenment, and as its most visionary figure.

While Hegel cannot be exonerated of the charge of being a metaphysical thinker, by seizing upon those features of his thought that return it to our grasp whenever it threatens to spin out of control, Dallmayr's argument about Hegel's theory of modernity proves the indictment of metaphysician too well-worn and facile. This is only one of the many great strengths of

Dallmayr's outstanding study from its first to its last thought. In the construction of this argument Dallmayr foregrounds Hegel's *Philosophy of Right* and related writings, forging an inquiry that draws Hegel out of transcendental regions of experience into a direct and intense engagement with modernity, an engagement that shows Hegel to be brilliantly situated at the center of the debate about modernity and its future. Along the way Dallmayr interweaves contemporary theoretical voices, not only as parties to whom Hegel speaks, but as coconspirators who realize the intent of Hegel's political theory even as they attempt to improve upon it. At the same time, Hegel's work is appraised in light of and defended against a variety of charges leveled by contemporary schools of thought which are themselves at war with each other's interpretation of modernity. In *G.W.F. Hegel: Modernity and Politics* Dallmayr achieves nothing less than a Hegelianism "transformed for political life" that can unlock the promise and potential of modernity.

I am especially grateful to Stephen Wrinn of Rowman & Littlefield for shepherding **Modernity and Political Thought** through the transitional stages to our new publisher and home, and for his thoughtfulness and professionalism that make it possible for editor and authors alike to produce their best work. And while each of the authors of series volumes will earn rewards and punishments commensurate with his or her contribution, as the hidden architects of the series each must also share credit with me for launching **Modernity and Political Thought.**

—Morton Schoolman
State University of New York at Albany

Notes

1. William E. Connolly, *The Augustinian Imperative: A Reflection on the Politics of Morality*; Richard E. Flathman, *Thomas Hobbes: Skepticism, Individuality, and Chastened Politics*; Michael Shapiro, *Reading "Adam Smith": Desire, History, and Value;* Tracy B. Strong, *Jean-Jacques Rousseau: The Politics of the Ordinary*; George Kateb, *Emerson and Self-Reliance;* Jane Bennett, *Thoreau's Nature: Ethics, Politics, and the "Wild"*; Thomas Dumm, *Michel Foucault and the Politics of Freedom*; Stephen White, *Edmund Burke: Modernity, Politics, and Aesthetics* (Lanham, Md.: Rowman & Littlefield, 2002).

2. **Modernity and Political Thought** was first published by Sage Publications, Newbury Park, Calif. Volume 1, William E. Connolly, *The Augustinian Imperative: A Reflection on the*

Politics of Morality (1993); Volume 2, Richard E. Flathman, *Thomas Hobbes: Skepticism, Individuality, and Chastened Politics* (1993); Volume 3, Fred Dallmayr, *G.W.F. Hegel: Modernity and Politics* (1993); Volume 4, Michael Shapiro, *Reading "Adam Smith": The Politics of Desire* (1993); Volume 5, Stephen K. White, *Edmund Burke: Modernity, Politics, and Aesthetics* (1994); Volume 6, Tracy Strong, *Jean-Jacques Rousseau: The Politics of the Ordinary* (1994); Volume 7, Jane Bennett, *Thoreau's Nature: Ethics, Politics, and the "Wild"* (1994); Volume 8, George Kateb, *Emerson and Self-Reliance* (1994); Volume 9, Thomas Dumm, *Michel Foucault and the Politics of Freedom* (1996); Volume 10, Seyla Benhabib, *Hannah Arendt's Reluctant Modernism* (1996).

3. Fred Dallmayr, *Twilight of Subjectivity: Contributions to a Post-Individualist Theory of Politics* (Amherst: University of Massachusetts Press, 1981); *Critical Encounters: Between Philosophy and Politics* (Notre Dame, Ind.: University of Notre Dame Press, 1987).

4. Fred Dallmayr, *Between Freiburg and Frankfurt: Toward a Critical Ontology* (Amherst: University of Massachusetts Press, 1991). My discussion is confined for the most part to the third chapter, "Critical Theory and Reconciliation."

5. I have in mind Max Horkheimer's and T. W. Adorno's *Dialectic of Enlightenment* (New York: Herder and Herder, 1972), originally published by Fischer Verlag, 1944.

Preface

This book was first published about a decade ago. At that time, I almost felt like apologizing to readers for the chosen topic. I began the preface of that first printing with the question, "A book on Hegel?" and proceeded to recount a conversation with a prominent colleague in which the latter had categorically dismissed the relevance of Hegel for contemporary philosophy and political thought. As it happened, the colleague's comments were not far from capturing the intellectual mood or climate prevailing at the time—something of which I was fully aware. In the meantime, however, the intellectual mood has changed or shifted—though surely not in a radical way. In some philosophical quarters, and also among some political theorists, one finds a renewed sensitivity or receptivity for Hegel's work, coupled with attempts to explore his contemporary relevance. However, the extent of the change should probably not be exaggerated. In a time of a globally triumphant market liberalism or neoliberalism, the primary intellectual accent tends to be placed on private-individual interests and negative freedoms, rather than on global equity and ethical life (*Sittlichkeit*) along loosely Hegelian lines. Simultaneously, some radically "postmodern" trends are liable to marginalize or disavow the work of a thinker who, for good or ill, is considered a philosopher—even the quintessential philosopher—of "modernity."

Thus, despite some more favorable attitudes, Hegel's position still remains deeply ambivalent and contested—as it has been from the beginning. As I noted in the preface of the first printing, Hegel has been under a cloud virtually since his death, with successive generations eagerly trying to prove him wrong or shove him out of sight. For a century and a half, philosophers and theorists have untiringly tried to demonstrate the "collapse" of Hegel's thought and his inability to meet their expectations. However, as Martin Heidegger has rightly argued, the situation may be the reverse: Instead of asking whether Hegel lives up to our expectations (or those of his critics), the main question is whether and how we live up to his.

My chief ambition in this book is not to make Hegel a contemporary but to show the continued saliency of some of his key insights, chiefly in the field of politics and political philosophy. The end of the cold war and the collapse of the former Soviet Union have unhinged the stranglehold of a heavily regimented, bureaucratically controlled collectivism, thus clearing the way for free enterprise and liberal-constitutional forms of government. At the same time, however, these trends carry in their wake large-scale social dislocations and economic unemployment, thus throwing into relief the importance of social justice and welfare. In this situation, Hegel is liable to emerge as a crucial mentor. While celebrating individual freedom as the linchpin of an enlightened modern society, Hegel also insisted on embedding this freedom in a network of social relationships and, above all, in the fabric of public justice and civic virtue based on mutual recognition. Similar considerations apply to the upsurge of developing or third world countries in the world today. While initially absorbed by the struggle for national independence, these countries quickly get embroiled in the process of economic modernization and industrialization—a process that brings to the fore (perhaps in aggravated form) all the problems encountered by European, or Western, societies in the early stages of the industrial revolution. Again, it was Hegel who, more cogently than anyone else, pinpointed the agonies as well as the glories and promises of modernization, which give relevance to his work far beyond its native place of origin.

My approach to Hegel is guided, to some extent, by these broader considerations. It is not a goal of this book to present a completely new or unheard of Hegel; nor have I been animated by the detective's zeal to unearth a previously unknown manuscript or letter. This book is one in a series whose overall title or theme is "Modernity and Political Thought." A specific instruction of the series editor was to write a study, limited in length, which would be intelligible to a general readership as well as being accessible to students in advanced undergraduate and graduate courses or seminars. Taking this instruction to heart I have tried to produce a manuscript which, while faithful to Hegel's arguments, keeps to a minimum, or to a manageable level, the scholarly apparatus customary in academic monographs. In the case of Hegel, the available scholarly literature is daunting and formidable. Without shortchanging scholarly standards, one of my main endeavors has been to keep this study lean and unencumbered, and to present Hegel's teachings in a crisp and readable form.

Partly due to the theme of the series and partly to limitations of space, the range of the study is necessarily circumscribed. The central focus is on Hegel's political philosophy as articulated in his *Philosophy of Right* and in related writings both preceding and succeeding that text. Without neatly segregating the political dimension from the rest, this focus implies a relative neglect or deemphasis of other important domains of his work, including issues relating to logic, aesthetic, the philosophy of religion, and the like. Apart from this broad demarcation, my approach is distinct by placing the accent on Hegel as philosopher of *modernity* and a modern *polis*, that is, as a theorist of a viable political community in the context of modern life forms. In good measure, this accent derives from the current state of intellectual debate in the West. For a number of reasons, and in varying guises, the issue of modernity has become a centerpiece in contemporary discussions, with some participants extolling modern society as an unmixed blessing and others decrying its glaring and dehumanizing defects. In this situation, Hegel's philosophy can offer important guidance—by upholding what I would call the "high road" of modernity, that is, a road marked by the vision of a socially responsible human freedom. Both devotees and detractors of modernity, I believe, can learn or benefit from Hegel's teachings: the former by being reminded of their own better aspirations and the latter by being confronted with a storehouse of treasures that they seem too ready to abandon.

For all its deep admiration for Hegel's work, my study does not seek to vindicate any kind of orthodox Hegelianism. As I realize, life forms and modes of thought have changed dramatically in the time span separating us from his era. In the philosophical domain, our age has rendered dubious or suspect a number of key categories prevalent in traditional philosophy or metaphysics, including the categories of noumenal consciousness, subjectivity, and idea (or essence). In large measure, erosion of or suspicion toward these categories is the hallmark of contemporary postmodernity and a "postfoundational" mode of thinking. Given Hegel's prominent role in defining the character of modernity, his work necessarily is pertinent to, and a crucial reservoir in shaping, the meaning of *postmodernity* (notwithstanding the protestations of many of its practitioners).

Another distinctive feature of my book is the attention I give to the "effective history" (*Wirkungsgeschichte*) of Hegel's work, that is, to the critical reception and transformation of his legacy by successive generations of readers—from Kierkegaard and Marx through Nietzsche and existentialism to our present postfoundational period. Anyone approaching Hegel today is constrained to work his or her way somehow through the thicket of sedimented interpretations clustered around his work, in the hope of eventually emerging with a viable reading adequate for our time. Without endorsing a radical "constructivism" (which treats all readings as arbitrary fabrications), I hold that past teachings need to be approached and tested anew in each age from the angle of its peculiar concerns and agonies (which is one way of "philosophizing with a hammer"). Where these timely concerns are neglected, inherited treasures are liable to be transformed into museum pieces—something which Hegel would have utterly abhorred.

As I try to show in the concluding portions of this book, Hegel—like all great thinkers of the past—must be seriously engaged in our time, in order to bring out (as Heidegger said) the "unthought in his thought." In my view, the trajectory of his "effective history" does not point in the direction of a replacement of spirit by matter, of objective *Geist* by subjective inwardness, of universality by particularity, or of essence by contingency. In lieu of such simple reversals (often used to sideline his thought), something more subtle seems to have been happening: namely, a dissemination and sheltering of spirit in the capillaries of phenomena and a return of reason to its inconspicuous beginnings. Under the auspices of this happening, spirit is no longer—or at least no longer preeminently—embodied in the modern state, but has found refuge among ordinary people in the diverse lifeworlds around the world. This dispersal, I believe, still concurs with the deeper intent of Hegel's thought, as expressed in an early version of the

Philosophy of Right: "To find spirit in the concrete fabric of reality, to grasp the reconciliation of spirit with the world—this is our [the philosopher's] kind of worship."

Overall, the central hope of this study is to convey to readers some of the intensity and spirited élan of Hegel's work. I leave it to readers and reviewers to judge whether this aspiration has been fulfilled or even distantly approximated. Basically, my purpose has tended to militate against needless pedantry and esoteric jargon. Wherever possible, I have used available English translations of Hegel's texts but not in a slavish manner. Hegel may not always have been the greatest stylist. Yet, his prose is often considerably more eloquent and lucid than that of his translators. Thus, I have frequently reworded English renditions, preferring on the whole readability (faithful to meaning) to cumbersome literalness. The edge against pedantry also governs the method of annotation. To avoid cluttering the text with numbers, I have tended to assemble citations in notes placed at the end of paragraphs.

As always, authorship in the present case implies indebtedness. In preparing and writing the manuscript, I benefited from a number of scholars whose treatment of Hegel helped me to sort out my own thinking in this area. Above all, I want to acknowledge my indebtedness to Shlomo Avineri, whose *Hegel's Theory of the Modern State* stands out as a model of clarity and good sense. In nearly equal fashion, I am indebted to Charles Taylor, whose *Hegel and Modern Society* has been a source of sustained inspiration. In addition, there are a number of scholars whose comments or observations have helped me at various junctures of my study. Among these are Richard J. Bernstein, the late George Armstrong Kelly, and Michael Theunissen. Beyond this circle there is a broader group of colleagues whose steady companionship has tended to shape my views in more diffuse ways. Without any order of preference I want simply to mention here William Connolly, John O'Neill, Calvin Schrag, and Hwa Yol Jung.

In addition, there are other types of debt that need to be acknowledged. The manuscript has been typed and retyped with usual efficiency by Patricia Flanigan. I am particularly grateful to Morton Schoolman for his superb editorial work on the manuscript. The most pervasive debt of gratitude, however, goes to my wife, Ilse, to whom this book is dedicated. Without her loyal encouragement and support none of this endeavor would have been possible or worthwhile.

1

Introduction

Why Hegel today? Why in particular a book addressed to a broader audience beyond the narrow circle of professional experts? Is Hegel not the epitome of the insulated academic far removed from the concerns of everyday life? Does his work not have the reputation of being enshrouded in metaphysical complexities (as well as a forbidding Germanic style)? On a political level, does his thought not favor totalitarian designs or at least an idolatry of the state (particularly the Prussian state)—features that are impalatable and completely obsolete in our post-Cold War environment?

No one writing on Hegel can quickly brush these questions aside, especially not the issue of metaphysical complexity. On a closer reading, many of the cited apprehensions will turn out to be unfounded, but not the one regarding philosophical difficulty. To put matters simply, Hegel was the last great *systematic* thinker in the history of Western philosophy, a thinker who sought to render all facets of reality accessible to philosophical understanding and to integrate them into an intelligible

1

whole. No doubt his work is complex and difficult—but for a reason. Reality itself, he would have argued, is complex, multidimensional and resistant to facile explanations. A book devoted to Hegel's thought today thus faces a formidable challenge: the challenge not to popularize his work to the point of vitiating its integrity while simultaneously trying to rescue it from academic insulation or oblivion.

The reference to philosophical complexity already points out one facet of Hegel's relevance today, namely, that of a thinking grappling with reality on a broad scale. Under the sway of positivist empiricism, philosophy in our century has tended to be reduced to the position of a handmaiden or "underlaborer" of science, a role involving at most the sharpening of conceptual tools and procedures needed in empirical research. Philosophical inquiry from this vantage is marginalized because "facts" (one assumes) are able to speak for themselves without requiring philosophical interpretation and scrutiny. In opposition to empiricist myopia or fact centeredness, efforts are sometimes made to erect philosophy into the guardian of universal categories and principles, that is, of the transcendental or a priori premises undergirding human cognition as such. While valuable as an antidote, however, the strategy carries a price, the price of distancing if not divorcing thought from its subject matter, which is the concrete fabric of the world.

Between positivist obtuseness and transcendental abstraction, philosophical reflection seems stranded. It is precisely at this point that Hegel enters the stage by proposing a mode of reflection closely attentive to, and steadily nourished by, concrete-substantive experience. Empiricism, in Hegel's view, was only a preliminary stage of knowledge, a stage antedating the discovery of self-consciousness. But the discovery of self-consciousness, in turn, was only a gateway to the non-self, that is, to the exploration of others and the world. As he writes in his *Philosophy of Right*—a work that will occupy a central place in this study—philosophy, in being concerned with reason and consciousness, aims through this concern precisely at the "grasp of reality in its concrete presence," not at abstract principles separating form from content. For, he adds, what is called *form* is simply reason viewed as "conceptual comprehension," while *content* is reason seen as "substantive essence of ethical and natural reality." The confluence of the two is the core (or "idea") of philosophical inquiry.[1]

These comments carry over to another aspect of Hegel's thought about which much (perhaps too much) has been written and which is sometimes styled as his central contribution: the notion of *dialectics*. In both philosophical and popular literature, dialectics is often presented as an abstract schema or else as a handy formula (captured by the labels *thesis-antithesis-synthesis*)—a formula that readily can be superimposed on subject matter of any kind. This view, however, entirely misses the point. Far from denoting an empty schema, dialectics for Hegel signaled the innermost movement of reality and thought, a movement deriving from the fact that no thing or concept stands by itself but gains its meaning from its relationship to a whole web of other things and concepts, including the relationship to its own nonexistence (or negation). In the traditional language of philosophy, dialectics for Hegel thus occupied a metaphysical or *ontological* status; here *ontology* means concern with the essence of being, manifest in natural and historical reality.

This status tends to be ignored or obscured even in more sophisticated readings of Hegel's work. Thus from the vantage of Hegelian Marxists (that is, Marxists faithful to Hegel's teachings) a sharp distinction has to be made between the dialectics of history and the nondialectal domain of nature, a view that places nature beyond the pale of reflective understanding while simultaneously erecting history into a human product (or a product of subjective designs). In greatly refined manner, this view surfaces even in Taylor's magisterial study of Hegel, a work that more than any other in recent times has rendered Hegel accessible again to contemporary readers. While admiring both the scope and the verve of his study, I cannot quite concur with Taylor's distinction between *logical* (or ontological) and *historical* dialectics, where the first is tied to strict, logical proof and the second to a weaker mode of *interpretive* plausibility. It seems to me, separating logic from substantive experience means to tear asunder precisely what Hegel took pains to try to combine or bridge.[2]

The unifying or holistic character of Hegel's thought is widely recognized and accentuated, and sometimes even made into a term of reproach (I shall return to this point). But unity for Hegel, of course, was not simply a "given" fact or an immediately available situation that the mind could passively grasp or register. Like everything else in the world, unity was not directly present and understandable but was only the goal or endpoint of a complex process of development. The road to this goal was punctured by separation, differentiation, and even by opposition and contradiction (in the sense that every finite being viewed separately stands in contradiction with itself, and with others). Thus Hegel's philosophy amply acknowledged the divisions or diremptions (*Entzweiungen*) that human maturation and cognition inevitably seem to involve: the divisions between subject and object, between human being ("man") and nature, between individual and community, and between finite and infinite reality. Yet, his philosophy did not stop at this point, because division or contradiction could not be the final word.

Although divided and separated, subject and object, human being and nature were severed precisely in light of a relationship that undergirded and made possible their division. Realization of this relationship or bond was the stepping-stone to a mediated unity that did not nullify previous oppositions. Hegel spoke in this context of the "reconciliation" of opposites and of their "sublation" (*Aufhebung*) on a higher level where *previous stages are both preserved and transcended.* The ultimate force making possible this reconciliation and transcendence was called the *absolute spirit,* or the *world spirit* (*Weltgeist;* translated by Taylor as "cosmic spirit")—a spirit that is more than but not radically alien to human spirit. In Taylor's words, Hegel's response to the radical subject-object division was

> to throw down the barrier between man and the world in having the knowledge of finite subjects culminate in the self-knowledge of infinite subject. . . . Man separates from nature in the course of realizing his vocation as a rational being. But it is just this vocation fully realized, just the full development of rationality which shows him to himself as the vehicle of *Geist* and thus reconciles the opposition.[3]

For contemporary readers, the notion of a healing spirit promoting cosmic unity may seem difficult or alien (Taylor calls it "close to incredible"). I have to postpone this issue to a later context. In other respects, however, Hegel's vision still resonates strongly with present-day quandaries or dilemmas. On the political level, one of the most widely debated issues in Western democracies concerns the respective merits of individual freedom and social-political bonds—or (in current terminology) of *liberalism* versus *communitarianism.* Inspired by the legacy of Reformation and Enlightenment, champions of individual freedom consider the essence of politics to be the defense of personal rights and liberties against encroachments emanating from government or the public sphere; seen from this vantage, all community standards or shared public bonds appear questionable and possibly oppressive, namely, by imposing constraints on individual spontaneity or initiative. For at least 100 years now, this emphasis on civil rights has been buttressed by economic developments, particularly the emergence of a (capitalist) market economy wedded to free enterprise. Countering this liberal focus, advocates of community are quick to point to the corrosive effects of egotism and *possessive individualism* on moral and political life. In our time, such complaints are corroborated by philosophical arguments asserting the fragility of modern ego identity and even the impossibility of conceiving the ego outside of intersubjective bonds, that is, outside the formative influences of a common culture or shared tradition. One of the (possibly) appealing aspects of Hegel's political philosophy resides precisely in its attempt to reconcile and transcend this conflict, by integrating and preserving facets of both liberalism and communitarianism. As will be shown later, Hegel's *Philosophy of Right* constitutes a multifaceted edifice that makes room both for free individual initiative (on the level of *civil society*) and for shared moral bonds (on the level of the ethical state).[4]

Beyond the range of domestic politics, Hegel's vision carries import for prominent features of international politics in our age, particularly the long-standing conflict between superpowers (which now seems to be abating). Under the aegis of the Cold War, the international arena pitted against each other the free world and communist totalitarianism; the former is devoted to free individual enterprise and the latter to a governmentally imposed socialism or collectivism (as prelude to a future "classless" society). As it happens, both camps were heirs or descendants of the modern struggle for liberty and equality. But while one side construed these terms in a utilitarian-individualistic sense, the other side opted for a collective egalitarianism (presumably ensuring the freedom of the proletariat).

In a sense, this conflict had already announced itself in the French Revolution, an event that signaled both a bourgeois revolt designed to unleash individual enterprise and a *levée en masse* aimed at installing popular sovereignty or a collective general will. Hegel was an astute observer of these political developments of his time. Although initially attracted to the liberating impulse animating the French Revolution, he came to perceive both in rigid individualism and in popular collectivism a dangerous bent toward *abstraction:* a bent to abstract from the rich fabric of differences and mediating institutions operating in concrete political life. Hegel's political philosophy carefully sought to preserve—rather than obscure or suppress through the abstracting of—these differences and mediations, while simultaneously being attentive to the demands for liberty. Since Hegel's time, the bent to abstractness has steadily gathered momentum, until it finally surfaced in our age in the opposing tendencies of social atomism and totalitarianism. To quote Taylor again, Hegel discerned

> the two great disruptive forces which threaten the modern state. The first is the force of private interest, inherent in civil society and in its mode of production, which constantly threatens to overrun all limits, polarize the society between rich and poor, and dissolve the bonds of the state. The second is the diametrically opposed attempt to overcome this and all other divisions by sweeping away all differentiation in the name of the general will and the true society of equals, an attempt which must issue, Hegel thinks, in violence and the dictatorship of the revolutionary elite.[5]

In many respects, Hegel's philosophy—including his political philosophy—resembles a complex balancing act mediating conflicting tendencies bent on tearing modern society apart. While ready to give these tendencies their due, he was unwilling to let them run unchecked. Taylor defines the polar trends balanced in Hegel's thought as those of *expressivism* and radical *moral freedom.* The first trend—epitomized by Herder and early romanticism—emphasized human imagination and self-presentation in shared cultural meanings and institutions; the second—exemplified by Enlightenment and Kantian philosophy—focused on rational maturation and progressive emancipation from traditional bonds.

For a number of reasons, I find Taylor's label of expressivism limiting or misleading (one reason is its association with romantic subjectivism). In my view, a better label would be *holism,* or a holistic notion of the "good life," seen as antipode or complement to the desire for individual freedom. One advantage of this formulation is that it brings into view classical Greek thought with its centerstaging of the *polis* and the good life achieved through shared involvement in public affairs. Throughout his life, Hegel remained strongly attracted to ancient Greece and its model of politics, although he clearly recognized its drawbacks or limitations. While providing for moral unity and a shared cultivation of public virtues, the *polis* in his view was insufficiently differentiated or attentive to the diversification flowing from moral autonomy and the pursuit of individual freedom. Promotion of such autonomy was the unquestionable achievement of modernity, particularly of the Reformation and (strands of) the Enlightenment. In turn, however, modern individualism was one-sided by stressing only the exodus of individuals from traditional bonds—that is, the aspect of negative freedom—while neglecting the moral and cultural benefits derived from participation in a political community and the ongoing quest for the good life. On Hegelian premises, the task of political theorizing was precisely to seek the integration and transcendence (*Aufhebung*) of the respective merits of antiquity and modernity through the conceptual formulation of a *modern polis*.[6]

Through this integrative move, Hegel's thought inserts itself squarely into contemporary discussions about modernity or the continuing viability of the "modern project." Defenders of radical individualism are sometimes prone to dismiss Hegel simply as a traditionalist or a devotee of premodern life forms, a view that completely neglects his modern, revolutionary sensibilities (and also his sympathy for modern constitutionalism). More fairly and more plausibly, Habermas presented Hegel as a modernist and, in fact, as the chief instigator of the "discourse of modernity" (that is, of the modern type of argumentation). In Habermas's account, this modern discourse has three main features, all of which are anchored in individual consciousness (or subjectivity): the emphasis on critical rationality, moral autonomy, and creative self-realization. Prefigured in Kant's three Critiques, these features are said to undergird the domains of modern science, ethics, and art. As it happens, Habermas's study—while highlighting these aspects—found in Hegel's work a certain deficit or shortfall of modernism, a deficit deriving chiefly from his lingering holism or attachment to traditional metaphysics (evident in his celebration of spirit, or *Geist*).

As remedy for this shortfall, Habermas's study proposed recourse to the process of communicative interaction leading to a quasi-contractual agreement among participants. Yet, in relying on individual will-formation, his proposal threatens to upset or unhinge Hegel's mediating balance between individual and community in favor of modern predilections for radical individualism. What is neglected, in particular, is Hegel's role as both instigator *and* critic of the discourse of modernity. Long before the agonies and diremptions (*Entzweiungen*) of our age, Hegel discerned the *dialectic of Enlightenment,* that is, the propensity of modernity both to unleash human freedom and to undercut human well-being, or the good life. This insight, in his case, did not foster nostalgia for the past—for the presumed golden age of antiquity—but rather a sober attempt to restore modernity to its hidden promise or potential.[7]

Hegel's outlook, one might add, has implications also for another feature of contemporary international or global politics. Following the dismantling of colonial empires, a host of newly independent countries or regions has entered the world stage—countries that are frequently lumped together under the label of third world. Simultaneously, however, with this postcolonial upsurge, the world arena is undergoing a steady process of Westernization, a process spearheaded by Western science, technology, and production methods. In this situation, third world countries are faced with a grave dilemma: either to cling to non-Western and premodern traditions, but at the price of remaining underdeveloped and unable to compete with Western economic (and military) advances, or to assimilate Western models, but at the risk of losing their distinctiveness and their indigenous ways of life. The agonies of this dilemma are evident in the tensions pervading the non-Western world today, tensions that sometimes surface in the form of a fervent traditionalism and sometimes in the guise of a relentless modernism bent on rapid industrialization.

At this juncture, Hegel's dialectical thought may still offer a viable remedy for reconciling the past and the future. On Hegelian premises, tradition or indigenous culture is not a given thing or object that could be preserved unreflectively. Rather, precisely in order to grow, tradition needs to be exposed to critical reflection—the hallmark of Western modernity—and thus undergo the tribulations of divisiveness and diremption (between subject and object, self and nature). In turn, however, modern divisions are not a final goal but only the gateway to a situation in which tradition can be imaginatively recuperated and previous stages be transcended or sublated in a higher unity. Seen from this vantage, third world countries enter the path of modernization not for modernization's sake but precisely to recover their distinctive life forms—just as Western modernity only gains meaning through encounter with the non-West. In a sense, this correlation reflects the Hegelian dialectic of universalism and particularism, now projected onto a global scale. Briefly put, the particular or indigenous is viable only through mediation with the universal. But the universal, in turn, makes sense and is supportable only by being anchored in particular or local life worlds.[8]

Examples of Hegel's timeliness could be further expanded and elaborated. I realize, however, that my account conflicts sharply with a prevailing intellectual mood or climate. Bluntly stated, Hegel is out of fashion in many quarters, being considered either as obsolete or obnoxious (or both). Ever since Popper's indictment half a century ago, Hegel has tended to be viewed as an enemy of democracy and of the liberal "open society." This assessment has been greatly aggravated or intensified by recent philosophical trends—epitomized by poststructuralism—stressing fragmentation and the merits of social antagonism.

In light of these trends, Hegel's holistic leanings are seen as emblems of "total," if not totalitarian, designs, while his search for comprehensive understanding is accused of harboring a domineering impulse—the impulse of subjugating or expunging all modes of "difference" or "otherness" in favor of absolute knowledge. On the political level, Hegel's comments on the state as an ethical institution are denounced as idealist mystifications camouflaging both the centralized power of bureaucracy and the large-scale manipulation and corruption pervading the public domain. The same verdict obtains on the international level. Far from having anything instructive to teach to the non-West, Hegel's work is treated as part and parcel of Western imperialism bent on making the rest of the world over in its image. Viewed in this manner, Hegelian thought appears indeed as the culmination of modern Western philosophy—but a culmination revealing only the sinister aspects of that heritage as well as its rapid obsolescence. In lieu of Hegel's striving for a shared ethical life, or *Sittlichkeit,* critics now place the accent on radical diversity, incompatibility, and agonistic struggles for power. Instead of the fostering of public institutions, preference currently is given to individual (or group) separateness and at most to local or sporadic types of resistance to the all-perversive tentacles of political domination.[9]

Although splintered into many facets, contemporary thought is strangely united in this anti-Hegelian mood. When Hegel is not rebuked as protototalitarian, he is taken to task as a gnostic "sorcerer" intent on fusing immanence and transcendence. In my view, indictments of this kind are excessively harsh and precipitous, though not entirely groundless. My point here is not to turn a blind eye to the drawbacks of Hegel's philosophical system. As I shall try to show later, his work indeed reflects strands of traditional philosophical speculation that today have become dubious or unpersuasive. In our postmetaphysical era, no one can blithely endorse *foundational premises* or categories like *subjectivity, idea,* or *spirit.* Yet, acknowledgment of this fact does not amount to a simple negation or dismissal of Hegel's work. Basically, his thought cannot be simply overturned or put "right side up" (as Marx and Engels once suggested).

The reason for this impossibility resides in the immense richness and complexity of his thought, a complexity that uncannily seems to have anticipated most of the counterarguments that are advanced (often naively) by critics today. In mounting their various attacks, critics frequently can be shown to move along paths that Hegel himself had sketched out long ago. Thus, to take the case of poststructuralism, the emphasis on differentiation and local particularity is precisely the point that Hegel actually had directed against the abstractness of Enlightenment thought (including its Kantian variant). Similarly, the stress on singularity and individuality—first polemically initiated by Kierkegaard—follows in the footprints of Hegel's assault on universal categories not instantiated in human experience or concrete historical constellations. And if the accent is placed on conflict or antagonism, no one again has captured this aspect more eloquently than Hegel in his portrayal of the "struggle for recognition." Generally speaking, Hegel's edifice is bound to remain intact as long as priorities are simply exchanged or polarities simply reversed (from universal to particular, from unity to disunity, or else from immanence to transcendence); as part of a philosophical account, polar terms presuppose each other and cannot be one-sidedly unhinged or dislodged.[10]

Again, my point is not to vindicate Hegel's system as such. Yet, for criticism to get off the ground, this system must surely be taken seriously in all its richness and complex subtlety. Otherwise critical forays are likely to miss the target (or only hit a strawman). In my view, the only chance to make headway is by focusing on the level of metaphysics or ontology (concern with "being")—the level at which Hegel's thought is most genuinely at home. My own endeavor in these pages seeks to proceed along these lines. In doing so, I need to fasten both on the continued strength and importance of Hegel's insights and on their possible limitations in a postmetaphysical historical context.

Such an endeavor, to be sure, is not without precedent. Nearly a century ago, the Italian philosopher Croce wrote a book titled *What Is Living and What Is Dead of the Philosophy of Hegel.* In that study, Croce sought to disentangle the living core of Hegelian thought from its suspect, implausible, and possibly outdated encrustations. What Croce considered alive (or *vivo*) was basically the internal *logos* of Hegel's philosophical system, particularly its dialectical logic focused on the emergent synthesis of opposites (*coincidentia oppositorum*). By contrast, what he discarded as dead (or *morto*)—the "unburied bones" of the system—was a certain overbearing *panlogism* that subsumed all distinctions of degree and all differences of method to the single method of dialectics seen as the self-manifestation of spirit.[11]

What distinguishes my approach from Croce's—leaving aside the latter's unequaled erudition—is mainly a greater temporal and philosophical distance from the topic of inquiry. Notwithstanding his strong reservations and proposed revisions, Croce remained an idealist, wedded to the foundational axioms of German classical idealism, encapsulated in the metaphysics of spirit. Since the publication of his book, philosophical thought has undergone many profound transformations—from pragmatism and positivism through the "linguistic turn" to Heideggerian postmetaphysics and the contemporary upsurge of Nietzscheanism. In various direct or indirect ways, these transformations are linked with important changes in Western societies, changes that were far off or only embryonically present in Hegel's and Croce's times; among these are bureaucratization of governmental controls, the rise of welfare systems, and the informational revolution (spawned by computer technology).

To grasp the significance of Hegel today—to discern what is *vivo* and *morto* in his thought—it will be necessary to mediate his teachings carefully (and dialectically) with such evolving historical developments and with the thought patterns and experiences of our time. Given his emphasis on historical concreteness, this is an effort that Hegel himself would hardly have scorned. Historical mediation of this kind requires, above all, attentiveness to the historical effectiveness of Hegel's legacy, that is, to the engagement and struggle of successive generations of thinkers with that legacy in light of their own situation. This continuing engagement is basically what Gadamer termed *Wirkungsgeschichte.* As he points out in *Truth and Method,* the term refers not merely to the after effects of a work, that is, to the story of (mis)interpretations— something that historical scholarship has recognized and studied for a long time. Instead, *Wirkungsgeschichte* denotes the implication of both text and interpretation in a historical nexus of understandings and preunderstandings, a nexus from which neither text nor interpretation can fully extricate itself and that alone grants access to a work of the past (though not in the mode of neutral analysis). The notion, he states, "that *wirkungsgeschichtlich* inquiry is required whenever a work or legacy is to be lifted from the twilight of tradition into the clarity of its proper significance, is indeed a new or novel demand"—one raised by contemporary hermeneutics (in its Heideggerian sense).[12]

The present study aims to give at least some attention to such inquiry, which is not extrinsic to my subject matter. *Wirkungsgeschichte,* as Gadamer stresses, is intimately compatible and congenial with Hegelian thought, though it ultimately points beyond the horizon of his historical self-understanding. As is well known, Hegel considered his own work chiefly as a summation or capstone of Western metaphysical developments, a capstone in which opaque tendencies of the past finally reached their clarification and distillation. Comments to this effect are strewn throughout his writings, but are most emphatically phrased in his preface to the *Philosophy of Right.* As he notes there, the task of all philosophy is to grasp "what is" or the reality of being, but the reality of being is reason itself. Seen from this vantage, philosophy is simply "its own time comprehended in thought." Focused on "what is," philosophy cannot move beyond present reality or the existing world, just as little as an individual can "overleap his/her own age or jump over Rhodes." To these comments the conclusion of the preface adds a famous passage that seems to confine reflection entirely to a retrospective stance: "As the thought of the world, philosophy appears only at a time when reality (*Wirklichkeit*) has completed its formative process and stands ready in its prime." Hence, "whenever philosophy begins to paint its grey in grey, then a shape of life has grown old; and with philosophy's grey it cannot be rejuvenated but only comprehended. The owl of Minerva spreads its wings only with the onset of dusk."[13]

Although valuable as an antidote to a reckless utopianism or abstract moralism, Hegel's comments at this point tend to shortchange his historical sense or his own conception of temporality. For clearly, temporality cannot be restricted to the confluence of past and present, but also harbors a future dimension, which does not cancel the past. Buried in existing reality are multiple intimations of untapped possibilities—a host of anticipations, dreams, and concrete longings (what Ernst Bloch called the "principle of hope"). Moreover, a philosophy focused on dialectical movement must also make room for unexpected turns and twists, for the inroads of unfamiliar happenings and disclosures. When, as in Hegel's thought, *subjective spirit* is sent on a journey through alien lands in search of self-discovery, human experience must be open to encounters with radical otherness, which redefines previous self-understandings.

These considerations have a bearing on philosophical thought conceived as reflection on "what is" or the reality of being—where being does not coincide with the customary or habitual. As it seems to me, philosophical reflection cannot be limited to existing reality seen as a completed process, but must also venture into uncharted terrain thereby risking its premises and the comfort of ensured knowledge. In Hegelian language, philosophy cannot be entirely content with the grayness of aged retrospection or replicate the flight of the owl of "Minerva at dusk"; despite a preference for seasoning, its vistas remain forever youthful and impending. Precisely in focusing on "what is," philosophy also grants room to "Minerva at dawn"—with the owl spreading its wings toward imaginary horizons and toward distant, nearly imperceptible callings.[14] The structure of the present study is based on these observations.

The first part of the study tries to trace the evolution of Hegel's political thought, that is, his successive attempts to formulate the conception of a modern *polis;* these attempts stretch from his early theological and political writings to his *Encyclopedia* and his move to Berlin.

In the second part, I shall portray or recapitulate the main features of Hegel's mature political philosophy, concentrating primarily—though not exclusively—on his *Philosophy of Right.* Although, under hermeneutical auspices, this presentation cannot entirely abstract from my preunderstandings, that is, from my own historically formed interpretive dispositions, I shall rely largely on conventional wisdom (or traditional scholarship) regarding the substance of Hegel's teachings.

The third part turns to the story of Hegel's migration through time, that is, to the *Wirkungsgeschichte* of his thought. At this point, attention is given (albeit briefly) to the struggle of successive generations of thinkers with Hegel's legacy—from Kierkegaard, Marx, and the left Hegelians through Nietzsche and positivism to later manifestations of the linguistic turn; in view of the character of my own preunderstandings, special consideration is devoted to recent developments in Continental philosophy, including Gadamerian hermeneutics, Heidegger's postmetaphysics, and French deconstruction.

Informed by these philosophical perspectives, the concluding part resumes the interpretation of Hegel's work—now in a new, anticipatory key, honoring Minerva at dawn. My effort at this point will be to draw out the lessons of a transformed Hegelianism for contemporary political life, with an accent on the respective status of society and state and the relations of private and public domains. Faithful to dawn's herald, I also intend to sketch the broader implications of the study for the future of democracy and public ethical bonds (or *Sittlichkeit*) against the backdrop of a global setting.

Notes

1. G. W. F. Hegel, *Hegel's Philosophy of Right,* trans. T. M. Knox (Oxford: Oxford University Press, 1967), 10, 12. (In the above and subsequent citations I have altered the translation for purposes of clarity.) That Hegel's philosophy seeks to overcome both empiricism and transcendental formalism is a view developed, among others, by Bernstein; see Richard

J. Bernstein, *Praxis and Action: Contemporary Philosophies of Human Activity* (Phila-delphia: University of Pennsylvania Press, 1971), 233.

2. Charles Taylor, *Hegel* (Cambridge: Cambridge University Press, 1975), 218. For an abbreviated version of this comprehensive study see Charles Taylor, *Hegel and Modern Society* (Cambridge: Cambridge University Press, 1979), 64. For present purposes, I shall rely mainly on the latter version. Taylor does not actually believe that dialectics is amenable to logical proof, and he also recognizes his departure from Hegel's self-under-standing: "Hegel would never have agreed that any part of his system reposed on plausible interpretations as against strict argument, for this would be to abandon the conception of *Geist* as total rationality" (*Hegel and Modern Society,* 64). The chief representative of Hegelian Marxism is Lukács; see particularly Georg Lukács, *History and Class Con-sciousness: Studies in Marxist Dialectics,* trans. Rodney Livingstone (Cambridge: MIT Press, 1971).

3. Taylor, *Hegel and Modern Society,* 48-49.

4. Taylor, *Hegel and Modern Society,* 69. For statements of the liberal position see, e.g., Ronald Dworkin, *Taking Rights Seriously* (Cambridge, MA: Harvard University Press, 1977); John Rawls, *A Theory of Justice* (Cambridge, MA: Harvard University Press, 1971); and Friedrich Hayek, *The Constitution of Liberty* (Chicago: University of Chicago Press, 1960). Regarding the communitarian position compare, e.g., Alasdair MacIntyre, *After Virtue* (Notre Dame: University of Notre Dame Press, 1981); Michael Walzer, *Spheres of Justice* (New York: Basic Books, 1983); and Michael J. Sandel, *Liberalism and the Limits of Justice* (Cambridge, UK: Cambridge University Press, 1982).

5. Taylor, *Hegel and Modern Society,* 131.

6. Taylor recognizes this aspect when he writes

One of the most common ways of stating the problem was in terms of history, as a problem of uniting the greatest in ancient and modern life. . . . The beautiful Greek synthesis had to die because man had to be inwardly divided in order to grow. In particular the growth of reason and hence rational freedom required a diremption from the natural and sensible. . . . If the early Greek synthesis had been unreflective—and had to be, because reflection starts by dividing man with himself—then the new unity would fully incorporate the reflective consciousness gained, would indeed be brought about by this reflective consciousness. (*Hegel and Modern Society,* 7-8)

7. Jürgen Habermas, *The Philosophical Discourse of Modernity: Twelve Lectures,* trans. Frederick Lawrence (Cambridge: MIT Press, 1987), 4, 16-18, 40-43. For a critical review see Fred Dallmayr, "The Discourse and Counter-Discourses of Modernity," in *Margins of Political Discourse* (Albany: SUNY Press, 1989), 39-48. Habermas does not ignore the critical side of Hegel's position. As he writes, in fact, the principle of individual subjectivity "explained for him simultaneously the superiority of the modern world and its crisis character, in the sense that it represents both a world of progress and of alienated spirit. For this reason the first attempt to conceptualize the modern era was at the same time a critique of modernity" (*Philosophical Discourse of Modernity,* 18). Cf. in this context Lewis P. Hinchman, *Hegel's Critique of the Enlightenment* (Gainsville: Univer-sity Presses of Florida, 1984).

8. For some reflections along these lines see Bhikhu Parekh, *Colonialism, Tradition, and Reform* (New Delhi: Sage, 1989); also Ashis Nandy, *Traditions, Tyranny and Utopias*

(Delhi: Oxford University Press, 1987), and Fazlur Rahman, *Islam and Modernity* (Chicago: University of Chicago Press, 1982).

9. The notion of local resistances and of government as a pervasive (disciplinary) power or domination is associated chiefly with the work of Foucault; cf., e.g., Michel Foucault, *Discipline and Punish,* trans. Alan Sheridan (New York: Vintage Book, 1979). For a direct application of Foucault's poststructuralist perspective to Hegel's political philosophy see William E. Connolly, *Political Theory and Modernity* (Oxford, UK: Blackwell, 1988), 86-115. For an attack on Hegel along similar lines, cf. Jean-François Lyotard, *The Postmodern Condition: A Report on Knowledge,* trans. Geoff Bennington and Brian Massumi (Minneapolis: University of Minnesota Press, 1984). See also Karl Popper, *The Open Society and Its Enemies,* 5th rev. ed. (London: Routledge & Kegan Paul, 1966).

10. Regarding the struggle for recognition see G. W. F. Hegel, *The Phenomenology of Mind,* trans. J. B. Baillie (New York: Harper & Row, 1967), 228-240. Cf. also Karl Marx, "Afterword to Second German Edition of *Capital,*" in *The Marx-Engels Reader,* ed. Robert C. Tucker (New York: Norton, 1972), 197-198 and Eric Voegelin, "On Hegel: A Study in Sorcery," in *The Collected Works of Eric Voegelin,* Vol. 12, ed. Ellis Sandoz (Baton Rouge: Louisiana State University Press, 1990), 213-255.

11. Benedetto Croce, *What Is Living and What Is Dead of the Philosophy of Hegel,* trans. Douglas Ainslie (1906; trans., New York: Russell & Russell, 1969), 79, 203. As Croce observed, his overall goal was "to resolve the whole philosophy into a *pure philosophy of spirit* (or a logic-metaphysic, as it might then have been called)." For this purpose "it was necessary to draw forth the Hegelian thought 'from the sheath of its members,' that is to say, of its false members which had been badly attached to it; and to permit it to form its own members, answering to the nature of the primitive germ" (*What Is Living,* 203-204). In Croce's account, the "essential error" resided in the "confusion between the theory of distincts and the theory of opposites" from which arose "all that is philosophically erroneous in the system of Hegel" (*What Is Living,* 98-99).

12. Hans-Georg Gadamer, *Truth and Method,* 2nd rev. ed., trans. Joel Weinsheimer and Donald G. Marshall (New York: Crossroad, 1989), 300. Translation slightly altered for the sake of clarity.

13. Hegel, *Hegel's Philosophy of Right,* 11-13.

14. Cf. Ernst Bloch, *The Principle of Hope,* 3 vols., trans. Neville Plaice, Stephen Plaice, and Paul Knight (Cambridge: MIT Press, 1986). In my view, the deepest insight is expressed in this passage of Hegel's preface: "To recognize reason as the rose in the cross of the present and thereby to enjoy the present, this rational insight yields *reconciliation* with reality—a reconciliation which philosophy affords to all those who once have received the inward calling to *comprehend*" (*Hegel's Philosophy of Right,* 12).

2

Toward a Modern Polis:
Hegel's Evolving Political Thought

reat works rarely emerge suddenly in philosophy, as in the arts.
Commonly, such works are nurtured by a conducive climate of
opinion that, in turn, is preceded by a long line of guideposts
and precursors, preparing the ground for an exceptional initiative. This
does not mean that historical background or circumstances can account
for exemplary feats, which would reduce philosophy and art to the
status of epiphenomena. History holds no key to causal explanation. But
neither is philosophy (or art) an island onto itself.

In the case of Hegel, these considerations are particularly appropriate
given his self-perception as a latecomer, pulling together and bringing
to completion central strands of modernity, or the modern age—an age
marked by the unfolding of free spirit (or the freedom of spirit). In his own
view, this unfolding was prepared by the labors of many previous generations, from the Renaissance and Reformation through the Enlightenment

to German idealism (represented by Kant, Fichte, and Schelling).[1]
These labors, in turn, were rendered possible by the spirit of Christianity that had crystallized in the Middle Ages but whose inner substance
had been announced and formulated by classical philosophy in Greece.
Thus modernity, for Hegel, stood at the apex of a long teleology of
spiritual maturation—and it was the task of philosophy (his philosophy)
fully to comprehend and articulate its meaning.

Life and Times

Just as the spirit of modernity, Hegel's thought did not spring full-
blown from the head of Zeus. Like the age he sought to comprehend,
his philosophy—particularly his political philosophy—reflected a long
process of maturation and seasoning. Hegel was born in 1770 in Stuttgart, the son of a revenue official. He was a boy at the time of the
American Revolution and in his late teens at the outbreak of the French
Revolution. After having attended grammar school in his native Stuttgart, he went in 1788 to the seminary in Tübingen (*Tübinger Stift*) where
he studied for five years, concentrating on philosophy (especially Enlightenment philosophy), the classics, and theology. Thus the spirit of modern,
enlightened freedom, and the legacy of holism—deriving from Christianity
and the classics—were the formative pillars in his education.

Among his fellow students in Tübingen were Hölderlin and Schelling
with whom he formed long-lasting friendships. In 1789, the winds—or
rather the storms—of the French Revolution penetrated the tranquility
of the seminary, being greeted by many students with enthusiasm as the
beginning of a great political and intellectual resurgence. It is reported
that, jointly with Schelling, Hegel planted a "freedom tree" at the
university and that he also became involved in a political club es-
pousing French ideas, which hence was subject to police investigation.[2]

After leaving the seminary, Hegel did not join the ministry but
instead went to Berne in Switzerland as a tutor. There he devoted
himself in earnest to the study of Kantian philosophy. Kant's major
works—inaugurated by the *Critique of Pure Reason*—had just appeared
in the preceding decade and had managed to put Western thought on a

new footing under the auspices of the spirit of rational critique, a critique addressed both to traditional metaphysical assumptions and to outmoded social and political conditions. The impact of this reading on Hegel was profound. He wrote in a letter to Schelling in 1795: "From the Kantian system and its ultimate consummation I expect a revolution in Germany which will start with principles that are already there and merely require to be worked out and be applied to all hitherto existing knowledge."

In Berne and its surrounding regions, Hegel had occasion to observe at close hand—and criticize—old-fashioned feudal-aristocratic practices and institutions, which stood in sharp conflict with enlightened demands of individual freedom and modern principles of constitutional government. As he realized at the time, demands for freedom were closely linked with individual economic initiative and property rights. This insight led him to a study of (classical) political economy, focusing his attention on the writings of Sir James Steuart, the mentor and contemporary of Adam Smith. Under the impact of these writings, Hegel gained an appreciation of modern free enterprise and market economics, a familiarity that later was going to surface in more elaborate form in his conception of *civil society*. Yet, while recognizing the role of free enterprise, he also was critical or apprehensive of a narrow economism, that is, of an exclusive focus on private self-interest to the detriment of public and moral bonds. Largely under the influence of classical authors, Hegel opposed a purely economic liberalism and a contractually founded *night watchman* state, seeking to vindicate instead a community or polity of virtue as the framework for public freedom.[3]

From Berne, Hegel moved in late 1796 to Frankfurt, again as a tutor—a position that his friend Hölderlin had been able to secure for him. During the roughly four years he spent there, he became increasingly apprehensive of a certain abstractness beleaguering modern Enlightenment thought, including even Kant's critical rationalism. No doubt this apprehension was in part nurtured by the aftermath of the French Revolution, particularly the so-called reign of terror, which demonstrated to Hegel the dangers of an abstract, or noncontextual, conception of human freedom. Contextualizing human freedom meant attentiveness to concrete history, including its cultural and religious dimensions.

In developing this sensitivity, Hegel was again guided by various authors and mentors, including perhaps the proximity of Hölderlin. Most prominent, however, was the influence of Johann Gottfried Herder, who—a former student of Kant—had of late come to underscore the role of history, poetry, and culture and who, in doing so, had emerged as the main inspiration of early German Romanticism (*Sturm und Drang,* "storm and stress"). To some extent, this historical-cultural turn was evident in the sequence of Hegel's theological writings composed during this decade (referred to later).

In 1801, Hegel made his first attempt at an academic career, moving for this purpose to Jena where Schelling had already been teaching for a few years; earlier Jena had been a hub of *Sturm und Drang.* Following the writing of his Latin habilitation (or qualifying thesis), he was appointed a university lecturer and finally an extraordinary professor. It was in Jena that Hegel published his first philosophical treatise, an essay on the difference in the perspectives of Fichte and Schelling that sided largely with the latter's holism as against Fichte's radical individualism. Yet, these affinities for Schelling's views did not last very long, as Hegel soon grew disenchanted with certain intuitive and antirationalist tendencies that Schelling shared with the Romantics. It was also in Jena that Hegel composed a work that first established him as a major thinker: the *Phenomenology of Spirit.* As it happened, the book was completed in 1806 just at the time when Napoleon gained victory over Prussia in the battle near Jena—an event that Hegel still greeted as a liberating signal in tune with the progress of modern freedom.[4]

Because the university was closed, Hegel left Jena to become editor of a newspaper in Bamberg (Bavaria). Finding little challenge or satisfaction in this occupation he moved on to Nuremberg in 1808 to accept the rectorship at a classical secondary school (*Gymnasium*), a position he held for 8 years. It was in Nuremberg that both his personal life and his philosophical ideas began to stabilize and to assume distinct contours. In 1811, he married a woman many years his junior, laying the groundwork for a happy marriage and family life. Shortly afterward, he began publishing his *Science of Logic (Wissenschaft der Logik)* in two successive volumes or parts, a work that presented the basic logical or (rather) ontological premises of his evolving "system" of thought. Gaining almost instant recognition through these volumes, he received offers of professorships at various universities, among which he chose Heidelberg.

In Heidelberg, Hegel published—mainly for use in his own lecture courses—the imposing *Encyclopedia of Philosophical Sciences* (*Enzyklopädie der philosophischen Wissenschaften im Grundrisse*), which offered for the first time an overview and exposition of his system as a whole. Largely on the basis of this work, he received and accepted in 1818 a call to the university of Berlin, assuming a chair in philosophy that had been left vacant by Fichte's death. This move to Berlin inaugurated the most productive and influential period of Hegel's life—an influence only dampened or circumscribed by the largely restorative (if not reactionary) mood of the time. Students began to flock to Berlin from all parts of Germany and from abroad. A kind of Hegelian "school" started to emerge whose contours were broad and elusive but whose accents (on the whole) were set against both reactionary nostalgia and reckless progressivism.

During these years in Berlin, Hegel fleshed out his system in numerous directions, developing it into a comprehensive, nearly encyclopedic fabric of thought. Actually, not many works were published during this time. Hegel concentrated his efforts mainly on his lecture courses—the contents of which were published posthumously (largely on the basis of student notes). The early years of his career in Berlin saw the publication of his *Philosophy of Right* (initially titled *Naturrecht und Staatswissenschaft im Grundrisse* and later renamed *Grundlinien der Philosophie des Rechts*). Later during this period, a second and much enlarged edition of the *Encyclopedia* appeared, amplified by myriad explanatory notes. The truly comprehensive character of Hegel's thought was revealed in his lecture courses, which ranged from aesthetics to the philosophy of religion to the philosophy of history and the history of philosophy. These lectures throughout showed the imprint of his judicious, balancing mind. While his historical reflections tried both to salvage and to transcend legacies of the past, his comments on religion steered a middle course between a narrow rationalism (reducing faith to self-interest) and a more emotive-intuitive bent (associated mainly with Schleiermacher, his colleague in Berlin).

In 1829, Hegel was made rector of the university. The following year—punctuated by the July Revolution—was for him a time of anxiety.

Although in favor of constitutional reforms he feared the prospect of excesses reminiscent of the French reign of terror. His reformist leanings were amply evident in his last published work, an essay on the English Reform Bill of 1831 that—while criticizing its limitations—stressed the beneficial effects of this legislation on the dismantling of outdated privileges and feudal abuses. That same year of 1831 witnessed a cholera epidemic that swept through Germany. While working on a revision of his *Science of Logic*, Hegel in the fall succumbed to that illness (or else to a severe stomach ailment) and was buried in Berlin next to Fichte.

In the aftermath of Hegel's death, some of his friends and pupils busily began to assemble his writings and manuscripts. The result was a multivolume edition of his *Collected Works,* which contained many previously unpublished pieces, including his lectures on *Aesthetics* as well as his *Philosophy of Religion,* his *Philosophy of History,* and the *History of Philosophy.* Although impressive in scope, the edition was far from conveying a correct picture of the full range of Hegel's writings. In his Hegel biography of 1844, Rosenkranz (a former student) alluded to some "early" manuscripts he had seen and that were said to antedate the publication of the *Phenomenology of Spirit.* The reference was sufficiently intriguing for subsequent generations of scholars to search through Hegel's papers and manuscripts left at the University of Berlin. In 1905, Dilthey published a study on the young Hegel (*Die Jugendgeschichte Hegels*), concentrating on newly discovered manuscripts written before the Jena period. Two years later, his student Nohl edited a series of Hegel's early theological writings, making available for the first time manuscripts dating from Hegel's tutorial days in Berne and Frankfurt. Shortly afterward, further research revealed that the time in Jena had been much more productive than previously assumed. The year 1915 saw the publication of an early version of the *Encyclopedia* composed in Jena (sometimes termed his *first system*). Subsequent years brought to light other manuscripts of the Jena period, including versions of his *Logic* and his *Realphilosophie.* In the meantime, Lasson had begun (in 1907) a new edition of Hegel's collected works incorporating many previously unpublished manuscripts, an effort that was continued in subsequent decades, suspended during World War II, and resumed by Hoffmeister after the war. The effort overlapped to some extent with the reprinting (with slight changes) of the first collection of Hegel's writings, now as a centenary edition in 26 volumes under the direction of Glockner. At the present time, the Hegel Archives in Bochum are in the process of issuing a revised critical edition of Hegel's works, an undertaking that again yields many new discoveries, though hardly of the dramatic kind made in preceding decades.

Hegel's Philosophical System

As revealed in his collected works, Hegel's thought is an imposing and sprawling edifice, encompassing in intent all dimensions of knowledge and experience. In its comprehensive scope, his thought resembles the Aristotelian corpus and the *Summa* of Thomas Aquinas (as well as the *new science* of Vico). Yet, his work is impressive not only for its breadth of scope. Animating the entire edifice and rendering it habitable, there is a quasi-Platonic impulse pursued with gripping intensity and fervor. The affinity with Plato is evident in the centerstaging of dialogue—now restyled and systematized in the form of dialectics. More important, the affinity surfaces in their shared idealism, or their common focus on *idea* or *spirit*.

As in the case of Plato, idealism for Hegel did not mean a vague utopianism or a simple attachment to higher ideals. Instead, as Hegel repeatedly emphasized, idealist philosophy insists that only spirit or idea is truly actual or "real" (*wirklich*) in an ontological sense—with the result that idealism and realism begin to converge. This insistence, one should note, does not imply the rejection or denial of external reality or of such dimensions as matter or material objects. Rather, what idealism holds is that the essence, or inner sense, of matter and all (ontic) beings is idea or spirit. In a Platonic vein, there is here a distinction—although not a separation—between a contingent or finite reality and an essential or infinite reality, with the latter ultimately merging with *absolute spirit*. All contingent or finite modes of being, from this vantage, are basically a partial manifestation, or epiphany, of spirit—just as spirit requires contingent reality for purposes of self-disclosure and self-realization. The central aim of Hegel's philosophy was to demonstrate the role of spirit as the founding agency and animating truth in all reality. Given the religious overtones of this aim—the coincidence of absolute spirit with the divine—his work constitutes a monumental theodicy designed to vindicate the wholeness of being against all forms of fragmentation, corruption, and despair.

While akin in impulse or orientation, Plato's legacy was transformed by Hegel in numerous ways. First of all, Hegel construed spirit not simply as a pliant receptacle reflecting cosmic truth. Rather, following a central *motif* of modern philosophy—deriving from Descartes—he equated spirit or idea with subjectivity or consciousness and hence ultimately with freedom (although not in a private-idiosyncratic sense). Accordingly, self-disclosure of spirit involved for him a steady deepening of self-consciousness. At the same time, Hegelian philosophy—more than its Platonic precursor—was bent on mediation and "sublation" (*Aufheburg*). Like Aristotle before him, Hegel sought to build a teleological bridge between the two worlds of experience, that is, between the domain of essential-infinite being and that of contingent reality, or between essence and existence. More precisely, he aimed to pinpoint the developmental process through which spirit, as essential being, unfolds out of contingent reality—or (figuratively put) to indicate the formative stages leading from the cave into the light of truth. This movement was the heart of his dialectics.

As previously indicated, dialectics for Hegel did not mean an abstract formula but an experiential-ontological occurrence. In dialectical terms, no contingent being or phenomenon stands or is able to stand by itself. Rather, every particularity points beyond itself to a larger web of meaning—which, in turn, intimates the disclosure of being in the epiphany of spirit. Such disclosure, one should add, does not simply mean a canceling of particularity. Under the auspices of sublation—that is, the simultaneous transcendence and preservation of levels of experience—every contingent or immediately given phenomenon is both true and false: false in its contingent separateness, but true as an anticipation (*Vorschein*) of essential spirit. Expressed differently, through negation of the false separateness, reflection leads to a higher, more holistic level of insight on which concrete particularity is both reflectively transcended and preserved or salvaged in its true being or meaning.

Dialectical movement of this kind pervades Hegel's philosophical system in its entirety or its comprehensive structure. In his *Encyclopedia,* Hegel differentiated between three levels, or stages, in the formative self-realization of spirit: *abstract immediacy, concrete self-alienation,* and *mediated synthesis in the self-knowledge of spirit.* On the level of abstract immediacy we discover the *science of logic,* which furnishes the basic categories and principles governing thought or consciousness as such. This is the level, or stage, of spirit for itself—a stage that hovers precariously between truth and falsity. Its categories are false in their abstract separateness but true in their intimation of a more fully developed mode of thought. The stage of pure abstractness is negated and transcended through a turn to the realm of contingency and finite reality, that is above all the realm of nature.

In confronting nature, reflection encounters the *otherness of spirit* and thus undergoes a process of self-alienation by becoming enmeshed in a domain of opacity and sheer externality (or a world in itself). Yet, although alien to pure thought, nature is not simply the negation of spirit but rather a mode of its self-realization or actualization (in the guise of externality). The task of the philosophy of nature is to break through this external opacity and to uncover in the processes of nature the concealed workings of spirit. Approached in this light, the laws of nature again are both true and false: the latter because of their external status, and the former because of their (disguised) realization of spirit.

In a renewed dialectical move, externality is in turn negated and transcended by a reflective shift to human consciousness as it unfolds in history, culture, and religion. Although human existence is embedded in nature, consciousness is able to extricate itself from nature's opacity and to perceive the entire world (including the human mind) as manifestation of a higher spirit whose dictates are inscribed in every finite being. In this manner, consciousness mediates between the abstractness of pure thought and the contingency of external nature. Moreover, in the mode of self-consciousness, consciousness offers a glimpse or window into fully self-realized spirit (that is, the stage of spirit in and for itself).

In addition to governing the system as a whole, dialectics also penetrated into the various stages of the formative process. Thus, on the level of logic or pure thought, we find a tripartite movement from being to essence to concept. In Hegel's view, being itself was a merely abstract and indefinite category. As such, the term is void of content and basically coincides with nonbeing (or nothingness). To overcome this void, thought has to move to the level of *becoming,* which preserves the truth of the (false) opposition because, in the process of becoming, a being both is and is not. In this process, indeterminacy (that is, lack of specific content) is transcended; by means of concrete or determinate negation, a distinct being profiles itself against pure being (and nonbeing). Hegel calls this emergent-determinate entity *Dasein,* or existence. Yet by itself, *Dasein* is again only a brute or nontransparent category. To render it transparent, a reflective act is required that discloses the inner truth of *Dasein* and hence the *essence* of becoming. Focus on essence, however, brings to the fore an internal conflict or rupture, namely, that between essence and appearance, universal and finite reality. This conflict can be healed only on the level of the *concept,* where essence and appearance are mediated and transcended in a concrete judgment.

Dialectics persists in the domain of nature or natural philosophy where Hegel traced a triadic movement from mechanics (stipulating basic categories like time and space) through inorganic physics to organic physics and biology—steps that signal nature's progressive transparency to mind. Hegel's *dialectical imagination* reached its fullest and most subtle expression in the field of actual consciousness, that is, the philosophy of spirit. Here the sequence leads from subjective spirit, seen as an immediately given datum (partially amenable to psychological inquiry), to the levels of objective spirit and absolute spirit, with the former subdivided, in turn, into the phases of abstract right, morality, and ethical life (*Sittlichkeit*), and the latter comprising the dimensions of art, religion, and philosophy. Because Hegel's political thought is located chiefly on the level of objective spirit, I leave further details here to a later discussion.[5]

The preceding comments, to be sure, only convey a sketch, or skeleton, of Hegel's philosophical system, a sketch belying the immense richness and nuanced shadings of his work. Moreover, there are many areas or facets of this work that have not yet been alluded to (and cannot be explored in this context) where his dialectical subtlety yields a rich harvest of insights (usually along the triadic path of factual immediacy, reflectiveness, and concrete actuality). An example is his philosophy of history that presents mankind as evolving from a stage of natural savagery through a stage of externally (often violently) imposed law and order to a level at which humans can freely understand and accept the rationality of civilized rules and public life (a level that, for Hegel, coincided basically with modernity). Similarly, his philosophy of religion traced a movement from natural mythology to revealed legislation to a form of inner-directed religious life (exemplified by Christianity, chiefly in its Protestant form). Resonances of this sequence can also be found in his aesthetics or philosophy of art where art forms are differentiated along the rubrics of mythical-symbolic, classical, and Romantic modes of expression.

No doubt, Hegel himself was sometimes carried away by his systematizing bent—in the direction of compressing the vital momentum of dialectics into a lifeless schema. Among many others, Croce has been eloquent in spotlighting and bemoaning this occasional tendency. Croce wrote:

> The Hegelian dialectic has so often been satirized, but no satire can compare with that which the author himself unconsciously gives of it, when he tries to think Africa, Asia, and Europe, or the hand, the nose, and the ear, or family patrimony, paternal authority, and the last will and testament, with the same rhythm with which he had thought being, nothingness, and becoming.

For Croce, triadic schematism of this kind—which surfaces sometimes in historical accounts but "runs riot" in natural philosophy—was no ground for indicting Hegel's system as such. Instead, insight into the workings of that system, he noted, might instill a "feeling of admiration for that closely-knit web of errors [in specific application]—for the method of that madness, as Polonius would have said."[6]

Early Political and Theological Writings

The breadth of Hegel's philosophical system needs to be constantly kept in mind, even when attention is given to a distinct facet or area of his thought. As in a richly woven tapestry, all facets of his work are closely interconnected and no strand can be pulled out or sharply isolated without damage to the rest. The present study focuses on Hegel's political thought, but it does so in full awareness of these interconnections. In the case of Plato and Aristotle, it is commonly accepted that their political writings cannot be properly understood apart from or outside their broader metaphysical framework. This rule applies even more aptly to the Hegelian opus. The categories and principles laid down in the science of logic form the groundwork animating the entire sprawling edifice—from natural philosophy to the crowning apex of the philosophy of spirit where these principles are not discarded but rather fully developed and actualized.

Students of politics in particular need to be reminded of the grand holism of Hegel's work—as an antidote to professional myopia or deformation. Politics, for Hegel, was not a master-discipline dominating or embracing all other modes of life (to this extent, his approach was clearly not totalitarian). In his philosophy of spirit, political institutions were overarched and complemented by more "absolute" modes of thought, like art, religion, and philosophy. While not all-embracive, politics also could not neatly be segregated or isolated from other domains of experience. Hence, Hegel's teachings on the topic were not confined to specifically political treatises but were often interspersed with other issues. This is particularly true of his early writings in which political and religious reflections frequently coalesce.

As previously indicated, Hegel's tutorial years in Berne were devoted to an intensive study of Kantian philosophy seen as the culmination of Enlightenment thought and of the modern spirit of (inner) freedom. Under the influence partly of Kant and partly of works on classical economics, Hegel during this period undertook a study of the political and economic conditions in Berne—a study that unfortunately has not survived. What is preserved from the time, however, is a German translation with a preface, written by Hegel, of a French pamphlet on the situation in the so-called Pays de Vaud, which was administered by Berne.

The comments and notes, attached to the translation, are suffused with liberal Enlightenment principles and their insistence on constitutional or legal safeguards and reforms. Both in the political and the economic domains, Hegel attacked the feudal and oligarchical structure

of the Bernese administration, a regime devoid of any guidelines promoting individual rights and equity. The strongest strictures were addressed at the absence of written legal codes (particularly a penal code)
and the lack of even a semblance of separation of powers (evident in the
absorption of legislative and judicial functions by executive authority).
While endorsing Enlightenment principles, Hegel's comments took
exception to a narrow economic type of liberalism—sometimes bran-
dished in defense of Berne—a type bent on reducing public freedom to
property rights and citizenship to economic self-interest. According to
apologists of Berne, the city's regime was vindicated by its low level
of taxation, said to correspond to a high level of individual freedom.
Taking a strongly political stance (inspired partly by the classics),
Hegel rejected this equation of freedom and self-interest. As he pointed
out, the equation was completely invalidated by the example of England,
a country where a high level of taxation coincided with a high degree
of public freedom and a strong sense of citizenship. In Hegel's view,
public freedom was measured not by the level or quantity of taxation
but by the criterion of whether taxes were self-imposed. As he added in
an intriguing side glance at developments in America,

> The duties which the English Parliament imposed on tea imported into
> America were extremely light; but what caused the American Revolu-
> tion was the feeling of the Americans that with this totally insignificant
> sum, which the duties would have cost them, they would have lost their
> most important right.[7]

Easily, the most intriguing and revealing writings dating from the
same period deal with religious issues, particularly with the issue of
civil religion (or folk religion), seen as a leaven animating public life.
In large measure, the writings reflected Hegel's need to bridge or
reconcile his theological training in Tübingen with his fervor for Enlightenment ideas and especially for Kantian ethics predicated on moral
self-legislation. As one may note, Enlightenment for Hegel did not
signal a simple turn to secularism (or secularization) but rather a
gateway to purified religious belief divorced from clerical structures
and congruent with the demands of inner-directed morality. As he
observed in an essay composed at the end of his Tübingen period,
popular or civil religion (as the complement of individual piety) had to

satisfy a number of requirements. Its teachings had to be "founded on universal reason," although "imagination, the heart, and the senses must not go away empty-handed in the process." Moreover, its scope had to be such "that all of life's needs, including public and official transactions, are bound up with it." These demands in his view, were fulfilled in a properly construed Christian community (purged of *fetishistic* dogmas)—as they had been in the public life of the Greeks, whose faith "was based on a profoundly moral demand of reason and lovingly animated by the warm breath of their feelings."

Similar sentiments emerge in manuscripts written during the early years in Berne (and preserved only as fragments). Relying on the distinction between legality and morality, Hegel commented there that "since there are no institutions specifically intended to promote respect for the moral law and the disposition to fulfill it in keeping with its spirit . . . we are not inclined to dissociate religion and morality, but on the contrary consider the latter to be the primary purpose of religious institutions." Public religion, from this vantage, was even more crucial than civil legislation, for "man's highest purpose is morality, and among the various natural tendencies that promote it, man's religious instinct is one of the most important." To be sure, to fulfill its moral purpose, religion had to be inner directed and not externally imposed as a dogma:

> Making objective religion subjective: this great undertaking the state must assume. To this end its institutions must be compatible with freedom of conviction; they must not violate conscience and liberty, but exert only an indirect influence on the motives of the will.[8]

Still from the Berne years we have an essay that is perhaps the most spirited (and inspiring) piece of the young philosopher. Called "The Life of Jesus," the essay presented Jesus as the embodiment of pure inner-directed morality and thus of the highest aspirations of Kantian ethics. Commenting on the opening lines of John's gospel, Hegel equated *word* with reason, even pure reason—noting that "pure reason, transcending all limits, is divinity itself," and that "through reason man learns of his destiny, the unconditional purpose of his life." It was John the Baptist who reawakened the people to this purpose or destiny—"not as to something alien, but rather as to something they should be able to find within, in their true self."

Jesus himself displayed this inner spirit from early childhood to his adult years and manifested it steadily in word and deed. A high point of his adult teaching was the Sermon on the Mount where, among other things, he also commented on the relation between legality and morality, asserting the superiority of the latter. "I have not come to annul what the laws demand," the essay has him say, "but rather to make them complete, to breathe spirit into these lifeless bones. Heaven and earth may pass away, but not the demands of the moral law nor the obligation to obey them." The crucial thing was not to get bogged down in empty rituals and external (heteronomous) observances: "You must not remain satisfied, like the scribes and Pharisees among you, with observing the mere letter of the law"; instead, "you must act out of respect for duty and in the spirit of the law." A later part of the essay paraphrased and expanded on Jesus' words regarding the coming kingdom, uttered at one point on the Mount of Olives. Discounting entirely the notion of an external savior or reliance on strange happenings and signs, Jesus in Hegel's account placed the emphasis squarely on inner moral growth or the spiritualization of humanity:

> Divine plans are not confined to a single people or faith, but embrace the entire human species with unpartisan love. Only when reason and virtue instead of names and slogans are recognized and practiced all over the earth may you declare the divine plan to have been accomplished. It is unwavering loyalty to this hope for mankind . . . that will keep you free of sectarian sentiment and keep you forever upright and courageous.[9]

Hegel's concern with religious ethics or a Kantian-style moral religiosity is also amply manifest in another manuscript composed roughly at the same time (though a concluding part was added later): the essay called "The Positivity of the Christian Religion." The chief aim of the essay was to show how Christ's teachings could have assumed the garb of *positivity* (a term roughly equivalent to externality or heteronomy). In Hegel's account, Jesus grew up in a faith context that had become overburdened with legalism and external ritual. In stark opposition to this background, his effort was "to raise religion and virtue to morality and to restore to morality the freedom which is its essence." Basically, he urged or preached not a virtue "grounded on authority," but rather "a free virtue springing from man's own being."

Despite this strenuous effort, positive-heteronomous features gradually and steadily crept into Christianity, and this for a number of reasons. To some extent, Jesus himself had to accommodate his teachings to the peculiarities of his environment and to the limited understanding of his followers. Among many of his disciples and followers, for example, there was a tendency to value and venerate more highly the person of Jesus rather than his teachings regarding virtue and (inner) truth. As a consequence, even the latter teachings came to acquire mysterious and authoritarian qualities—in contrast, for instance, to the philosophical teachings of a Socrates. These tendencies were aggravated by the missionary expansionism of Christianity and finally by its elevation into a state religion and the resulting assimilation to Roman imperial structures. In Hegel's words:

> This development of Christ's teachings into the positive faith of a sect gave rise to most important results both for its external form and also for its content. These results have continually and increasingly diverted it from what we take to be the essence of any true religion, including the Christian religion: that is, from having as its purpose the establishment of human duties and their underlying motives in their purity and the use of the idea of God to show the possibility of the *summum bonum.*

The elevation to a state religion, in particular, was dangerous and counterproductive. Because it is "not as a state, but only as a moral entity" that a state can "demand morality of its citizens"; on the other hand, it is impossible for a state "to force men to act out of respect for duty even if it calls religion to its aid."[10]

Hegel's move to Frankfurt—and his proximity there to Hölderlin—ushered in subtle changes in his outlook that, in due course, surfaced in his writings. While still opposed to legalism and to positivity seen as external heteronomy, Hegel during this time also grew disenchanted with strict Kantianism, particularly with the formalism of Kantian ethics and its reliance on categorical duty (as opposed to human inclination). This does not mean, as is sometimes asserted, that Hegel abandoned Kant's moral fervor (or that he "suddenly broke" with

Enlightenment thought, as Kroner has claimed). Rather, the change in outlook was more subtle.

Without relinquishing the spirit of his previous mentor, Hegel came to realize the one-sided abstractness of inner-directed duty and hence strove to find a path bridging and reconciling the inner and outer domains and also the realms of finite (phenomenal) and infinite (noumenal) reality. During the years in Frankfurt, he found the central resource or cornerstone for such a bridge in *love*—a love that, again, was instantiated in exemplary fashion in Jesus. The essay "The Spirit of Christianity and Its Fate" clearly reflects this subtle shift of accent. In the footsteps of previous writings, the essay again denounces traditional legalism and heteronomy. In a new departure, however, its pages also criticize duty-centered *morality* (a term used to designate Kantian ethics).

The Sermon on the Mount serves Hegel, once again, to illustrate this ethical point. In Hegel's portrayal, the sermon does not teach "reverence for the laws" but rather exhibits something "which fulfills the law while annulling it as law." At the same time, the sermon rises above the commands of strict duty—commands that "presuppose a cleavage" between reason and inclination and hence a "domination" of rational rules (*thou shalt*) over the latter. Kant's interpretation of Christ's central injunction—to "love God above everything and thy neighbor as thyself"—in the sense of a "command requiring respect for a law which commands love," involved for Hegel a "profound reduction" of its meaning to a command or imperative. As Hegel pointed out, seen as love inclination is a virtue or synthesis in which law or duty "loses its universality and the subject its particularity." In fact, both law and the individual subject "lose their opposition," while in Kant's conception the opposition remains and "the universal becomes the master and the particular the mastered." In the fulfillment of law or duty, he added, moral disposition ceases to be (abstractly) "universal, opposed to inclination," just as inclination ceases to be "particular, opposed to law"; in turn, this correspondence of law and inclination "is life and, as the relation of differents to one another, love."[11]

Both in their lively style and their content, the preceding essays showed the influence of, or at least an affinity with, the thinking of Hegel's seminary friends and also aspects of Romanticism. This affinity was openly underscored in a programmatic statement written by Hegel just before his departure from Berne (and apparently meant as a joint manifesto). In the manner of Hölderlin and Schelling, the statement advocated a close liaison of philosophy and aesthetics and hence an alliance of truth, goodness, and beauty. "The philosopher," we read there, "must have as much aesthetic power as the poet," a unison through which both activities are ennobled: "In this manner poetry acquires a higher dignity and thus becomes again what it was in the beginning—a teacher of mankind." At the same time, philosophy had to make room for concrete (or sensual) folk religion, in accordance with the maxim "monotheism of reason and heart, polytheism of imagination and art."

Regarding the political implications of this program, the statement noted somewhat boldly that compared with the spirit of humanity

> there is no idea of the state, for the state is something purely mechanical—and there is no [spiritual] idea of a machine. Only what is an object of freedom may be called "idea." Therefore we must transcend the state! For every state must treat free men as cogs in a machine. And this is precisely what should not happen; hence the state must cease to exist.

This cessation of the state would usher in the "absolute freedom of all spirits" and ultimately the "equal development of all capabilities, those of the individual and the community"; this would mean "the reign of universal freedom and equality of spirits." The political postulate of freedom and equality continued to reverberate through Hegel's writings in the Frankfurt years—with particular attention to economic dangers besetting the harmony of public life. "In the states of modernity," Hegel wrote at the time, "security of property is the hinge on which all legislation turns and to which most of the rights of citizens relate." Pointing to examples in Periclean Athens, in Rome during the period of the Gracchi, and in Florence under the Medici, Hegel tried to show how "the disproportionate wealth of a few citizens can threaten even the best type of constitution and thus destroy freedom itself." In light of these experiences, the French *sansculottes* were perhaps unjustly maligned when one ascribed "to rapacity alone their attempt to reach a more equal distribution of property."[12]

The Constitution of Germany

Seen together, Hegel's early writings were a spirited defense of enlightened freedom—though freedom was not identified with self-interest (or even with private morality) but seen as an emblem of nonrepressive public life where reason, imagination, and sensibility blend. The outlook animating these writings is sometimes attributed to a certain youthful élan or Romantic exuberance—an élan that was completely abrogated or canceled in the work of the "mature" Hegel. This assessment, in my view, is entirely mistaken, or at least badly overstated. To be sure, these writings were often more suggestive than rationally persuasive, more filled with fertile glimpses or vistas than with fully developed arguments. To achieve a more coherent articulation and development of his ideas was precisely Hegel's life-long goal, but a goal that was not essentially inconsistent with his early inspiration. Thus his concern with civil or folk religion as a social bond was not simply abandoned in his later writings in favor of a bland secularism, but rather expanded and transformed through the conception of an ethically suffused citizenship. Religion in this conception was not simply discarded—although, in tune with his early insight, it could not be mandated by public power and hence had to remain independent (though not completely separated) from the state.

Similar considerations apply to the bonding and reconciling power of love extolled during the Frankfurt years. Again, Hegel's later work did not simply renege on this notion and replace it with coldhearted, logical calculation. Taken in its strong sense, it is true, love tended to be confined later to the private domain; yet its animating spirit continued to reverberate throughout his entire philosophical system. In a way, the notion of dialectics with its process of diremption and sublation of opposites was a rational explication of love's potency—quite in line with an early manuscript in which Hegel had portrayed love's movement as the sequence of union, separation and differentiated reunion.[13] Seen in this light, I believe Hegel's popular image needs to be revised. Far from being the abstruse pedant, as he is sometimes pictured, Hegel throughout his life was basically an *erotic* philosopher, in tune with the legacy deriving from Socrates and Plato.

As previously indicated, Hegel in 1801 moved from Frankfurt to Jena to begin his academic career. There he had occasion to ponder and ripen some of the more embryonic or undeveloped elements of his thought. Much of this pondering occurred on a strictly philosophical level (seemingly) removed from the clamor of events of the day. Schelling's presence in Jena prompted Hegel to sort out his position regarding his friend's work and regarding German idealism in general. His treatise on the difference between Fichte and Schelling—written just before he joined the university—tried to steer a course between Fichte's *subjective idealism* (with its separation of ego and nature) and Schelling's more *holistic-intuitive vision.*

While leaning somewhat in the direction of Schelling, Hegel (as mentioned) came to regard his friend's approach as marred by instantaneous synthesis and by neglect of the differences and diremptions marking human life and requiring intelligible mediation. But how was it possible to combine or bridge the valid demands of subjective rationality with the desire for holistic unity? To articulate his views on the matter (mainly to himself), Hegel during his first year in Jena composed an ambitious manuscript—the so-called *first system*—which offered a rough sketch of his evolving system of thought in a manner anticipating his later *Encyclopedia* (although without thematizing fully the philosophies of nature and spirit). The main accent of the manuscript was on logic or logical knowledge—with a twist. *Logic,* in Hegel's treatment, did not simply mean mental acrobatics but the inner movement of thought itself, a movement reflecting the ontological parameters of reflective life. In line with classical teachings, logic still resonated with the Greek notions of *logos* and "idea," notions now filtered through the media of modern rationality and Kantian critique.[14] Thought's movement was seen as an unfolding dialectic of oppositions, in a manner distantly akin to the pattern of Platonic dialogues. The deeper wellspring of this movement, however, was *spirit,* an agency capable of bridging and progressively sublating the distinction between thought and being and between immanence and transcendence.

Given its ontological bent, philosophical logic from Hegel's vantage could never be neatly segregated from substantive, worldly contents—including social and political reality. In the midst of trying to design his philosophical system, Hegel found time in 1802 to complete a manuscript on which he had been working for a few years and which has been titled (by editors) "The Constitution of Germany." The essay offered an astute diagnosis of political conditions in Germany, particularly of the status of the old German empire (still seen as continuation of the Holy Roman empire). The final verdict of the diagnosis was terminal illness—a verdict anticipating by several years the actual dissolution of that empire. In Hegel's analysis, the basic source of the illness was the absence of anything resembling a "public realm," more specifically, the appropriation (or colonization) of that realm by feudal customs and estates; by the vast array of duchies, kingdoms, and principalities; and generally by private-particularistic interests. As he wrote in a draft that dates from the Frankfurt years, "It is a pretty commonly shared conviction that, apart from despotic (that is, non-constitutional) states, no country has a more deplorable constitution than the German Empire."

The ground for this deplorable situation was the old-fashioned and outdated character of the imperial structure—a structure that was "the work of past centuries" but that was no longer carried or animated by the "life of our contemporary time." As an outgrowth of long-vanished ideas and beliefs, the old empire could not offer nourishment or an occasion for lived engagement to people of a postrevolutionary age: "The edifice with its pillars and decorations now stands in the world isolated from the spirit of the time." What was left of the public or political domain was an amalgam of rights and privileges vested in princes, estates, and corporations. Public legal principles were not founded on concrete reason but were *abstractions* from empirical conditions: "In its original substance, German public law is thus basically private law, and political rights are a legal possession or property." To this, an early (draft) "Introduction" added the following: "The potent universality as source of all law has disappeared in the German Empire because it has become isolated and turned into particularity."[15]

The text of 1802 announced the verdict bluntly. "Germany is no longer a state," the opening sentence asserted. The demise of the German empire as a state was concretely demonstrated by the defeat of German princes at the hands of the armies of the French republic. However, to penetrate beyond surface phenomena and grasp the deeper causes or reasons of events, philosophical reflection was needed—a reflection encouraged and invited by the return of peace time. Hegel's essay had no other purpose than to contribute to such deepened reflection:

> The thoughts contained in this essay, when published, can have no other aim or effect save that of promoting the understanding of what is and thus a calmer insight and also a moderate acceptance of it in word and deed. For it is not reality (what is) that makes us irascible and resentful, but the thought that it is not as it ought to be. But once we look beyond chance or hazard to the compelling reasons of reality, then we recognize also that it is as it ought to be.

For Hegel, the meaning of public or political events could not be grasped through reliance on abstract norms or principles divorced from actual experience; nor was it sufficient to cling to empirical phenomena or details. In the case of the German empire, it was hopeless to try to comprehend its status by focusing on abstract rules or legal artifacts, which precisely tended to camouflage or shield from view the internal decay and dissolution of the state. On the other hand, the tendency of some legal and political theorists to fasten onto empirical description was nothing but an admission of defeat and of a pliant willingness to adjust to existing conditions (of decay). In opposition to both approaches, Hegel insisted on the need of *conceptual* understanding, that is, an understanding geared toward the inner reason or idea of reality. Viewed in this light, the status of Germany could not be in doubt: "The question how the German constitution should conceptually be defined is no longer in dispute. What can no longer be conceptually grasped, has ceased to exist."[16]

Regarding the meaning of statehood, Hegel basically took his bearings from the structure of modern European states, particularly that of England and France (though minus the excessive centralization of power evident in the latter). "In order for a multitude to constitute a state," the essay noted, "it is necessary that it form a system of common (military) defense and of public authority." Public authority implied a structure of supreme governance and the existence of general or universal laws, as distinguished from particularistic customs or strictly private interests. In view of discouraging recent experiences in battle, Hegel put considerable emphasis on the system of military defense—not simply as a vague postulate but as the actual instantiation and expres-

sion of a shared public will. As he stated in another conceptual definition: "A multitude of human beings can only call itself a state if it be
united for the common defense of the entirety of its property." The
emphasis here, as one should note, was not simply on good intentions
but on the actual unity of the public will. Another feature that should
be highlighted is the reference to property. In line with developments
in modern Western society, Hegel made property relations an integral
part of a constitutional order. Yet, on the level of the state, his concern
was not strictly with private property rights but with the *entirety* of
public property, that is, with a shared standard of life.

Both in terms of public authority and a common will, the German
empire did not measure up to the criterion of statehood. A state, in
Hegel's words, requires "a universal center, a monarch and estates,
wherein the various powers, foreign affairs, the armed forces, finances
relevant thereto etc., would be united," a center that would not only
direct but would also have "the power necessary for asserting itself and
its decrees, and for keeping the individual parts dependent on itself."
Such a center did not exist in Germany due to the near-chaotic dispersal
of rights and privileges throughout the realm. In view of this situation,
the German political edifice was "nothing but the sum of rights which
the individual parts have wrested from the whole," and the essence of
its constitution was a legal system "carefully seeing to it that no power
was left to the state."[17]

While stressing the need for a political center, Hegel's conception of
the state did not envisage the complete uniformity or standardization of
all dimensions of social and public life. Outside the sphere of public
law and common defense, his view allowed for a great diversity of
political arrangements as well as of local and regional customs and ways
of life; far from being crucial or determining, such features were marginal
or incidental to the nature of the body politic. In his study on Hegel's theory
of the modern state, Avineri provides a succinct list of these incidental and
politically noncrucial features. The list includes items like these: the
number of wielders of public authority; whether their status is hereditary
or elective; the degree of participation by citizens and estates in the process
of legislation; the structure of administration; the type of taxation; the
homogeneity or heterogeneity of citizens in terms of customs, ethnicity,
and language; and the presence or absence of a shared religious faith.

In this list, the last two items are particularly striking and noteworthy.
The acceptance of ethnic and linguistic diversity places Hegel in contrast to some theories of the nation-state that identify statehood and
ethnic nationality. In Avineri's words, "It is most significant to note
that it is precisely in the *modern* state that Hegel sees ethnic-linguistic
ties as unnecessary." Hegel's own statements on the issue are unambig-
uous. "In our day," his essay stated,

> the tie between members of a state in respect of manners, education, and
> language may be rather loose or even non-existent. Identity in these
> matters, once the foundation of a people's union, is now to be reckoned
> among the accidents whose character does not hinder a multitude from
> constituting a public authority . . . [In fact,] the dissimilarity in culture
> and manners is a necessary product as well as a necessary condition of the
> stability of modern states.

Whatever disadvantages arose from ethnic or linguistic diversity
could, in Hegel's view, be remedied "by the spirit and art of political
institutions." A similar consideration applied to the issue of religious
belief. Since the time of the Reformation, German principalities had
maintained a system whereby the religious denomination of the prince
determined the religion of his subjects (*cuius regio eius religio*). This
principle, however, has been rendered obsolete by modernization and
a mobile culture steadily promoting religious diversity. "Here in religion at least," we read, "an identity might have been thought necessary;
but this identity too is something which modern states are managing to
do without." As experience has taught, religious uniformity "has no
more presented wars or united peoples into a state" than religious
diversity "has in our day rent the state asunder."[18]

As reflected in the essay, Hegel's conception of the state involved a
combination of limited central power with decentralized and diversified
modes of life and with a broad scale of local and individual freedom.
In his portrayal, the strength or virtue of the old German regime resided
precisely in its cultivation of local and regional autonomy; its system
of rights and privileges had not been imposed from above but was
historically grown and the result of particularistic initiative. The defect
besetting this system was its destruction of the public sphere. For Hegel,
the task of a properly modern state was to restore the balance between

public authority and local autonomy, in a manner leaving broad room to civic freedom. As he wrote in an eloquent passage:

> This is not the place to argue at length that the government as the center of public authority must leave to the freedom of its citizens whatever is not necessary for the goal of organizing and maintaining authority and thus for domestic and external security. In fact, nothing must be as sacred to it as to permit and protect the free activity of citizens in all such matters, irrespective of all thoughts of utility; for this freedom is sacred in itself.

The balance of freedom and authority was reaffirmed in another context in which Hegel praised "those people as fortunate to whom the state gives a free hand in subordinate general activities"—just as public authority could be termed "infinitely strong if it is supported by the free and unregimented spirit of its people." As it happens, in some modern states, the balance was badly disrupted, in favor not of local particularism but of excessive centralization of power. In such states, and in the theories supporting them, the state was viewed as "a machine with a single spring which imparts movement to the entire infinite clockwork." Where this model prevailed—and France and Prussia were for Hegel outstanding examples—we find a "pedantic craving to determine every detail," an "illiberal jealousy" of individual and corporate rights, and a "mean carping at any independent citizen action." The price to be paid for this centralized paternalism was the decay of civic spirit and freedom: "A mechanical hierarchy, super-rational and devoted to 'higher' ends, shows no confidence whatever in its citizens and hence can expect none from them."[19]

The bulk of Hegel's essay probed in detail features of the old German regime, including its finances, its territorial structure, and its legal order, features that must be bypassed in the present context. One aspect that deserves mention, however, concerns the role of "estates" (*Stände*) and specifically the changing fabric of social bonds produced by the modernization of society. Hegel in this respect made explicit reference to the rise of the bourgeois middle class (*Bürgerstand*) with its emphasis on individual freedom, private property, and economic initiative—an emphasis that was bound to transform the entire social structure and the meaning of politics or public authority itself.

As he noted, during the early days of the old regime the prevalence of local and regional particularism was perhaps less troubling due to the persistence of a common religion and also to bonds of feudal vassalage and of kinship (among princes). "As long as religion was uniform," we read, "and as long as the nascent bourgeoisie had not yet introduced great heterogeneity into the social fabric, princes, dukes and lords could regard one another more readily as a whole and accordingly could act in unison." This unity, however, was ruptured with the rise of bourgeois individualism and the growing division of labor, a development that required a reconstitution of the public sphere on a new basis:

> But when through the growth of imperial cities the bourgeois sense gained ascendancy—a sense which cares only for individual particularity without regard for public order or the needs of the whole—at this point the individualization of dispositions would have demanded a more general or universal and more affirmative bond.

In lieu of the formation of such a bond and hence the construction of a modern state, however, the old German particularism was only aggravated and compounded by the proliferation of individual self-interest. This development was very different from that occurring in other Western societies, notably in England. There the numerically largest part of citizens, that is, the bourgeoisie, came to look out more and more "for their own necessities and livelihood," just as each individual became steadily preoccupied with "his own needs and private affairs." At the same time, the complexity of social and economic life increased in the same measure as foreign relations gained greater independence from the country's domestic affairs. As a result of these changes, the management of public authority "became more and more closely concentrated in a center consisting of monarch and estates" (and their representative assemblies).[20]

In view of the decay of the old German order, the conclusion of Hegel's essay pleaded for the construction of a modern German state (in a manner distantly reminiscent of Machiavelli's plea for the unification of Italy at the end of *The Prince*). In looking around for a possible agency or unifying vehicle, Hegel saw little hope for political regeneration through Prussian efforts. In fact, Prussia appeared to him at the time as the epitome of mechanistic, centralizing paternalism—a system devoid even of the liberating spirit pervading republican France. Somewhat derisively, a passage early on in the essay spoke of the "sterility" of Prussian life and of the "utter lack of scientific and artistic genius" characterizing the country. Resuming this critique, the conclusion chided Prussia for its authoritarian regime and the demise of representative institutions. "The interest of German freedom," Hegel wrote, "naturally seeks protection from a state which itself rests on this system of freedom." This desire, however, could not presently find any sustenance in Prussia where the provincial estates had "lost their significance owing to the predominance of royal power."

In these circumstances, Austria under the Habsburgs provided a more likely focus for German hopes. Citizens as well as cities and corporations had "a natural interest to look to the imperial court and to expect support there for whatever is meant now by German freedom." To be sure, Austria itself needed to be reformed to serve as a suitable vehicle for a modern state. Apart from the renunciation of old imperial pretensions, Hegel emphasized particularly the need for a reorganization of the judicial system, of the structure of military defense, and of the old "imperial diet" to be transformed into a broadly representative assembly, partly elected on the basis of new territorial divisions. As Avineri comments judiciously:

> The greatest achievements of the late eighteenth-century Habsburgs lay in their transformation of what originally amounted to a haphazard collection of dynastic domains, linked together only through personal ties of allegiance to the family, into rationally organized crownlands, measuring up to modern criteria of political organization. . . . Austrian reformism went hand in hand with a liberalizing policy towards Protestants and Jews, an aspect which certainly did not escape Hegel's attention, since religious tolerance figured so strongly in his discussion of the modern state.[21]

Knowledge, Faith and Natural Law

Hegel's stay in Jena was a very productive period, as reflected in the large number of published and unpublished manuscripts written during those years. Roughly at the same time as completing his constitutional study, he composed an essay on the relation between philosophy and religious belief and (shortly afterward) another one on natural law. In a sense, both essays were tentative steps toward articulating aspects of his philosophy of spirit, which was to become the crowning part of his system. The first essay, titled "Faith and Knowledge," was clearly a further attempt on Hegel's part to come to terms with both his seminary years and his Enlightenment leanings. It is also evidence that religious tolerance for him was not equivalent to religious indifference and that the issue of positively established faith had to be sharply distinguished from the spirit of religion itself.

As presented in the essay, the two terms of its title were not simply externally juxtaposed but intimately intertwined. Under the impact of Enlightenment teachings, the conviction was spreading that philosophy could safely be confined to the level of a secular rationalism, in a manner relegating religion to the domain of private (and arbitrary) belief. In Hegel's view, this assumption was untenable—for the simple reason that the expelled element (religion) inevitably returned to trouble the comfortable safety of reason. Far from finding within itself a secure anchor, rationalism continued to be haunted by its exiled partner—in the form of the persisting conflict between appearance and essence and between finite and infinite reality. Thus the issue presumably resolved through a simple division of intellectual labor resurfaced as a basic dilemma intrinsic to philosophical reflection. In the words of the essay, "The contrast between faith and reason is in our time a contrast within philosophy itself."[22]

Historically, in the confines of Western Christianity, the separation between faith and reason was introduced by nominalism and confirmed by the Reformation. Opposing the confident rationalism of the scholastics—their attachment to an all-embracive, substantive metaphysics—Protestant reformers proceeded to sever the bonds linking knowledge and faith, reason and revelation. On the side of philosophy, a similar segregation was promoted by Enlightenment thinkers from Descartes to Kant and particularly by the latter's confinement of philosophy to the task of critique performed within the limits of (finite) reason alone. In Hegel's view, these developments signaled an undeniable advance in human maturation and reflectiveness. By emphasizing inwardness, Protestant and enlightened thought involved a refinement of human subjectivity and moral autonomy, in opposition to external-paternalistic constraints and dogmas of the past. Yet, the advance was purchased at a price: the price of the growing separation of subject and object, of man and nature, and of immanence and transcendence.

In Reformation thought, this separation still had a tragic quality, as the gulf between human and divine reality was a source of suffering and agony. Subsequently, however, this agony was progressively muffled and subdued—especially to the extent that Enlightenment rationalism turned complacent by extolling as goal a purely secular-mundane happiness. "The sublime subjectivity of Protestantism," Hegel commented wryly, "is transformed by Enlightenment into an empirical subjectivity, and the poetry of its grief . . . into the prose of a satisfaction with this finite world." In more subtle form, this tendency persisted even in the writings of Kant and Fichte, with their endorsement of a rationalist humanism that treated "man and mankind" as absolute principles rather than "a reflected splendor of eternal beauty." According to Hegel's essay, it was time again to face up to the tragic grandeur of Reformation teachings—though not as an end in itself. Modernity or modern maturation, in his view, inevitably entailed divisiveness and diremption. Yet, in understanding the motives of diremption, philosophical reflection also prepared the ground for a healing of conflicts and oppositions. As he wrote, philosophy had to confront and try to comprehend "absolute suffering," "infinite grief" and even the "godlessness" of a purely secular world. Only in this manner—along the path of a "speculative Good Friday"—was it possible for wholeness to be restored "in all its seriousness and out of its deepest ground, and into the most joyous freedom of its true form."[23]

Hegel's reflections on diremption and wholeness were continued in his essay on natural law, formally titled "On the Scientific Methods of Studying Natural Law." In a way, the title of the essay is misleading, because its subject matter is not confined to natural-law doctrine in the narrow sense but extends to embrace much of modern jurisprudence and political theory. As on other occasions, Hegel's argument pursues a balanced course, and one escaping eclecticism by virtue of its metaphysical grounding. Just as the preceding manuscript had steered a path between secular rationalism and established faith, the new essay navigated precariously between Kantian and Fichtean formalism, on the one hand, and unprincipled empiricism (or positivism), on the other. Neither of the two approaches, the essay claimed, could yield a coherent grasp of social and political reality. "Empiricism," we read, "presents detailed contents confusedly and in connection with other details that, in their essential reality, would form an organic and living whole; but this whole is destroyed by dissection and by empiricism's elevation of inessential and isolated abstractions to the rank of ultimacy." To be sure, empiricists willingly use concepts or schemata to order their data; however, by treating these concepts in turn as contingent-empirical factors, they leave their cogency and inner connection obscure.

To remedy empiricist confusion through conceptual unity was precisely the aim of German idealist philosophy and particularly of Kant's transcendental rationalism. By focusing on the necessary or a priori conditions of experience, Kant sought to lay the groundwork for a unified framework encompassing all phenomena. As before, Hegel willingly acknowledged in this effort an advance of rational reflectiveness over the profusion of sense data, granting that there was no road leading back behind Kant's critique. Admission of this advance, however, was again severely qualified by insight into its shortcomings, particularly its inability to live up to its promise of unity. By expelling all empirical or a posteriori phenomena outside the bounds of reason, Kant's framework remained in effect purely abstract or formal and its synthesis basically contradictory or divided against itself, namely, by virtue of the form/content split. In Hegel's words, "although practical reason postulates the identity of idea and reality, the latter remains strictly opposed and external to reason. . . . While speaking of the absolute identity of idea and reality, moral theory thus does not live up to its claim; rather, moral reason is in essence the non-identity of the two elements."[24]

The defects of these discussed approaches were clearly evident in the domain of jurisprudence and political theory. While German idealism postulated absolute moral principles, these (noumenal) principles were carefully screened from contact with concrete political experience. Concern with the latter was the chief hallmark of the tradition of legal and political empiricism (especially as formulated in the British context). As is the habit of empiricism in general, empiricist political thought was by no means adverse to resorting to conceptual categories, all presumably culled from empirical data. Natural-law theories couched in this tradition were, in fact, replete with a host of diverse concepts, ranging from the *state of nature* through *natural rights* to the *social contract* and notions of royal or popular sovereignty.

Yet, in the absence of an intelligible and coherent framework, these concepts remained randomly juxtaposed and even potentially in conflict with each other. Thus the premise of a presocial, or natural, freedom was barely if at all compatible with the notion of a constituted public authority; likewise, the privileges of popular or local assemblies seemed completely at odds with royal (or executive) political prerogatives. In Avineri's words, "to Hegel, natural law theories failed to find a middle way between Hobbes and Robespierre" or between despotism and anarchy. Even in Rousseau's refined version of the natural-law model, it was by no means clear how individual will related to general will or how the general will "becomes necessarily real in individual subjects." What was lacking was attention to the issue of mediation or the interconnection of public and private life. Nor could mediation be mechanically provided or institutionally secured—as Fichte had attempted through the notion of an *ephorate,* that is, a board of control meant to supervise governmental actions. As Hegel observed, this notion was a hybrid liable to do more harm than good. For either the board was dependent on the government, and hence unable to control it, or else independent and thus a kind of countergovernment.[25]

Moving beyond transcendental rules and empiricist proliferation, Hegel's essay sought to pinpoint the holistic bond lacking in natural-law doctrines and found it in the living spirit of a people or a political community. Civic spirit, in his view, resolved or sublated the dilemma of idea and reality, of inclination and duty. Not reducible either to private interest or to abstract norms, such spirit was in effect the embodiment of "absolute ethical life" (*absolute Sittlichkeit*). In adopting this focus, Hegel clearly drew inspiration from the classical tradition of the *polis*, or *res publica*. Yet his essay was keenly aware of the impossibility of a simple return to the classical tradition—a return blocked by the modernization of Western society and the growing sway of individual initiative (sometimes, as in Germany, bordering on the complete privatization of social life).

The main carrier of this modernization was the middle class or bourgeoisie—an estate to which Hegel in this context again devoted close attention. In his portrayal, this estate was basically governed by economic self-interest and hence only distantly concerned with public life. Enmeshed in exchange relations in business and commerce, members of that class were satisfied with a minimal government and with a system of general or formal rules protecting property and insuring the performance of contracts. "The status of this estate," we read,

> is so characterized that it consists in possession as such and in the legal rules safeguarding possession. The estate forms an interrelated system [of exchange]; and by virtue of the fact that property relations are integrated into this formal unity, every individual who is capable of holding possession relates to all others on the level of generality—that is, as a *bourgeois* (*Bürger*). As a compensation for the political insignificance deriving from their position as private individuals, members of this estate enjoy the fruits of peaceful business and the complete security of such enjoyment.

Although, due to their preoccupation with private economic interest, bourgeois individuals could not fully participate in ethical life (or *Sittlichkeit*), they were not completely unaffected by ethical standards or devoid of moral rules. In fact, Hegel saw the bourgeois estate as the appropriate target group of a system of abstract-formal principles in the Kantian sense; in contrast to absolute ethics, such a system could be termed *relative morality* (namely, relative to empirical conditions). On this level, he noted, we find "the formal abstraction from specific conditions, and hence the morality of the *bourgeois* or private person for which the difference of conditions is fixed and which relies or depends on them."[26]

In contrast to the simplicity of the classical *polis*, public life in the modern age could not be holistic in an immediate or substantive sense. Under conditions of modernity, Hegel argued, ethical life had to be mediated or filtered through the welter of property relations and economic self-interest—just as absolute spirit could only come into its own by undergoing the trials and agonies of finite reality. At this point, Hegel returned to the themes of tragedy and the speculative Good Friday struck in the earlier essay. Public life seen from this angle, he noted,

> is nothing but the staging of that ethical tragedy which the absolute eternally performs with itself, in the sense that it eternally gives birth to

external objectivity in which shape it surrenders itself to suffering and death—only to rise again from the ashes into its glory. The divine in its shape and objectivity has hence a double nature, and its life is the absolute unity of these natures.

Transposed to the sphere of public life, the two natures of the spirit (or the divine) surfaced in the correlation of two social estates, one more self-interested, the other more public-spirited. Next to and superimposed on the bourgeois class, Hegel's essay recognized another class or estate: the "estate of free men" whose members are "individuals of absolute ethical life (*absolute Sittlichkeit*)." Instead of toiling in particular projects, this estate had as its task or aim "the being and maintenance of the wholeness of the ethical order."

Yet, although devoted to wholeness, free citizens of this kind were still an estate or part and hence not directly synonymous with public unity. In terms of the essay, the public, or absolute, estate could perform its function only by allowing itself to be mediated by society with its cauldron of economic interests and private initiatives; this mediation involved a complex learning process, a process signaling the slow emergence, or becoming, of public spirit. Seen as an unfolding movement, public life was not marked by instant synthesis or identity but rather by the complex interweaving of identity and difference, of universalism and particularism. Only such complex interweaving could capture the sense of public wholeness in our time. Only in light of the concrete "individuality of the whole" and the "distinctive character of a people" was it possible to perceive something like public unity. Only in this way could one see "how all parts of the constitution and of legislation, all aspects of ethical relations are permeated by the whole and thus form one edifice."[27]

Labor, Economics and Public Life

Aspects of the preceding arguments were fleshed out in greater detail in a series of manuscripts written in Jena in the years immediately following the natural-law essay (but not published during Hegel's lifetime). Foremost among these manuscripts for present purposes are the *System der Sittlichkeit* (*System of Ethical Life*) and the *Jenaer Realphilosophie* (comprising elements of his system exceeding the framework of logic). A chief aim of the *System der Sittlichkeit* was to elaborate the mediating steps, or the process of transition, leading from particular self-interest to public or absolute spirit—what Hegel later would call the movement from natural to real (or absolute) consciousness. The starting point of the study was natural intuition, that is, a preconceptual and internally undifferentiated mode of natural life. As an intuitive mode, this condition is basically a state of *feeling,* but a feeling that is at the same time purely singular and particular. Due to its singularity, this feeling soon discovers its opposition to other singular phenomena, that is, the separation of life into inside and outside or subject and object. This discovery engenders the impulse to overcome the separation, by integrating objects into oneself. In Hegel's words: "The feeling of separation is *need* (*Bedürfnis*); feeling as separation superseded is *satisfaction* (*Genuss*)." Yet satisfaction achieved through integration or consumption occurs on a purely intuitive-immediate level; although a given object may be removed or negated, the world of objects and hence the separation of subject and object still remains intact and unchanged.

A different and superior mode of dealing with the world, according to the *System,* is "labor" (*Arbeit*), an activity geared toward the production of durable goods intended for later satisfaction or enjoyment. To secure such later satisfaction, the laboring individual has to take hold of the product and claim possession of it. Thus possession (*Besitz*) arises here as a direct implication of the pursuit of satisfaction through labor (although in a prelegal sense). Another result, however, is still more important for Hegel. In the production of goods, he notes, a subtle dialectic is unleashed. While meant to transform the world, labor simultaneously transforms the laboring individual into a conscious agent deliberately designing or fabricating products (and also fashioning tools for this production process). Hence, natural intuition begins to make room for conceptualization, with both laborer and product emerging as conceptually distinct and differentiated.[28]

Laboring production, however, is only an initial step on the long road toward ethical public life. Human beings, for Hegel, are not only tool makers (*homo faber*) for the fashioning of external goods. They are, more important, self-fashioning creatures, in the sense that they are able to make themselves into "tools of reason" by subordinating natural inclination to the life of the spirit. Strictly speaking, the latter change involves not so much instrumental fabrication as rather a complex process of learning and "formation" (*Bildung*) predicated inevitably on interaction with other human beings. This interaction is already evident in individual labor bent on production of self-serving goods. For in taking possession of such goods the individual laborer necessarily excludes others from such possession—and hence acknowledges at least indirectly human interdependence.

To raise such implicit acknowledgment to the level of explicit awareness—and thereby to promote conscious reciprocal "recognition" (*Anerkennung*)—is the task of social learning and education. By virtue of this learning process, individual agents are gradually raised from the stage of natural particularity to the plane of rational universality (and ultimately to a condition fusing particularism and universalism). In the words of the *System*, through labor the individual is able to become "a universality for the other, just as the other is for him." Laboring, in this sense, implies a "universal reciprocity and formation (*Bildung*) of mankind," a process leading to "reciprocal recognition, entailing highest individuality as well as differentiation." In Avineri's instructive commentary on this process,

> It is from these considerations that Hegel derives the transsubjective, non-individual nature of property: *property pertains to the person as recognized by others,* it can never be an intrinsic quality of the individual prior to his recognition by others. While possession relates to the individual, property relates to society.[29]

Regarding the further maturation of consciousness or reason, the *System der Sittlichkeit* elaborates a sequence of stages in complex detail—not all of which is crucial for present purposes. Basically, the sequence leads from a kind of natural or immediate reciprocity represented by the family, through the formal and generalized reciprocity of the market to the concrete universality of the state, or public life. At each stage and between stages, a subtle dialectical movement occurs, rendering transitions intelligible. On the level of the family—held together by love—the father constitutes the more universalist and the mother, the more particularist element; the child provides the mediation and sublation of the two components. Exiting from the narrow circle of the family on reaching maturity, the child enters the broader realm of society and market relations, a sphere predicated on reciprocal recognition of property, production of commodities, and their exchange. The mediation between particularist activities here is provided by formally universal rules guaranteeing the performance of contracts and, ultimately, by money as medium of exchange. While on the level of business and commerce individuals remain basically separated and a contrast prevails between particularism and abstractly universal rules, the opposition is overcome on the plane of the state where citizens recognize each other as concrete "universals," namely, as participants in a shared public life. This is the stage of "absolute ethical life" (*absolute Sittlichkeit*) familiar from the natural-law essay.

Along the way, Hegel makes reference to a number of important issues, at least some of which deserve brief mention. One of these has to do with the role of language and speech in human education and the maturation of reciprocity. For Hegel, the "totality of speech" extends from the more "unconscious" modes of gesture, mien and glances of the eye through signs and symbols to written and spoken language. In discussing individual relations in society, Hegel also alludes to inequalities of power and influence, especially those occurring between *lord* and *bondsman,* although without developing the theme at length. Just before turning to the public sphere, the *System* pays attention to the "negative as freedom," as manifest in violent crime, combat, and other activities governed more by the negation than the affirmation of life.[30]

The stage of the *polis,* or public sphere—seen as absolute ethical life—represents the convergence of intuition and concept and also the coincidence of individual particularity and universality. In Hegel's words,

Ethical life (*Sittlichkeit*) is characterized by the fact that the living individual, as life, is equal with the absolute concept, that his empirical consciousness is one with absolute consciousness, and that the latter is itself concrete-empirical consciousness, that is, internally differentiated intuition. . . . In ethical life the individual exists in an eternal mode; his empirical being and doing is something basically universal: for it is not his individual aspect which acts but the universal absolute spirit in him.

Regarding the modalities of public life, the *System* distinguishes between the public "at rest" as embodied in the "constitution of the state," and the public "in motion" as represented by the "government," a distinction that may briefly be expressed as the difference between regime or polity, on the one hand, and governing or public policymaking, on the other.

Under the first rubric, Hegel deals with absolute ethics itself (where grief and suffering are sublated), with the instantiation of this ethics in the system of virtues. Hegel deals next with relative ethics, or morality, as manifest in bourgeois integrity, or "honesty" (*Rechtschaffenheit*), and finally he deals with "trust" (*Zutrauen*) as a natural or elementary form of ethics. The different types of ethics are correlated with different social classes or estates, specifically with these three: the absolute estate, which has "absolute and pure ethical life" as its principle; the bourgeoisie, or class of rectitude, whose principle lies in "work for needs, in possession, gain, and property"; and finally the peasantry as the class of "crude ethical life," whose labor is geared not so much to the production of durable goods as the provision of a livelihood dependent on soil and animal husbandry. Under the rubric of the government, the discussion ranges from legislation and public administration to adjudication, regulation of the economy, and education. The study is rounded out by a differentiation between *free* and *unfree* types of government, the former being subdivided into monarchy, aristocracy, and democracy.[31]

In Hegel's evolving perspective, the *System der Sittlichkeit* occupies an important place by anticipating or foreshadowing many of his later, more developed arguments. Yet, in some respects, the manuscript remained sketchy and elusive—a feature that prompted the need, keenly felt by Hegel himself, to fill in gaps and to provide a more coherent and detailed formulation of his overall framework. This task was tackled during the immediately ensuing years in a number of lecture courses and in manuscripts (composed for these courses) that have come to be known as *Jenaer Realphilosophie*. Since the first publication of these manuscripts half a century ago, it has become customary to distinguish between an earlier version (dating from 1803-1804) and a later version (written in 1805-1806) or simply between *Realphilosophie I* and *Realphilosophie II*. Although this juxtaposition has more recently been challenged owing to the fragmentary state of the former text, I shall follow here the established custom for the sake of convenience.

Building on the *System der Sittlichkeit,* the first version of *Realphilosophie* traced the maturation of human reciprocity from family through society to public life, locating the crucial precondition of reciprocity again in mutual recognition (*Anerkennung*). It is with regard to this reciprocal acknowledgment that the text introduced an important amplification, namely, by presenting recognition as potentially a struggle of life and death. In Hegel's portrayal, this struggle resulted from the conflict or contradiction inherent in the process of recognition: the insistence of the individual agent on his or her particularity (uniqueness) coupled with the demand to be recognized as more than an isolated atom (that is, as a universality). "Recognition of singularity," we read,

> is absolute internal self-contradiction. For, recognition means the existence of consciousness as a whole in another consciousness. But insofar as it is achieved, this process cancels the other consciousness; and thereby recognition is canceled too. The latter is not actualized but rather ceases to be in its very happening.

The process of recognition thus carries in its train the "nothingness of death"—both of the other and the self. Only by passing through the portals of this death can recognition emerge as shared consciousness, namely, in the mode of spirit *sublating* singularity and universality: "This state of sublation of singular totality is totality as absolutely universal, or as absolute; it is spirit as absolutely real consciousness. Here, singularity perceives itself as ideal and sublated."[32] Put differently, individual consciousness is threatened with extinction by another consciousness in the very act of recognition; yet in clinging to its own singularity, it remains unrecognized and denied. Hence, genuine recognition has to perform the feat of sublating (transcending *and* preserving) individuality on a universal plane.

Another important amplification in the text had to do with labor and the economic market. While the *System der Sittlichkeit* had portrayed labor chiefly as an advance in consciousness and (reciprocal) self-realization, the new text pointed to the darker underside and effects of economic exchange, namely, alienation and possible exploitation. At issue is basically the abstractness of the system of exchange and the growing distance of commodity production from concrete human needs. Whereas labor is undertaken initially for the (indirect) satisfaction of individual needs, economic exchange establishes a formal and abstract mechanism that is increasingly estranged from and even opposed to the concerns of individual producers. The individual, Hegel notes, "labors no longer for what he needs, and needs no longer what he has produced." In place of the reality of the satisfaction of needs there remains only the possibility of such satisfaction; hence labor becomes "formal, abstractly general, and isolated." Differently phrased, the general framework of production into which individual need and labor and their correlation are integrated or elevated is a purely *formal universality.*

As the text still insists, labor and production signal an advance in consciousness. But consciousness here is a simplified and abstract rationality that coexists with the dissection of concrete life into separate activities and processes and hence with the emergence of an "empirical infinity of particularities." The latter result is particularly evident in the growing division of labor, a division that increases the volume of manufactured goods but also the separation and isolation of individual workers. Quoting Smith, Hegel writes:

> In an English factory eighteen people work on the production of a needle. Each has a specific part of the work to do and only that. A single individual would probably not produce 120 needles, perhaps not even one; however, these eighteen jobs divided among ten people produce 4,000 per day.

The increased quantity diminishes the quality of individual labor. In comparison with the work of artisans, the skill of the factory worker is vastly more limited and the consciousness of the laborer is reduced to "the last extreme of dullness."[33]

The dialectic of consciousness is coupled with the dialectical reversal of freedom. Basically, modern economic production is geared toward the transformation and subjugation of external objects and hence toward human supremacy over such objects and over nature in general. Yet by erecting an abstractly formal mechanism, modern production in effect engenders and intensifies lack of autonomy. In seeking to subject nature to control, the individual laborer "only increases his dependence on it." This dialectic is aggravated by the use of tools and especially by the development of machines. By means of tools and machines, the laborer seeks to gain distance from external reality, while subjecting the latter increasingly to anatomical dissection and manipulation. As Hegel notes, however, this dissection rebounds on the laborer, namely, by transforming labor steadily into a lifeless and "deadening" process. The tool, we read,

> removes from the worker his material assault (on things); but it remains his formal means and thus his activity directed toward a lifeless target—in the sense that this activity destroys things by tearing them out of their living context and positing them as something to be annihilated. In the machine the laborer cancels this formal activity by letting the machine alone do the work. Yet, this deception which he perpetrates upon nature . . . takes revenge on him. For, the more he takes away from nature, the more he subjugates her, the baser he becomes himself.

The use of machines does not remove the necessity of labor; it only aggravates the distance and estrangement of the laborer from his work. Labor is increasingly stripped of its creativity and intrinsic liveliness and transformed into something mechanical, machinelike, and basically dead. The machinelike character of work is replicated in the mechanical system of economic interaction and exchange—a system epitomized by money (*Geld*) seen as the "existing concept" and formal unity of all things needed. In Hegel's account, the fabric of economic exchange in a modern nation forms an "immense system of communality and mutual dependence," but it is a dependence that is lifeless and atomistic, "an internally circulating life of death which, in this circulation, moves hither and thither in a blind and elemental way, and like a wild animal calls for strong continual control and curbing."[34]

Realphilosophie I stopped short of developing the implications of its arguments for public life in the state. This gap was remedied in the later version (of 1805-1806). Actually, *Realphilosophie II* moved again through the entire gamut of human maturation and reciprocity—a movement that need not be recapitulated here. Along this route, the text brings again a number of intriguing modifications and additions. One such addition connects alienation with economic inequality and oppression. As before, Hegel starts from labor and the mechanical system of rules deriving from commodity production. "Generalized labor," he writes, "means division of labor." Each individual as individual labors for "a need," but the target of this labor "transcends *his* need"; rather, he labors "for the needs of many, and so does everybody else." In this way, labor becomes "abstract"; and given this abstractness of labor, the individual behaves "as an abstract ego and in the manner of objects," and not in the manner of "a concrete and circumspect spirit who controls and masters a broad scope (of affairs)." Labor simultaneously becomes lifeless and mechanical, and the only movement possible is of a quantitative and spatial-temporal sort, which is accomplished by the machine. In Hegel's words, the multiplication of needs leads to division of labor and the segregation of laborers in an abstractly general framework. In this process, taste for consumption is refined through constant innovations. At the same time, however, due to the abstractness of labor, human life becomes

> more mechanical, duller, and devoid of spirit. Spirit which is a fulfilled and self-conscious life gives way to empty ritual. The power of the self resides in its richly comprehensive grasp; but this is lost. The individual can delegate some work to the machine; but his own activity becomes all the more formal. His dull laboring confines him to one small point; and labor becomes all the more perfect the more it is one-sided.[35]

It is at this point in his account that Hegel explicitly links the division of labor with the emergence of social and economic inequality. Normally, he observes, the skill of an individual determines the possibility and effectiveness of self-preservation (and the preservation of family life). Yet, under complex market conditions, commodity production is exposed to the hazards and accidental fluctuations of the entire system. As a result,

> a mass of the population is condemned to stupefying, unhealthy, and precarious labor in factories, manufacturers, mines, etc. Moreover, whole branches of industry which supported a large class of people suddenly collapse because of a change in fashion or because the value of their products fell due to new inventions in other countries, etc. Thus, whole masses are abandoned to poverty which cannot help itself. A contrast emerges between vast wealth and vast poverty—a poverty that finds it impossible to make any headway. Like any other quantity, wealth erects

itself into a power. Further accumulation of wealth takes place partly by
chance, partly through the universal mode of production and distribution.
Wealth becomes a point of attraction . . . collecting everything around
itself, just like a large mass attracts to itself the smaller one. To them that
have, shall be given.

As a consequence of these developments, the text adds, the social
fabric threatens to be torn asunder; economic exchange gives way to
class conflict and radical enmity. "This inequality between wealth and
poverty," we read, "this need and necessity turn into the utmost diremption of will, into inner indignation (*Empörung*) and hatred." This conflict can be remedied only on another level of human reciprocity: that
of the public sphere. In Hegel's view, public authority has the obligation to step into the situation and to alleviate—however cautiously—
economic disparities by means of poor taxes and institutions, by curbing excessive profits and by securing a minimum standard of living for
the underprivileged. As he writes, government "comes onto the scene
and must see to it that every sphere is preserved"; it must provide
"means or remedies," find "new outlets for products in other countries,"
and "discourage some activities if they are too detrimental to others."
To be sure, freedom of commerce must be maintained and intervention
should be "as inconspicuous as possible." Still, government has the
general overview while individuals are "buried in particularity."[36]
Government's role, however, is not limited to mitigating the disparities of wealth and status, which would reduce it to a tool of economics.
For Hegel, public life—as embodied in the constitution and government—has a higher, more intrinsic goal: the task of mediating and
sublating particularity and universality, individual and general will. It
is on the level of public life that private individuals are rescued from
atomistic dispersal, segregation, or oppression—not through some external power or miracle. They are rescued through participation in the
workings of the absolute spirit, which is essentially their own (on the
level of purified or essential selfhood). According to *Realphilosophie
II,* "the state as the rich manifold is the sublation of both particularistic
existence and of the pure self-being of the person. Humans have their
genuine being and thinking in law—which is absolute authority." Such
sublation is endemic to the nature of spirit, which appears on one level
as particular *personal consciousness* and, on another, as *pure con-*

sciousness, reflecting (ontological) reality. In the public sphere, sublation operates in the notion of the general will, seen as mediation of particular wills. The general will, Hegel writes in a subtle modification of Rousseau's teachings, "is the will of all jointly and each individually."

This general will has to constitute itself first "out of the will of the individuals," so that the latter appears as "the elementary principle" of the general will. But, on the other hand, the general will is really "primary and essential" and individuals have to "make themselves into a universal through self-abnegation, sublimation and educational formation *(Bildung).*" Seen from this vantage, the state provides the solution to the riddle or antinomy of subject and object, autonomy and heteronomy, namely, by representing a higher synthesis. The unity of individuality and universality, we read,

> exists in a dual way: on the one hand, there is the pole of universality which is itself an individuality (namely, the government—which is not an abstract feature of the state, but an individuality which has the universal at its end); and on the other, the pole geared toward singularity. Both individualities coincide. The same individual takes care of himself and his family, labors, signs contracts, etc.; and simultaneously he works for the universal, taking it as his end. From the first viewpoint he is called *bourgeois,* from the second *citizen.*[37]

As should be noted, public life, or the state, for Hegel is not a compact unity but only a mediated synthesis or a sublation of unity and difference, in which universality is filtered through individual freedom and self-consciousness. This reliance on individual initiative, in his account, is basically a modern feature. As he says, it is "the higher principle of modernity which was unknown to the ancients, including Plato." *Realphilosophie II* at this point offers a broad sketch of political development or of the evolution of public life in Western society—a sketch that involves basically a three-stage sequence leading from ancient tyranny through classical democracy to the modern mediation of the individual and public spirit as embodied in constitutional monarchy. In Hegel's view, public authority had initially to be imposed on barbaric peoples from above, namely, by lawgiving tyrants who enforced public rules as a curb on stubborn selfishness. With the consolidation of the public sphere, this external imposition became increasingly superfluous—

and was consequently abolished or overthrown by democratic peoples bent on self-government. This was preeminently the period of classical democracy or the Greek *polis*, which witnessed the complete fusion of popular will and government. But the fusion occurred in a manner that was unmediated and direct and that hence tended to particularize public affairs while simultaneously submerging the individual entirely in the city. This, Hegel writes,

> is the beautiful happy liberty of the Greeks which has been and is admired so much. The people is at the same time dispersed into citizens while also constituting *one* individual, the government. It only interacts with itself: the same will is particular and universal. . . . In ancient times, beautiful public life was the ethos of all; beauty was the immediate unity of the universal and the particular, a work of art in which no part separates itself from the whole but forms a genial unity of self-knowledge and expression. Yet, absolute self-consciousness or absolute self-being of the individual was lacking. Like the Spartan state, Plato's republic signals the disappearance of self-conscious individuality.

It is the mark of modernity to have unleashed self-consciousness and thereby to have engendered a "greater diremption and learning process" and also a "deeper spirit," which inhabits the realm of ethical life (*Sittlichkeit*). By virtue of this diremption, the individual is able to descend into his or her inwardness, to discover selfhood and self-will as autonomous from universality, while simultaneously grasping self-consciousness or subjectivity as the gateway to the absolute. In modern constitutional government, this mediated unity is instantiated in the monarch who is both natural subject and public authority.[38]

Having stipulated the character of modern government, *Realphilosophie II* proceeds to delineate the differentiated structure of the modern state as revealed in the variety of estates. This structure reflects in turn the maturation of consciousness, from simple trust through diremption and relative morality to ethical life. As before, the peasantry is introduced as the class of unreflective consciousness, as "the estate of immediate trust and raw concrete labor." Being unreflective, this estate embodies a trust "lacking in individuality" or that derives its individuality simply from "the unconscious individual (which is) the earth." The relation between work and its fruits depends here on "the unconscious domain of nature," which governs agriculture in accordance with seasons.

The next class, that of the bourgeoisie, is subdivided in the text into the bourgeois estate in the narrow sense (*Bürgerstand*) and the business estate (*Kaufmannstand*). The former is composed chiefly of artisans who fashion durable goods in a deliberate way. Selfhood here "transcends the earth" and unconscious nature, and the governing moral standard is honesty. The business class is engaged in commodity exchange, which is "neither natural nor artificial production or fabrication." Exchange is something spiritual, a mediation that is "liberated from use and need as well as from immediate labor." Consciousness in this class is extricated from external objects and fastens onto an abstractly rational principle, that of money and exchange value. The standard of behavior resides in formal law.

The third class is the universal class, or the public estate—an estate that works directly "for the state" as a whole. According to the text, this estate represents "the intervention of the universal into all forms of particularity," in a manner resembling "the arteries and nerves" that run through and animate the body. The moral standard here is the fulfillment of duty in accordance with absolute ethical life. The discussion of public structure is rounded out in the text by a brief allusion to two quasiuniversal estates: those of the academic intellectual (*Gelehrter*) and the soldier, the former marked by universalism of thought; the second, by the risking of singularity. In an important concluding section, the text demarcates the boundaries of the state by pointing to regions transcending its dominion. Returning from its objectification in historical reality, spirit here reaches full "contemplation of itself"—specifically in the modes of art, science (or philosophy), and religion.[39]

Phenomenology of Spirit

Both the *Realphilosophie* and the *System der Sittlichkeit* remained confined to Hegel's desk. Shortly before leaving Jena, Hegel completed a larger manuscript on similar topics, which was published soon afterward and established his broader fame; its title is *The Phenomenology of Spirit*. The term *phenomenology* in this context meant roughly "study of the modes of appearance"—a study here focused on the modes of appearance of spirit. In greater detail and with greater depth than the preceding manuscripts, the study traced the unfolding of consciousness from immediate sense perception, need and desire through the emergence of self-consciousness and reciprocal recognition to the epiphany of pure spirit, first in the realm of ethical life and next in the domains of philosophy and religion. To grasp this unfolding process it was necessary to move beyond both shallow empiricism and abstract formalism—that is, beyond random accumulation of data and the imposition of abstract schemata—and to uncover the inner life spring of the movement. In the words of the justly renowned preface to the study, reality is not confined to its "telos" but resides crucially in its "realization," just as the sheer "result" is not the real whole that is seen only when outcome is taken together with its unfolding or "becoming" (*Werden*). Considered apart from becoming, *telos* was a "lifeless generality," and *result,* a mere "corpse" suitable for a postmortem.

The inner life spring of becoming was formulated by Hegel in this lapidary statement: "In my view—a view which the developed exposition alone can justify—everything depends on grasping and expressing truth not only as *substance* but also as *subject* or *subjectivity.*" *Substance* here meant reality in itself or in its immediacy; *subjectivity,* however, denoted consciousness or negation of sheer immediacy, hence diremption or alienation of subject and object, reflection and world—a diremption that could only be overcome through self-recognition in otherness. In this manner, truth emerged as "the process of its own becoming, as the circle which has its purpose both as its end and as its beginning." The (mediated) correlation of substance and subjectivity, of beginning and end was captured in the notion of spirit—that "most sublime concept which belongs uniquely to modernity and its religion," and according to which spirit alone is real in the mode of *other-being* and *self-being* (or as being in and for itself). The study of the unfolding of spirit through consciousness and reason, however, was the specific aim of the "phenomenology of spirit."[40]

In examining the becoming of spirit, Hegel's *Phenomenology* is in a way a modern type of pilgrim's progress. It reports the story of the "long and laborious journey" undertaken by consciousness on its way to absoluteness (or the story of the *itinerarium mentis ad deum*). This story can be grasped as a learning process (*Bildung*) or as a formative experience that consciousness undergoes or makes with itself. As the preface states, the study of this path is the "science of the experience (*Erfahrung*) undergone by consciousness"; for consciousness "knows and comprehends nothing but what falls within its experience." The subject matter of experience, however, is spirit—for spirit is precisely "this movement of becoming an other (an object) for itself and of sublating in turn this otherness," that is, the movement of "estrangement" (*Entfremdung*) and its overcoming.

Every individual has to undertake this journey of experience, in a way retracing or replicating the stages already passed through by previous generations and centuries (thus linking ontogenesis with phylogenesis). As regards the content of experience, we read, the individual "has to go through the stages through which general spirit has passed," but now "as shapes already discarded by spirit, as steps along a road which has been elaborated and smoothed out." The driving agent prompting the movement and differentiating the end from the beginning of the (circular) process is reflective subjectivity and its built-in negativity, which is called the "most wondrous, greatest or rather the absolute power." Seen as self-enclosed and resting in itself, the preface observes,

> the circle is an immediate relation of elements in their unity and hence not particularly wondrous. But that a particularity separated from its context—that a contingent and only contextually real element—should gain individual existence and autonomous freedom: this is the immense power of the negative; it is the energy of thought, of the pure ego. Death, as we may call this unreality, is the most terrifying thing, and to be able to hold on to death demands the greatest strength. Weak and sapless beauty hates reason, because the latter requires of it what it cannot supply. But the life of spirit is not one that shuns death and keeps clear of destruction; rather, it endures death and in death maintains its being. Spirit gains its truth by finding itself in the midst of utter dissolution (*Zerrissenheit*).[41]

To be sure, the entire effort of phenomenological inquiry would be in vain if (ordinary) skepticism were correct in confining consciousness to sense perception and thus barring its access to the realm of spirit. This confinement is operative even in Kantian critical philosophy, with its rigorous separation of subject and object, of human reason and reality "in itself." This barrier is radically challenged in the *Phenomenology*'s introduction, which is one of the most difficult and most exhilarating philosophical pieces ever composed.

As Hegel notes there, modern philosophy relies heavily on epistemology, that is, an approach specifying a rigorous methodology of cognition, one in which knowing (as an instrument) is sharply separated from the target of knowledge. While modern philosophy is prompted by the distrust of absolutes and the fear of lapsing into error, he adds, it is worth pondering whether this approach is not deeply flawed—whether the fear of erring here is not itself an error or a "fear of truth" and whether critical distrust should not itself be distrusted. What foments this distrust is the role of consciousness in the stipulated epistemology and in philosophical reflection in general. For clearly, both knowledge and error are modes of consciousness, and so are the method of knowing (or the knowing subject) and the target of knowledge and its truth. If this is so, however, cognition cannot proceed through a separation of subject and object, as epistemology demands, but only through a study of the modes of consciousness and its formative learning process (*Bildung*). As Hegel explains, "the series of shapes which consciousness traverses on this road is the detailed history of its formation and elevation to genuine knowledge." Along this road, to be sure, natural or immediate consciousness is bound to come to grief; ordinary skepticism hence has to be replaced by a more radical doubt that questions and disrupts the complacency of natural beliefs. In the words of the introduction, natural consciousness

> on this path loses its own truth. For this reason, the road can be regarded as the path of doubt or, more properly, as the highway of despair. For what happens there is not what is usually understood by doubting, namely, a questioning of this or that supposed truth followed by a disappearance of doubt and a return to the original truth and the previous state of affairs. Rather, there arises the conscious insight into the untruth of appearing knowledge [in the mode of natural consciousness]. . . . Directed at the whole range of appearing or phenomenal consciousness, such skepticism prepares the mind for the task of judging what is true—by inducing a despair of all so-called natural beliefs, thoughts, and opinions.[42]

In further detailing the path of consciousness, the introduction strikes a dialectical theme. In undermining natural beliefs, radical doubt does not simply create a clean slate, but induces a process of maturation; shunning abstract denial (or a cult of pure nothingness), this maturation proceeds through *determinate negation,* which raises consciousness to a new level. By means of such negation, Hegel observes, we witness the emergence of a "new form" or shape and a transition is made, "ushering in a progress through a whole sequence of (further) shapes." Similar dialectical considerations apply to the yardstick, or criterion, of knowledge. From the vantage of epistemology, such a yardstick is the precondition of cognition (that is, a presupposed condition of the possibility of knowledge), or else the yardstick is placed in the target of knowledge, in an objective truth in itself (apart from the process of knowing). As Hegel is able to show, these assumptions are untenable because of the rootedness of both the precondition and the target of knowledge in the dialectical unfolding of consciousness. "But the nature of the topic we are examining," we read,

> surmounts this separation or this semblance of separation and presupposition. Consciousness furnishes its yardstick in itself, and our inquiry becomes hence a comparison of consciousness with itself; for the distinction previously made [between knowing and known] falls inside itself. . . . Thus in what consciousness by itself declares to be the essence or the truth (in-itself) we have the standard which it erects itself in order to measure thereby its knowledge.

Application of this standard, however, is not simply an abstract or formal methodology. Seen as a process of maturation, learning transforms both consciousness itself and its content, both the knower (or subject) and the object of knowledge; in applying its own yardstick, consciousness thus undergoes the purgatory of experience. "This dialectical process," Hegel states, "which consciousness performs on itself— on its mode of knowing and on its object (insofar as it engenders the new and true object)—is precisely what we call experience." Far from involving the smooth operation of a method, such experience entails a genuine reversal or "conversion" (*Umkehrung*) of consciousness itself.[43]

The body of the *Phenomenology* itself is a sprawling structure that resists brief summary; a few highlights must suffice in the present context. Basically, the text proceeds in a three-stage sequence from immediate consciousness through self-consciousness to the realm of reason and spirit. The starting point is immediate *sense certainty*, that is, the perception of a given thing through sensory organs. Although important as a first step, this "certainty" is shown to be fragile, or uncertain, because the object cannot be stabilized by sense organs alone (the *here* becomes a *there*, the *now* becomes a *then*). To stabilize sense impressions, a new step of focused "perception" (*Wahrnehmung*) is needed whereby an object is given fixed or determinate shape. In turn, however, this step is ambivalent and internally contradictory because the distinct shape of the object is achieved through differentiation from other objects (hence the in-itself status of the object depends on its difference). The conflict of fixity and difference is sublated through rational "understanding" (*Verstand*), which grasps the conflict as the basic relationship between essence and appearance, between supersensible (noumenal) and sensual reality. Supersensible reality is seen as a world of laws governing contingent flux. In the words of the text, the gaze is lifted to "the law (*Gesetz*) seen as the stable picture of unstable appearance"; the supersensible emerges as the "tranquil realm of laws," which—though transcending the sensual world—is nonetheless "present in the latter as its immovable copy or image." This contrast between essence and appearance, however, is in itself a merely immediate and nontransparent opposition, until self-consciousness arises and discovers itself as the source of the distinction between sameness and difference, permanence and flux. What happens here is a breakthrough to inwardness, piercing the veil covering subjectivity. Self-consciousness, Hegel writes,

> is the difference (or differentiation) of sameness. I distinguish myself from myself, and I realize immediately that the distinguished element is not distinct. I, the self-same being, separate myself from myself; but what is posited as differentiated and unlike me, is (in being distinguished) no difference for me. . . . The curtain hiding the inner self is here withdrawn and the self is able to gaze into its inwardness; this gazing at a self-sameness which separates itself from itself and posits itself as different while realizing at the same time the non-difference—this is meant by self-consciousness. What emerges here is that behind the so-called curtain covering inwardness nothing is to be found unless we ourselves step behind it.[44]

As portrayed in the *Phenomenology*, the discovery of selfhood is a difficult venture, fraught with many unsuspected hazards. The first step of this venture takes the shape of self-certainty, for which selfhood is manifest in immediate desire and need. In trying to ensure its certainty, the self seeks to satisfy its needs by internalizing or consuming objects; yet satisfaction of needs through consumption precisely perpetuates dependence on external objects whose multiplicity persists. The quest for selfhood next turns to labor and the process of reciprocal recognition (*Anerkennung*). This sets the stage for the discussion of "lordship and bondage"—the most celebrated part of the *Phenomenology* (and perhaps of Hegel's entire opus).

To become truly autonomous, the self realizes that it has to be recognized as such by another self, which can only happen in a radical struggle in which life and death, being and nonbeing hang in the balance. In this struggle, the stronger party subdues the weaker party and forces the latter to labor as a slave, or *bondsman,* and to produce goods destined for the satisfaction of the master, or *lord.* While seemingly ensuring the master's freedom (from labor), the relationship leads to a curious dialectical reversal. In devoting himself to leisure and the consumption of goods, the master actually remains dependent on external objects and on the labor of the bondsman; while the former only consumes and gratifies needs, the latter through labor creates or produces goods. In working and thereby postponing gratification (and even transferring gratification to the master), the bondsman discovers the potential for creative freedom—although this potential remains clouded and circumscribed by "fear" (*Furcht*), namely, fear of the master in whose service labor is performed. Labor, we read,

> is desire restrained and checked, consumption delayed and postponed; in other words, labor shapes or fashions goods. The negative relation to the object passes into the *form* of the object, into something permanent—because it is for the worker that the object has independence. . . . The toiling and laboring consciousness thus grasps through the apprehension of the independent thing *its own* independence.[45]

Finding their quest for autonomy still frustrated, both master and slave retreat into complete inwardness, thereby presumably avoiding both domination and dependence on needs (and external objects). This is the stage that Hegel calls Stoicism or Stoic consciousness where inner thoughts and principles are seen as a bulwark against outward pressures. In his account, however, this move is unsuccessful; while seeking refuge inside, consciousness in effect becomes cloistered while leaving external reality unperturbed. Noticing this dilemma, consciousness radicalizes its retreat by embracing complete skepticism, that is, a position negating the independent existence of external reality and thus presumably liberating the self from external bonds. Again, however, the move is foiled and even backfires by embroiling consciousness in contradiction: while denying the existence of any independent reality, skepticism presupposes the reality of consciousness as agent of denial (thus failing to apply skepsis to itself).

Pondering this quandary, consciousness eventually comes to perceive the contradiction not simply as a conflict between itself and outside reality but as an internal contradiction. Differently phrased, consciousness perceives itself as internally divided, as an *estranged* consciousness, alienated from itself. In this stage of *unhappy consciousness,* the self undergoes (or suffers through) the experience of the separation of its own particularity from the rest of reality of which it is and remains conscious. This conflict can be sublated only through the reconciliation of particularity and universality, that is, through the discovery of particular or natural consciousness as a gateway to "real" consciousness (or to itself as consciousness of universal reality). This step signals the emergence of "reason" (*Vernunft*), where reason means the insight that "consciousness, in its particularity, is inherently and essentially absolute and hence is all reality."[46] In its broader implications, the insight reflects the reversal (or conversion) of consciousness, that is, the breakthrough to the epiphany of spirit as absolute reality. Hegel's *Phenomenology* pursues the work of real consciousness, again in several stages, from the observation of nature through the articulation of inner morality to the realm of ethical life (in family and society). The study culminates in a discussion of absolute spirit as manifest in philosophy and religion.

From Jena to Berlin

Shortly after completing his *Phenomenology,* Hegel moved to Bamberg and from there a few years later to Nuremberg. In Bamberg he served as editor of a pro-French newspaper—an outlook that was entirely congenial to him. As one should recall, Hegel throughout these years was staunchly in the corner of republican France, that is, in favor of the modern political ideas embodied in the French republic—although not necessarily of its centralized administrative structure. As his writings during that period reveal, his attitude was entirely free of any German nationalist fervor, especially of any sentimental attachment to the old regime in Germany (symbolized by the defunct Holy Roman empire). On the eve of the Battle of Jena, Hegel in a letter described Napoleon as the "world soul" (*Weltseele*) riding through town "on horseback." A subsequent letter portrayed Napoleon as "the great constitutional lawyer in Paris" who was bent on teaching German princes or principalities the meaning of "the concept of a free monarchy." At the same time, Hegel was apprehensive lest attention in this modernizing process was focused solely on the French administrative apparatus, which represented only one half (the lesser half) of a properly modern state. "It is the other half," he wrote, "which is the most noble one—the liberty of the people, its participation in elections and decisions, or at least presentation of governmental regulations before the opinion of the people." In a chapter devoted to these turbulent years, Avineri succinctly pinpoints Hegel's political outlook. What characterized Hegel's attitude in Jena, he observes,

> as well as during his subsequent periods in Bamberg and Nuremberg, was his firm support for the French, his rejoicing at the Prussian defeat at Jena, his opposition to the German nationalist anti-French upsurge in 1813 and, above all, his admiration for Napoleon, the great modernizer of Europe and of Germany. Much more than mere infatuation with Napoleon, which was quite common among intellectuals at the time, was involved . . . his [Hegel's] political views were related to a fundamental theory about the historical significance of what was happening in Germany.[47]

As rector of a renowned school in Nuremberg, Hegel had the opportunity to participate actively in the process of transformation. Bavaria at the time was one of the German states, or principalities, undergoing rapid political and educational reforms, largely under the influence of French ideas. One of Hegel's friends, Immanuel Niethammer, was educational minister in the new Bavarian government and in this capacity offered Hegel the position in Nuremberg. Hegel accepted the post for both philosophical-educational and political reasons. As he stated in a letter written at the time of his move: "A new world may arise in Bavaria; one has hoped for this for a long time." As rector, he took over the teaching of all philosophy classes in his school, convinced that by providing enlightened philosophical instruction he could also contribute to the broader aims of modernization. This hope or conviction was succinctly expressed in a letter to Niethammer dating from the same period: "Daily do I get more and more convinced that theoretical work achieves more in the world than practical. Once the realm of ideas is revolutionized, ordinary reality cannot withstand."

Avineri gives an instructive overview of the development of Hegel's philosophical and political views during the Nuremberg years, focusing especially on his annual rectorial addresses. As he shows, these addresses almost invariably linked philosophical education with the nurturing of citizenship or civic spirit in the context of a modern state. Avineri also documents Hegel's firm opposition to the upsurge of German nationalism culminating in the anti-French insurrection of 1813. In Hegel's view, this nationalism—often fueled by a nostalgic-sentimental kind of Romanticism—was not so much a harbinger of liberation or emancipation but rather a retrograde movement liable to jeopardize the process of modernization and the (modest) accomplishments netted by political reforms. The defeat of Napoleon at Waterloo and his capture were for Hegel occasions not for rejoicing but for sober reflection tinged with apprehension and concern—concern about anti-French euphoria and the onset of reactionary politics threatening reformist gains. As he noted in his rectorial address in 1815:

> We must oppose this mood which always pointlessly hankers and yearns for the past. The old should not be deemed excellent just because it is old; and from the fact that it was useful and meaningful under different circumstances, it does not follow that its preservation is commendable under changed conditions—quite the contrary. . . . The world has given birth to a new epoch.[48]

As previously mentioned, the major philosophical work completed by Hegel in Nuremberg was his *Science of Logic,* whose two parts were published successively in 1812 and 1816. Conceived as the foundation of his entire system, the work reflected the subtle dialectical spirit animating Hegel's philosophical perspective as a whole. Broadly speaking, dialectics in the study involved a movement from abstract immediacy through reflective differentiation and diremption to the conceptual mediation and sublation of divisions. More briefly put, dialectics entailed a movement from the ontology of being (and nonbeing) through the theory of essences (and their distinction from appearances) to the level of the concept seen as actualized mode of thought (reconciling identity and difference). As Hegel did not fail to indicate, this movement was not only an internal-mental process but corresponded to the larger development of Western philosophy, namely, from classical Greek ontology through the abstract-reflective categories of the Enlightenment to the actualization of these categories in modern public life. To this extent, Hegel's *Logic* was meant to serve as capstone and distillation of a long-term historical teleology, although this meaning was obstructed and occluded both by a prevailing skepticism and a narrow preoccupation with everyday praxis.

As the preface of 1812 observed, both skepsis and common sense had produced "the strange spectacle of a cultured nation without metaphysics—like a temple richly ornamented in other respects but without a holy of holies." Yet thinking or theorizing could not permanently be stifled and was actually more "practical" than mere agitation. Echoing one of the earlier letters, the preface observed that "once the substance of the spirit has inwardly reconstituted itself, all attempts to preserve the forms of an earlier culture are in vain: like withered leaves they are pushed off by the new buds already growing at their roots." Cultivation of these buds, however, required sustained effort and intellectual discipline. In Hegel's view, the revolutionary era had ushered in a period of creative fermentation, which now had to give way to, or be supplemented by, rigorous philosophical inquiry:

> There is a period in the culture of an epoch as in the culture of an individual, when the primary concern is the initiation and assertion of the principle in its undeveloped intensity. But the higher demand is that it should become systematic knowledge.

The *Science of Logic* sought to satisfy this higher demand by showing the self-development of spirit from sense certainty to knowledge. More specifically, spirit for Hegel unfolds through differentiation and the determinate negation of immediacy to the eventual sublation of differentiated particularity in universal correlation by means of conceptual mediation.[49]

Publication of the *Logic* earned Hegel in 1816 a call to the university of Heidelberg, where he stayed for two years before moving on to Berlin. Philosophically, the Heidelberg years were highlighted by the publication of the *Encyclopedia of Philosophical Sciences* in 1817 (a work later repeatedly revised and expanded). Intended as a synoptic outline for his students, the study ranged broadly over the spectrum of topics treated in his lecture courses at the university, proceeding from logic through the philosophy of nature to the philosophy of spirit (subdivided into subjective, objective, and absolute spirit). The motivation guiding the publication was again clearly articulated in the Preface of 1817. Basically, the goal was to rescue philosophy from two dangers that for too long had "duped the earnestness" of readers: on the one hand, a freewheeling intuitionism sponsored by some brands of Romanticism and, on the other, a shallow skepticism deriving from Enlightenment thought. Of the two, the former was less grievous. Romanticism, Hegel wrote,

> may partly be considered as the outcry of a youthful joy, greeting a new epoch which has arisen in both the theoretical and the political realm. This joy saluted the dawn of a rejuvenated spirit with exuberance; however, it sought immediately to enjoy the fruits of the idea without laborious cultivation, and reveled in hopes and prospects which the new age promised.

While youthfulness excused Romantic exuberance, skepticism was "more repulsive" because it signified "weariness and impotence" and a proclivity "to find fault with philosophers of all centuries and to gloss them over with its own arrogance." In contrast to both tendencies, the *Encyclopedia* aimed to rekindle the proper concern of philosophical thought, namely, the "genuine love of wisdom," a concern that "alone bestows on humanity its dignity." This aim, in turn, was congruent with the aspirations of modern political and ethical life (*Sittlichkeit*), for which freedom is not only abstractly affirmed but established as confluence of individual and public freedom, as attribute of a "comprehensive general will, actual in all wills which know and determine themselves, mediated by a national constitution."[50]

Notes

1. For the background of Hegel's philosophy, see esp. George Armstrong Kelly, *Idealism, Politics and History: Sources of Hegelian Thought* (Cambridge: Cambridge University Press, 1969). The study concentrates on Rousseau, Kant, and Fichte.

2. See Karl Rosenkranz, *Georg Wilhelm Friedrich Hegels Leben* (1844; new ed. Darmstadt: Wissenschaftliche Buchgesellschaft, 1963), 29. Cf. also Wilhelm Dilthey, *Die Jugendgeschichte Hegels* (Leipzig: Teubner, 1921); and Joachim Ritter, *Hegel and the French Revolution*, trans. Richard D. Winfield (Cambridge: MIT Press, 1982).

3. Regarding the letter to Schelling, see Walter Kaufmann, *Hegel: Reinterpretation Texts and Commentary* (Garden City, NY: Doubleday, 1965), 303. Cf. also Paul Chamley, *Économie politique et philosophie chez Steuart et Hegel* (Paris: Dalloz, 1963). In the words of Avineri, "Alone among the German philosophers of his age, Hegel realized the prime importance of the economic sphere in political, religious and cultural life and tried to unravel the connections between what he would later call 'civil society' and political life." See Shlomo Avineri, *Hegel's Theory of the Modern State* (Cambridge, UK: Cambridge University Press, 1974), 5.

4. See G. W. F. Hegel, *The Phenomenology of Mind*, trans. J. B. Ballie (New York: Harper Torchbooks, 1967); also G. W. F. Hegel, *The Difference between Fichte's and Schelling's System of Philosophy*, trans. H. S. Harris and Walter Cerf (Albany: SUNY Press, 1977).

5. The term *dialectical imagination* is borrowed from Jay; see Martin Jay, *The Dialectical Imagination* (Boston: Little, Brown, 1973).

6. Benedetto Croce, *What Is Living and What Is Dead of the Philosophy of Hegel*, trans. Douglas Ainslee (New York: Russell & Russell, 1969), 175, 185, 190-191. Croce attributed this defect to the precipitous imposition of universal categories on concrete reality and historical developments.

7. Johannes Hoffmeister, ed., *Dokumente zu Hegels Entwicklung*, 2nd ed. (Stuttgart: Frommann-Holzboog, 1974), 149-152. That Hegel was not completely satisfied with the English parliamentary system, as it operated at the time, results also from his comment that "the nation can be represented in such an incomplete manner that it may be unable to get its voice heard in parliament." In these citations I follow Avineri's reliable translation; see Avineri, *Hegel's Theory of the Modern State*, 6-7.

8. See G. W. F. Hegel, *Three Essays, 1793-1795*, ed. and trans. Peter Fuss and John Dobbins (Notre Dame, IN: University of Notre Dame Press, 1984), 49-51, 78-79.

9. Hegel, *Three Essays*, 104, 111, 151. At another point, confronted and challenged by the Pharisees, the essay reports Jesus as saying,

> As for yourself, I cling only to the untainted voice of my heart and conscience; whoever listens to these honestly receives the light of truth. And all I ask of my disciples is that they heed this voice too. This inner law is a law of freedom to which a person submits voluntarily, as though he had imposed it on himself. It is eternal, and in it lies the intimation of immortality. (*Three Essays*, 127)

10. G. W. F. Hegel, *Early Theological Writings*, trans. T. M. Knox (Philadelphia: University of Pennsylvania Press, 1971), 69, 71, 86, 97-98. Reflecting on the moral

foundations of Christianity in the context of a universal state church Hegel added, "Because this church has become a church which is universal throughout a state, their essence is disfigured; they have become contradictory and unjust, and the church is now a state in itself" (*Early Theological Writings*, 104). His strictures against state religion were not reserved to Catholicism but extended to Protestantism as well: "However much the Protestants have fought against the name ('state'), they have never defended anything so gloriously and so vigorously as the thing itself" (*Early Theological Writings*, 107).

11. Hegel, *Early Theological Writings*, 212-215. See also Richard Kroner, "Introduction," in Hegel, *Early Theological Writings*, 8. While in Frankfurt, Hegel also wrote the essay "Love," which is preserved only as a fragment. In this essay we read:

> True union, or love proper, exists only between living beings who are alike in power and thus in one another's eyes living beings from every point of view. . . . This genuine love excludes all oppositions. It is not the understanding (*Verstand*), whose relations always leave the manifold of related terms as a manifold and whose unity is always an amalgam of opposites. It is not reason (*Vernunft*) either, because reason sharply opposes its determining power to what is determined. Love neither restricts nor is restricted; it is not finite at all. (*Early Theological Writings*, 104)

12. Hoffmeister, *Dokumente zu Hegels Entwicklung*, 219-221, 268-269; see also Avineri, *Hegel's Theory of the Modern State*, 9, 11.

13. Hegel, *Early Theological Writings*, 308. The claim that Hegel's mature writings left behind his early inspiration has been advanced, among others, by Habermas in Jürgen Habermas, *The Philosophical Discourse of Modernity: Twelve Lectures*, trans. Frederick Lawrence (Cambridge: MIT Press, 1987), 31-34.

14. In Kroner's words,

> Hegel renews, on the level of Kant and with his reflective insight, the ontology and metaphysics of Aristotle. . . . It is the glory of Hegel's philosophy that he resumed the ancient tradition without relapsing into its errors and illusions: he reconciled the old truth with the new, Greek methods with the idealism of Kant and Fichte. ("Introduction," in *Early Theological Writings*, 32, 34)

15. G. W. F. Hegel, *Politische Schriften*, epilogue by Jürgen Habermas (Frankfurt-Main: Suhrkamp, 1966), 18-21; Avineri, *Hegel's Theory of the Modern State*, 37-38. As early as 1798 Hegel had written a brief essay "On the Recent Domestic Affairs of Württemberg" where we read: "How blind they are who hope that institutions, constitutions, laws which no longer correspond to human manners, needs, and opinions, and from which the spirit has flown, can subsist any longer; or that forms in which intellect and feeling now take no interest are powerful enough to be any longer the bond of a nation!" See *Politische Schriften*, 12; also *Hegel's Political Writings*, trans. T. M. Knox, with introduction by Z. A. Pelczynski (Oxford, UK: Clarendon, 1964), 244. (In the above and subsequent citations I have slightly altered the translation for purposes of clarity.)

16. Hegel, *Politische Schriften*, 23-26; *Hegel's Political Writings*, 143-146.

17. Hegel, *Politische Schriften*, 29-32; *Hegel's Political Writings*, 150-154. As Avineri comments:

Hegel's dissatisfaction with German circumstances is an application of a general critique of the old patrimonial state which viewed political power as nothing more than an expression and extension of personal property rights. It is the same criticism which he waged, following Cart, against the old Bernese system and which he would wage later once again when polemicizing during the Restoration against the Historical School of Jurisprudence and Ludwig von Haller's idea of a patrimonial state, when he claimed that property is not the base of the state. (*Hegel's Theory of the Modern State,* 44)

18. Hegel, *Politische Schriften,* 32-37; *Hegel's Political Writings,* 155-159; Avineri, *Hegel's Theory of the Modern State,* 45-46. As Avineri adds, "The form of political framework which emerges out of Hegel's discussion of the nature of the modern state is a highly sophisticated and differentiated pluralistic system, where the state authority is basic and necessary—but minimal" (*Hegel's Theory of the Modern State,* 47).

19. Hegel, *Politische Schriften,* 38-44; *Hegel's Political Writings,* 159-164. Hegel, Avineri comments, is here able "to combine a critique of the centralizing, authoritarian consequences inherent in the principles of the French Revolution with a recognition of its liberating effects" (*Hegel's Theory of the Modern State,* 48).

20. Hegel, *Politische Schriften,* 74-75, 92-93; *Hegel's Political Writings,* 189-190, 202-203. According to Hegel, the system of representation derived from the old feudal order and was only transformed by the rise of the bourgeoisie. In any case (especially in view of their size), representation was "the system of all modern European states."

21. Avineri, *Hegel's Theory of the Modern State,* 58; Hegel, *Politische Schriften,* 43, 131-132, 136-137; *Hegel's Political Writings,* 164, 235-236, 239. Despairing somewhat of constructive reform, Hegel in the end appealed to a Rousseauan "legislator" or "German Theseus" as founder of the state; but this Theseus, he insisted, "would have to have magnanimity to grant to the people he would have to fashion out of dispersed elements, a share in matters that affected everyone." See *Politische Schriften,* 139; *Hegel's Political Writings,* 241.

22. G. W. F. Hegel, "Glauben und Wissen," in *Sämtliche Werke,* Vol. 1, ed. Hermann Glockner (Stuttgart: Frommann-Holzboog, 1958), 279. For an English version, see G. W. F. Hegel, *Faith and Knowledge,* trans. Walter Cerf and H. S. Harris (Albany: SUNY Press, 1977), 55. The paragraph containing the cited phrase continues somewhat later:

The question remains whether triumphant reason has not suffered the very fate that the triumphant strength of barbarous nations usually suffers from the defeated weakness of cultured nations: retaining the upper hand as far as external dominion is concerned, while being defeated in spirit by the vanquished. The glorious triumph of enlightened reason over what . . . it took for the faith that opposed it, looks different when examined in this light: neither is the positive element that it fought religion, nor has that which triumphed remained reason; and the offspring . . . posing as the common child of peace uniting both, contains as little reason as genuine faith. (Kaufmann, *Hegel: Reinterpretation,* 97)

23. Hegel, *Sämtliche Werke,* Vol. 1, 286, 291, 433; Hegel, *Faith and Knowledge,* 61, 65, 190-191. Kroner refers to a fragment dating from the same time in which Hegel saw

philosophy as contributing to "a new religion in which the infinite grief and the whole gravity of its discord is acknowledged, but is at the same time serenely and purely dissolved. . . . To embrace the whole energy of the suffering and discord that has controlled the world and all forms of culture for some thousand years, and also to rise above it—this can be done by philosophy alone" ("Introduction," in *Early Theological Writings*, 38).

24. G. W. F. Hegel, "Über die wissenschaftlichen Behandlungsarten des Naturrechts," in *Frühe politische Systeme*, ed. Gerhard Göhler (Frankfurt Main: Ullstein, 1974), 110-111, 126. For an English version, see G. W. F. Hegel, *Natural Law*, trans. T. M. Knox (Philadelphia: University of Pennsylvania, 1975), 59-60, 72. I sometimes depart from this translation for purposes of clarity.

25. Hegel, "Über die wissenschaftlichen," 118-122, 140-145; Hegel, *Natural Law*, 66-69, 84-88; Avineri, *Hegel's Theory of the Modern State*, 83.

26. Hegel, "Über die wissenschaftlichen," 163, 176; Hegel, *Natural Law*, 103, 114-115.

27. Hegel, "Über die wissenschaftlichen," 159, 164-165, 177, 193-194; Hegel, *Natural Law*, 99-100, 104-105, 115, 128-129. For a fuller development of Hegel's views on tragedy see *Hegel on Tragedy*, ed. Anne and Henry Paolucci (New York: Harper & Row, 1975).

28. G. W. F. Hegel, "System der Sittlichkeit," in *Frühe politische Systeme* ed. Gerhard Göhler (Frankfurt Main: Ullstein, 1974), 18-22; for an English version, see Hegel, *System of Ethical Life (1802/3) and First Philosophy of Spirit*, ed. and trans. H. S. Harris and T. M. Knox (Albany: SUNY Press, 1979), 103-108. I sometimes depart from this translation for purposes of clarity.

29. Hegel, "System der Sittlichkeit," 24-26; Hegel, *System of Ethical Life*, 109-111; Avineri, *Hegel's Theory of the Modern State*, 88.

30. Hegel, "System der Sittlichkeit," 27-31, 36-42, 48; Hegel, *System of Ethical Life*, 112-116, 122-127, 132.

31. Hegel, "System der Sittlichkeit," 60-61, 63-76, 102; Hegel, *System of Ethical Life*, 143, 145-163, 176.

32. G. W. F. Hegel, "Philosophie des Geistes," in *Frühe politische Systeme* ed. Gerhard Göhler (Frankfurt Main: Ullstein, 1974), 324-326; Hegel, *System of Ethical Life*, 240-241. The so-called *Realphilosophie I* is in these editions termed Hegel's "first philosophy of spirit," seen as the third part of his encyclopedic system.

33. Hegel, "Philosophie des Geistes," 332-334; Hegel, *System of Ethical Life*, 247-248.

34. Hegel, "Philosophie des Geistes," 332-334; Hegel, *System of Ethical Life*, 246-249.

35. G. W. F. Hegel, "Jenaer Realphilosophie (1805/06)," in *Frühe politische Systeme* ed. Gerhard Göhler (Frankfurt Main: Ullstein, 1974), 235, 250-251.

36. Hegel, "Jenaer Realphilosophie," 251-252. To some extent I follow in the above citations the translation offered by Avineri; see Avineri, *Hegel's Theory of the Modern State*, 96-99.

37. Hegel, "Jenaer Realphilosophie," 260-263, 266. In this context, Hegel rejects as one-sided *social contract* theories (including the one formulated by Rousseau) which derive public spirit simply from the agreement of (private) individuals ("Jenaer Realphilosophie," 263).

38. Hegel, "Jenaer Realphilosophie," 264-265, 267-269.

39. Hegel, "Jenaer Realphilosophie," 271-278, 280. As before, Hegel argues here for the correlation (which is neither unity nor strict separation) of religion or church and state, while philosophy is seen as the understood sublation of all spheres. Regarding the structure of classes or estates (terms that Hegel does not clearly distinguish), cf. Avineri's astute observation: The account "enables Hegel to combine a differentiated social struc-

ture . . . with a highly integrated political system. The estates described by Hegel are not the old medieval guilds: there is nothing restrictive about them, and their principle of organization is functional and rational, based on social morality, not on heredity or ascription." Avineri also points out an omission in Hegel's structure—the absence of industrial labor: "Obviously the worker is not part of the peasantry nor does he belong to the civil service. But neither does the commercial estate, the class of businessmen, include him: in Hegel's account . . . one finds the small, independent artisan, but as for the worker, he is conspicuous by his absence." See Avineri, *Hegel's Theory of the Modern State,* 108-109.

40. G. W. F. Hegel, *Phänomenologie des Geistes,* 2nd ed., ed. Eva Moldenhauer and Karl M. Michel (Frankfurt-Main: Suhrkamp, 1975), 13, 22-23, 28, 31; Hegel, *Phenomenology of Mind,* 69, 80-81, 85-86, 88. In the above and subsequent citations I have changed the translation slightly for purposes of clarity. Regarding the circular character of truth, Hegel adds: "The life of God and divine intelligence may hence be expressed very well as love disporting with itself *(Spielen der Liebe mit sich selbst);* but this idea degenerates into edification and even insipidity if it lacks the seriousness, the suffering, the patience, and the labor of the negative" *(Phenomenology of Mind,* 81).

41. Hegel, *Phänomenologie des Geistes,* 31-32, 36, 38-39; Hegel, *Phenomenology of Mind,* 88-89, 93, 96. While emphasizing the role of subjectivity, Hegel adds that the notion of radical subjectivity or the pure ego has already been sufficiently elaborated in modern philosophy (from Descartes to Kant); hence the task now was to return reflection to reality and to "realize and spiritualize the universal" *(Phenomenology of Mind,* 94). For a detailed commentary on the preface see Walter Kaufmann, *Hegel: Texts and Commentary* (Notre Dame, IN: University of Notre Dame Press, 1977), 6-111.

42. Hegel, *Phänomenologie des Geistes,* 68-70, 72-73; Hegel, *Phenomenology of Mind,* 131-133, 135-136.

43. Hegel, *Phänomenologie des Geistes,* 74-79; Hegel, *Phenomenology of Mind,* 137-143. Cf. in this context Avineri's comments:

> Hegel returns to the classical Aristotelian position that reality is intelligible. Kant's *Ding-an-sich* ultimately left human knowledge knocking, to no avail, at a closed door. Hegel, however, tried to do away with the Kantian distinction between the noumenal and the phenomenal. Hence the title *Phenomenology of Spirit,* which implies that ultimate reality, *Geist,* is manifest in its phenomenological appearances and intelligible through them. Yet while the classical Greek tradition viewed the *logos* as given, Hegel sees it as unfolding in the process of human manifestations—in history. *(Hegel's Theory of the Modern State,* 65)

44. Hegel, *Phänomenologie des Geistes,* 120, 134-135; Hegel, *Phenomenology of Mind,* 195, 211-212.

45. Hegel, *Phänomenologie des Geistes,* 153-154; Hegel, *Phenomenology of Mind,* 238.

46. Hegel, *Phänomenologie des Geistes,* 177; Hegel, *Phenomenology of Mind,* 267. For perceptive reviews of the arguments of the *Phenomenology* cf. Judith Shklar, *Freedom and Independence* (Cambridge, UK: Cambridge University Press, 1976); and Merold Westphal, *History and Truth in Hegel's Phenomenology* (New York: Humanities Press, 1982).

47. Avineri, *Hegel's Theory of the Modern State,* 63. In the above citations I follow largely Avineri's translation (from pp. 63, 66-67). For the text of the German letters see

Johannes Hoffmeister, ed., *Briefe von und an Hegel,* Vol. 1 (Hamburg: Meiner, 1952), 120, 185, 197.

48. Hoffmeister, *Briefe von und an Hegel,* 235, 253-254; Johannes Hoffmeister, ed., *Nürnberger Schriften* (Leipzig: Meiner, 1938), 370-373. Regarding Hegel's defense of liberal reforms Avineri comments aptly:

> The order Hegel is now beginning to defend is not the old order he had so radically attacked in 1801. It is not Hegel's views which have changed in the crucial decade between 1805 and 1815, but the whole fabric of German social and political life which has been transformed under the tremendous jolt it had received from the Napoleonic wars. The German system Hegel appears to be defending around 1815 is precisely the system he wished to see established in 1802. (*Hegel's Theory of the Modern State,* 70)

49. G. W. F. Hegel, *Hegel's Science of Logic,* trans. A. V. Miller (London: George Allen & Unwin, 1969), 25-28. In one of the most insightful commentaries on the *Logic,* Theunissen presented the work as a philosophy of both *freedom* and *eros* (or love). The aim of the *Logic,* he wrote, is to show

> that there cannot be a genuine relation to the Other which is not also a self-relation, and that no self-relation can claim truth for itself if it does not include relation to the Other. Against mere heteronomy as well as the abstraction of immediate autonomy (for-itself), Hegel vindicated a being-in-relation which—as *self*-being-in-the-Other—means freedom and—as self-being-in-*the-Other*—means love.

See Michael Theunissen, *Sein und Schein: Die kritische Funktion der Hegelschen Logik* (Frankfurt-Main: Suhrkamp, 1978), 49. Cf. also Errol E. Harris, *An Interpretation of the Logic of Hegel* (Washington, DC: University Press of America, 1983).

50. G. W. F. Hegel, *Encyclopedia of Philosophy,* trans. Gustav E. Mueller (New York: Philosophical Library, 1959), 55-56, 245. The last quote is taken from the section on objective spirit (par. 430).

3

Minerva at Dusk:
Hegel's *Philosophy of Right*

In 1818 Hegel moved to the University of Berlin, following an invitation based largely on his recently published works (especially his *Encyclopedia* and *Science of Logic*). This move inaugurated the most productive period in Hegel's life, a period during which he was able to flesh out his philosophical system in all directions—from aesthetics and the philosophy of religion to the philosophy of history and political philosophy. Time and place were propitious to this undertaking. The Congress of Vienna had marked the end of the turbulent Napoleonic wars, ushering in a more tranquil era conducive both to economic recovery and theoretical reflectiveness, or soul-searching. While giving rise to restorative and even reactionary tendencies, the era was still too close to the earlier turbulence to cast aside entirely the spirit of enlightened reform. Persistence of that spirit was particularly evident in Berlin and Prussia that—like some of the southern German states—had pursued modernizing reforms for well over a decade. As we may recall, Hegel in his essay on the German constitution had severely castigated the mechanical pedantry of the old Prussian bureaucracy; but times and conditions had changed. In the aftermath of Jena and other Napoleonic battles, Prussia had embarked on a reformist course under the able leadership of such ministers as Hardenberg and vom Stein. In moving to Berlin, Hegel thus could in large measure remain faithful to his convictions. As Avineri observes succinctly:

> The point is that the Prussia with which Hegel became associated in 1818 was not the Prussia of 1848, let alone 1914. It was a reformed Prussia, as it emerged after the Napoleonic wars from the modernizing and liberalizing efforts of vom Stein and Hardenberg. . . . Berlin University, founded in the post-1806 reforms, was one of the symbols of this transformation of the old, barren, militaristic Junker Prussia into a modernized, rationally organized, relatively liberal monarchy.[1]

Assuming the university position previously held by Fichte meant for Hegel both a philosophical and a political challenge or opportunity. His inaugural lecture in Berlin underscored eloquently the confluence of philosophical and political motives. As Hegel observed at the time, historical circumstances were auspicious to his new role: "Peace in Europe after the Napoleonic wars may favor a rebirth of philosophy," so that the latter, after its near extinction, might again "raise its voice and hope to receive attention and love." The calamities of the war years, he added, had entirely absorbed the energies of the people in the struggle for self-preservation and sheer survival. Understandably, that struggle had precluded the "quietude and leisure in which the inner life of the spirit pursues its absolute concerns." Now, however, the storm had blown over, peace had returned, and the time had come when free inquiry could again "blossom forth in its freedom from or vis-à-vis the state," that is, the prevailing political regime.

Actually, however, inquiry should assert its freedom not only from but also for and in the state, particularly in a state such as Prussia that had "ennobled itself by giving priority to the spirit" and that thus had "gained on integrity and cultural power, making it equal to other states (which are superior in external power)." In a modern context, cultivation of knowledge was an "essential value in a sound political life," and philosophy was the chief agent of this cultivation. As the center of a modern political state, the University of Berlin had to accord crucial importance to philosophical inquiry—and to support such inquiry against all kinds of fashionable trends, from reactionary traditionalism over skepticism to Romantic intuitionism. In terms of Hegel's address, these currents of "un-philosophy" were only "shells of former conditions" quite incompatible with the spirit of modern thought. "I appeal to this new spirit and salute its dawn," he concluded.

> Withal, I appeal to the spirit of the young generation. It is a beautiful period of life when you are privileged to participate in the freedom of inquiry without being hampered by material needs and distracted by momentary interests; and you are not yet corrupted by skeptical smugness. A sound heart still has the courage to demand truth; and the realm of truth is the home of philosophy at which she constantly works and which we share when we dedicate ourselves to her service.[2]

The correlation of philosophy and modern politics remained a recurrent concern throughout Hegel's years in Berlin. As indicated, the period brought to fruition all the many seminal ideas that he had tentatively sketched in his earlier writings. In his lecture courses at the university, Hegel dealt in detail with all the diverse facets comprised by his sprawling encyclopedic system. A crucial ingredient and center pillar of that system, however, was his political philosophy, whose mature statement and elaboration is contained in the *Philosophy of Right,* first published in 1820. As is true of all the Berlin manuscripts, the 1820 publication was only the outgrowth and culmination of a long process of intellectual gestation and maturation. Some stages of this learning process were discussed in the Chapter 2 (especially in the sections dealing with the German constitution, the *System der Sittlichkeit,* and the *Jenaer Realphilosophie*).

The most important stepping-stone on the road to the *Philosophy of Right,* however, was the Heidelberg period. It was in Heidelberg that Hegel first offered a lecture course on this topic—and lecture notes dating from this time have recently been made available to the public. These lectures have to be seen in conjunction with other efforts in the field of political philosophy undertaken in Heidelberg. The *Encyclopedia of Philosophical Sciences* contained an important section on *objective spirit,* which ranged over such themes as law (or legality), ethical life (*Sittlichkeit*), and constitutional government. As it happens, the same years also witnessed Hegel's intensive intellectual engagement in the political affairs of his home state, Württemberg, which at the time was undergoing the travails of constitutional reform. Because many of his observations in this context spilled over into, or provided the concrete backdrop to, his university lectures, brief attention needs to be given here to this episode.

Prelude: The Württemberg Estates

Like Bavaria and Prussia, Württemberg was one of the German states deeply influenced by progressive-liberal ideas. In 1815, the king of Württemberg (a country that had been reconstituted and greatly enlarged in the wake of the Napoleonic wars) submitted to the assembly of estates a new constitutional charter, which the traditional estates promptly rejected, ushering in a constitutional crisis. In 1817, roughly at the time of the appearance of the *Encyclopedia,* Hegel published a lengthy commentary on the proceedings of the Württemberg Estates, which had met during the preceding two years. In his essay, Hegel plainly sided in favor of the royal charter (with some modifications) and against the traditionalism of estates hankering for a return to the old feudal order. As he observed, a new era was beginning to emerge out of the ruins of the past. After the demise of the phantom called the Old German Empire, countries like Württemberg were embarking on the task of developing into a modern state. "Rare are such epochs and equally rare are those individuals," he stated, "to whom destiny has assigned the privileged lot of founding a state."

Normally, such founding acts were shrouded in the darkness of prehistorical times; later historical periods would show mostly a tinkering with institutions or a subtle shift of political power from some classes or estates to others. The French Revolution, however, had brought to the fore a new conception, namely, the *idea of the state* as a rational unity; and the intervening years, though turbulent, had seen many experiments designed to capture the idea in institutional form. In the case of Württemberg, the war years and the Vienna Congress provided the opportunity for a fresh new start. Hence, the king was "placed into the position—unique in history—of being able to issue a constitution *out of whole cloth.*" This opportunity was indeed seized by the king in 1815 when, in the presence of the assembled estates, he solemnly announced and pledged himself to the new charter. "There can hardly be a greater spectacle on earth," Hegel commented,

> than the scene where a king modifies the power which initially is his alone by adding the basic new provision whereby he accepts his people as an integral participant of the regime. . . . In the presence of such a scene— where outer appearance and inner substance of majesty so closely con- cur—the observer may justifiably wish to linger, savoring the august and invigorating moment.[3]

In line with other progressive constitutions in Europe, the royal charter provided for an assembly for estates, composed partly of nobil- ity and partly of elected representatives, with eligibility granted to Christian subjects 35 years and older (excluding certain professions) and electoral rights extending to all citizens at age 25 (subject to a nominal property qualification). After reviewing the provisions of the charter, Hegel turned immediately to the reaction of the assembled estates, noting the curious phenomenon of an assembly that while basing itself on preconstitutional, feudal prerogatives claimed never- theless the right to participate in the emerging constitutional order. In adopting this stance, Hegel noted, the assembly took a position opposed to the "real situation in the world," one directly in conflict with the new arrangements sanctioned in Vienna by "all European powers." Inspired by preceding events, these arrangements placed in the foreground public or civic rights in a rationally constituted state—something com- pletely foreign to the estates. The assembly, we read,

> rejected the royal charter not on the ground that it was contrary to the rights that subjects can claim in a political constitution on the strength of the eternal rights of reason. . . . Instead, it rejected the charter simply because it was not the *old constitution of Württemberg*—not merely insofar as it was different therefrom (which was not examined), but flatly and explicitly because it was simply not the old constitution, because the act of its proclamation was not the restoration and revival of the past.— But the dead cannot be revived.

In demanding such restoration, the assembly was governed not by reason but by nostalgia—a sentiment that rendered it incapable of having an inkling of the problem that had to be solved. In Hegel's view, nostalgia was not a proper guide in political matters. As he observed, " 'Old rights' and 'old constitution' are such fine, grand words that it sounds impious to contemplate robbing people of such rights." Yet, old age was not a qualitative standard and could not determine whether old rights or a constitution were good or bad: "Even the abolition of human sacrifice, slavery, feudal despotism, and countless other infamies was in every instance a cancellation of something considered an 'old right.' "[4]

In Hegel's account, the basic issue ignored by the assembly was the transformation of a traditional feudal order into a modern constitutional state. In a feudal order, social relations—even relations between prince and subjects—were essentially private relations, couched in terms of private rights and obligations. Due to this character, such relations were basically governed by private law, and especially by contractual rules. Such a conception was deeply ingrained in the old German system and was difficult to dislodge both from politics and political thought. Even in more recent times, Hegel observed, when "truer ideas" have stepped into the place of older "thoughtlessly accepted" views—like the view that rulers or princes govern by divine right—the expression "state contract" (*Staatsvertrag*) still conveyed the false impression that the notion of contract was still properly "applicable to the relation of prince and subjects, of government and people" and that the rules of private law and private rights were still adequate to this context. "A little reflection suffices, however," he added,

> to realize that the relation of prince and subject, of government and people is founded on an *original substantive unity,* whereas in a contract the opposite is the case, in the sense that contracts proceed from the mutual independence and indifference of the parties vis-à-vis each other. An agreement reached by the parties is an accidental bond which arises from subjective need and arbitrary choice. A contract of this kind is essentially distinct from the nexus obtaining in a state which is an objective, necessary bond independent of private choice or whim.

While political life in a state is grounded on a public duty on which individual rights depend, contracts proceed from individual choice, which first establishes reciprocal rights from which obligations are derived. With the transition of a country from feudalism to statehood, the earlier primacy of private law was bound to be revised. Accordingly, the traditional contractual relationships were destined to become a thing of the past.[5]

For Hegel, the fundamental error of the estates was their invocation of traditional feudal rights, that is, their reliance on the sheer positivity, or the positively established and vested character, of such rights. Times, however, had dramatically changed, leaving only the empty shells of past privileges. In this respect, the estates resembled those returned French émigrés who (according to one observer) had "forgotten nothing and learnt nothing"; they appear to have "slept through" the preceding decades, possibly "the richest and most instructive period in world history." In blotting out these decades, the estates repressed or sought to erase the lesson of that period—the memory of "what began twenty-five years ago in a neighboring realm" (France) and which then "echoed in all heads," namely, that "in a political constitution nothing should be recognized as valid unless it accords with the norms of reason." In its application, to be sure, validity according to the norms of reason could easily spawn the danger of abstract and high-handed theorizing oblivious of concrete circumstances. While avoiding this danger, however, the Württemberg Estates merely lapsed into the opposite (and perhaps more damaging) peril of sacrificing reason to inveterate custom. Recapturing the pro-French sentiments of his youth, Hegel offered this pointed analysis of the situation:

> One must regard the start of the French Revolution as the struggle waged by rational constitutional law against the mass of positive legal rules and privileges by which it had been stifled. In the proceedings of the Württemberg estates we see the same struggle between these principles, only the roles are reversed. In France, the majority of the estates and the popular party asserted and reclaimed the rights of reason, while the (royal) government was on the side of privileges; in Württemberg, by contrast, the king placed his charter under the auspices of rational constitutional law, while the estates set themselves up as defenders of privileges and positive law. Moreover, the estates offered the perverse spectacle of pretending to act in the name of the people—against whose interests (far more than against the king's) these privileges were erected.

Protection of vested rights and privileges clearly was not synonymous with defense of popular rights, that is, the rights of public citizenship sanctioned in the charter.[6]

While on the whole favoring the royal constitution, Hegel's essay voiced a number of reservations—some of which derived from special conditions in Württemberg, others from broader political considerations. One reservation had to do with restrictions imposed on eligibility to the assembly, particularly the exclusion of civil servants and members of some professions. Pointing to the small size and relatively undeveloped character of the commercial middle class in Württemberg, Hegel noted that the exclusion left as eligible deputies chiefly the class of lawyers, or advocates, a class not well suited to this public role. In its training and mind-set, this class was tied primarily to "the principles of private and positive law," which are "opposed to those of constitutional law, that is, of rational public law which alone is relevant to discussion of a rational constitution."

For Hegel, a crucial quality required in deputies was a certain outlook or disposition that he called civic, or public, spirit (*Sinn des Staates*). This outlook, however, was not simply an idiosyncratic trait. Rather, it was typically acquired in the "habitual preoccupation with public affairs," an occupation that offered not only insight into the "infinite worth of the common (or universal) weal" but also experience of the "recalcitrance, hostility, and dishonesty of purely private interests," especially where the latter take the form of vested rights. In Germany, a young generation marked by the upheavals of the Napoleonic era had received academic training and subsequently entered the civil service, often imbued with high hopes for a better future; the rules of eligibility, however, barred them from the public or political sphere. "The great events of recent history," we read,

> have inspired the youth in our universities with a higher goal than the mere concentration on future bread-winning and a career. Some have shed their blood so that German countries might acquire free constitutions; and they returned from the battle field with the hope of participating some day in the political life of the state. Their academic training has equipped them for this purpose and destined them in the main for civil service. Now, along with the whole class of academically educated people who generally pursue the same course, are they to lose the capacity to become members of estates and hence representatives of the people?[7]

Another, still more serious reservation dealt with the electoral system, specifically with the provision for direct representation based on voting rights enjoyed by individuals qua citizens. In Hegel's view, this provision was one of the less desirable legacies of the French Revolution, one conducive to the privatization and atomization of society. In the electoral stipulations of the charter, he commented, the citizens appear on the scene "as isolated atoms" and the electoral assemblies as "unordered, inorganic aggregates," such that the people as a whole is "dissolved into a heap or mass (*Haufen*)." This, however, is a shape in which the commonwealth "should never appear in any undertaking," for it is a shape "most unworthy of it and most in conflict with its concept as a spiritual (*geistig*) order."

For Hegel, the role of an individual in a public order was closely linked with such criteria as office, status, craft, or occupation. In assigning to citizens the capacity as voters, the royal charter granted them a "lofty political right," but it did so without any reference to "other civic bodies" and hence promoted in this respect a situation more akin to the "democratic, even anarchical, principle of individual isolation (*Vereinzelung*) than that of an organic order." In sponsoring such isolation, moreover, the charter tended to undermine the importance or significance of suffrage as such, given that the exercise of a "wholly occasional and isolated calling"—like that of casting a ballot—easily "ceases to be of interest in a short time." The point was not to reintroduce feudal corporations and guilds or the panoply of vested rights and privileges; rather the task was to restore the lower estates to political respect and significance and—"purged of privileges and traditional injustices"—to integrate them into the state as an organic fabric. In the terms of a passage summing up Hegel's reflections on this issue:

A living relationship exists only in an articulated whole whose parts themselves form particular subordinate spheres. If this is to be achieved, however, the French abstractions of mere numbers and amounts of property must finally be discarded or, at any rate, must no longer be made the dominant qualification or even sole condition for exercising one of the most important political functions. Atomistic principles of that sort spell, in philosophy as in politics, death to every rational concept, organization, and life.[8]

Natural Law and Theory of the State

The essay on the Württemberg proceedings appeared in 1817. During the winter semester of 1817-1818, Hegel presented in Heidelberg a lecture course that contained the nucleus of his later *Philosophy of Right;* its title was "Natural Law and Theory of the State" (*"Naturrecht und Staatswissenschaft"*). One of the students attending the course, named Wannenmann, took extensive notes of these lectures, which have recently been published (after having been found in a Heidelberg bookstore half a century ago). In these lectures, Hegel defined *natural law* as a rational or philosophical kind of law, that is, a law congruent with the demands of reason or spirit.

According to the introduction, natural law deals "with the rational provisions of law and with the realization or actualization of this idea"; its source is thought or reason, "capturing will in its free self-determination," which points to its "divine, eternal origin." As a work of reason, natural law has to be distinguished from *positive* law, which happens to be binding at a given time and place. In Hegel's pithy formulation: "In the domain of positive law, right is what prevailing laws dictate. In philosophical law, by contrast, lawful or legal is only what is right; no (positive) law can be the yardstick for this rightness." Positive law may contain some rational ingredients just as, in its mode of actualization, rational law reverberates in the positive sphere; the contrast nonetheless remains. By appealing to rational free will, law in its philosophical essence has a transcendental or spiritual quality and a kind of sanctity lacking in ordinary prescriptions. Such law or right (*Recht*) is "holy" because it is founded on "freedom of will"—and freedom, or free spirit, is "the basic defining quality of God." Positive legal stipulations, on the other hand, have an ambivalent status and need to be judged in terms of rightness. As the lectures stated, resuming the argument of the Württemberg Estates, "The fact that something is a positive or old law, does not by itself make it right. Changes of circumstances help to terminate the rightness embedded in such law."[9]

Given the stress on philosophical or rational essence, the term *natural law* was dubious and actually misleading because of its appeal to a natural referent. In Hegel's presentation, this appeal was mistaken. As he observed:

The sphere of law (*Recht*) is not the domain of nature—certainly not of external nature, but also not of internal-subjective nature insofar as natural human will remains on the level of natural needs and desires. Rather, the sphere of law is the realm of spirit and of freedom. In the latter realm, nature also is involved to the extent that freedom actualizes or externalizes itself; but freedom remains the foundation and nature only has a dependent role.

According to the lecture course, the term *natural law* deserved to be abandoned and to be replaced by a phrase like "philosophical jurisprudence" (*philosophische Rechtslehre*) or "theory of objective spirit." In its traditional use, it is true, the term *nature* carried a dual meaning by pointing either to the essence or essential concept of a phenomenon or else to unconscious nature as such. As Hegel commented, however, modern natural law tended to place the accent on the second meaning, that of "immediate nature." This accent gave rise to the notion of a state of nature, a condition claimed to exist before the emergence of society and the establishment of a political state. This notion, in turn, brought to prominence the "false conception" that society is something "not truly adequate or germane to the life of spirit, but rather a kind of artificial construct or (necessary) evil"—an evil hampering the sway of "genuine freedom." For Hegel, this conception was both false and contradictory: for either the state of nature is a condition of brute, immediate nature—a condition marked by the absence of right and wrong, justice and injustice, because spirit has not yet reached the level of these distinctions—or else, given that "man is essentially self-consciousness endowed with the concepts of good and evil," the state of nature denotes a state of unfreedom and injustice that must be transcended to erect the reign of "real freedom."[10]

In its philosophical or essential meaning, right or law (*Recht*) for Hegel was predicated on rational free will, that is, a will grasping itself "in its free self-determination." Not every will, however, was free in this sense. Following in the footsteps of earlier writings, the lecture course distinguished between natural will, prompted by impulses and needs, and rational free will, guided by freedom. In the former case, willing as a subjective act stands opposed to the array of objects chosen to secure satisfaction. In Hegel's words, natural will is "arbitrary choice, or will on the level of desires, instincts, inclinations which aim at some external or mental target and thus at a finite good." The objects of such willing may be consumed or destroyed—but only to be replaced by other objects, in fact by an infinite string of such objects (that is, by the "bad infinity" of finite things). Free will, by contrast, has itself as its object and hence wills its own freedom.

Yet, free will does not instantly reach fulfillment but unfolds in a complex dialectical process, leading from immediacy over diremption or division to mediated identity. Initially, free will is only an abstract notion, a purely "formal" entity without differentiation or determinate contours. This, according to the lectures, is the sphere of "abstract right," subdivided into the rubrics of property, contract, and illegality (or crime). In its next move, free will gains determinate existence that presupposes a process of differentiation, juxtaposing an inward act of individual willing to the object of that willing (the freedom or good of that individual). This is called the sphere of "morality" where behavior is guided by inner conscience and by freely and individually chosen yardsticks. The final step is the realization of inner freedom on the level of the general will, that is, in the context of "ethical life" (*Sittlichkeit*) and the state. In that last step, the contrast of law and conscience is sublated or mediated; what occurs here is "not only the realization of abstract law, but the realization of the idea of goodness—in a manner which actualizes that idea whose soul is the concept of freedom."[11]

The body of the 1817-1818 lecture course developed in detail the stages of the self-realization of will, from abstract right through morality to ethical life, subdividing the latter in turn into the three dimensions of family, civil society, and the state, properly speaking. However, I shall forego further discussion of this lecture course, because the same scheme, with slight variations, was preserved in subsequent presentations of the course and also in its published version under the title *Philosophy of Right*.

In 1818, Hegel moved to Berlin to assume a chair at the university. During the winter of 1818-1819, he lectured again on the same topic, still using as the title of the lectures "Natural Law and Theory of the State." The student who had produced the Heidelberg manuscript followed Hegel to Berlin and again took notes of the course; however, these notes are fragmentary and limited to the introductory part. As it happened, another student attending the course, Homeyer by name, took very extensive and detailed notes that (having been discovered a few decades ago) are now available in print. Apart from many revealing annotations, Homeyer's manuscript contains a preface to the lectures that, in its spirited character, resembles Hegel's inaugural address in Berlin. The preface opened with a sharp distinction between nature and spirit, between natural necessity and freedom through law. Spirit, Hegel noted, is not a natural entity, but rather the product of rational self-realization or self-actualization. In this process of actualization, nature is only a starting point; but the goal of spirit is to transcend natural immediacy in an act of self-creation. The latter act is an emblem of freedom that becomes manifest in law or rightness (*Recht*). Individuals as well as nations must move from naturalness to free spirit—an insight that casts new light on the notions of the state of nature and civil state. The state of nature, we read,

> as a state of infancy, is a condition of unfreedom governed by arbitrary, accidental will. Still buried in nature, will can still depend on the will (or command) of others; hence we find in this state fear, repression, and coercion of individual will—a will directed not at universality but at singular objects. Man is subject to "the will of others" in faith or obedience. But from this repression of will there arises the yearning for freedom, the yearning to leave the natural for a higher state.[12]

In terms of the preface, the legal condition of a country was a yardstick of the country's enlightenment and emancipation. In Hegel's view, every people has to engage in the "struggle" of historical actuality and freedom, which in large measure is a struggle of positive and rational law, given that positive law always contains (next to rational ingredients) provisions "dating from a previous lower state" of development. Legal arrangements hence reflect the level attained by the "spirit of a people." Once that spirit has entered a higher stage, legal and constitutional provisions of an earlier stage are bound to wither: "they must collapse and no power is able to preserve them." Recognition of this process was hampered by many adverse tendencies of the age, including a positivist or historicist jurisprudence clinging to legal idiosyncrasies of the past, and also a certain "anemic" kind of philosophizing, reducing reason to "intuitive guesswork" (*Ahnen*).

In Germany, progressive legal thought was obstructed by additional features endemic to German history, particularly the influence of feudalism and of the Roman civil law. According to the preface, the reception of the Roman law prevented a smooth transition from naturalness (reflected in German common law) to reason, because a foreign law was established as master over social life. The chief defect of the reception was the divorce it created between legal expertise and popular conceptions—between lawyers trained in the Roman law and the tradition of local or indigenous jurisprudence (a defect obviated in England by the continuity of the common law): "Devoid of legal learning the people were deprived of jurisdiction, of the old arrangement of receiving justice from one's peers." Aggravating the situation, feudalism had a detrimental effect on the progress of both private and public law. In the private realm, feudalism prevented the full emergence of individual property (and hence of personhood) by tying property closely to the land and to various obligations of vassalage. At the same time, and more grievously, public life was assimilated to property relations and hence colonized by private privileges: "The rights of the state are transformed into private possession; through the heredity of offices, public duty is reduced to individual caprice."[13]

During the winter semester of 1819-1820 Hegel again repeated his lecture course, still using the title "Natural Law and Theory of the State." And once again, by good fortune a student attending the lectures took extensive notes (which were discovered only a few years ago in the library of Indiana University). The manuscript is significant for a number of reasons. First of all, in contrast to earlier notes of the course, the text is not divided or broken down into separate paragraphs or sections, but rather presents a continuous line of argumentation. In this manner (even more than in the published version of the *Philosophy of Right*), the reader is able to follow the unfolding pattern of Hegel's thought, appreciating especially the inner connections between the stages of free will's self-realization. Still more significant is the timing of the lecture course. The course opened shortly after the enactment of the so-called Carlsbad Decrees of August 1819, decrees that imposed severe restrictions on freedom of speech, press, and assembly and that, in doing so, marked a dramatic tightening of restorative or reactionary policies.

The immediate occasion for the decrees was the upsurge of insurrectionist activities sponsored by student fraternities (*Burschenschaften*), activities that culminated in the murder of the dramatist Kotzebue. In light of these developments, one might expect the lecture course of that year to be subdued or circumspect, perhaps even marked by dissimulation or retrenchment. This expectation would accord with a thesis formulated by Karl-Heinz Ilting, a renowned Hegel scholar, some three decades ago, to the effect that Hegel "changed his political position between 1817 and 1820," by moving from a liberal-progressive to a conservative stance. The thesis was advanced before the discovery of the Indiana manuscript, which not only raises some questions but strongly disconfirms the thesis. As Henrich, the editor of the manuscript, comments, Hegel's course in 1819-1820 does not differ from earlier or later courses by a presumed "favoring of restorative policies." In fact, the lectures even exceed other courses "by emphasizing factors which support a 'liberal' reading of his theory. There is no trace of an adaptation to dramatically unfolding circumstances of the time."[14]

The lectures opened with an intriguing introduction that in many ways anticipated—and helps to clarify—prefatory passages in the later *Philosophy of Right*. As before, Hegel started from the distinction between positive and philosophical jurisprudence. Philosophical inquiry, he noted, aims at grasping the concept of right (*Recht*), not merely at describing empirically or positively prevailing legal provisions. Guided by reason or spirit, philosophy hence does not coincide with an empirical science concerned with the flux of contingent phenomena. Yet, while deviating from empirical description, philosophical jurisprudence is also not content with postulating abstract norms, or an "ought" divorced from real life. Instead, the concept of right denotes the inner truth or spirit of legal and political reality. Akin to the divine, such truth is neither reducible to nor radically separate from empirical provisions. In Hegel's words:

> It is irreligious to say that truth or the divine only hovers beyond the blue sky or in the inwardness of subjective imagination. One commonly grants that nature is divine (or divinely ordered); but philosophical thought is assumed to be godforsaken (*gottverlassen*), entirely abandoned to worldly contingency. In fact, however, the idea is omnipresent—not in the manner of an indifferent spectator, but by animating everything, so that without it nothing could be.

In Platonic and Christian terminology, phenomenal reality can be called the *body* and spirit or idea the animating *soul*, and without the agency of the soul, the body would "disintegrate into dust." In the vocabulary of Platonic philosophy, the concept of law is coterminous with its *essence*, while positive provisions occupy the level of *appearances*. Reality, from this vantage, is twofold: comprising both an essential core, governed by spirit, and an external garment of phenomena. Contingent or empirical reality, in Hegel's account, resembles a "colorful tapestry" where a host of interests and purposes crisscross and collide with each other. While aware of these phenomena, philosophy shifts the focus to the essential core and inner unity of reality. In doing so, philosophy penetrates the profusion of phenomena "to their simple structure, to those quiet spaces free from particular interests"; although recognizing the right of the latter, it perceives in their rich diversity the guiding light of "universality."[15]

As one should realize, however, essence or universality for Hegel is not simply a static category—and hence does not entirely coincide with a Platonic idea. Essence is not properly timeless but rather is the inner spirit animating a given time and place. As he notes: "Philosophy is not meant to transcend its time, but rather to stand in time and to recognize (spirit's) presentness" or the present shape of spirit. This shape, however, undergoes changes in the course of history—as can be illustrated precisely in the case of Plato's philosophy.

According to Hegel, Plato was able to grasp "the inner reality of his world"; he did this by formulating "the principle of ethical life (*Sittlichkeit*) in its simple immediacy," which is the essence of the "Greek spirit." Yet, ethical life could not persist in this simple mode; following its own inner logic spirit had to develop and mature—and hence proceed to the mode of diremption (*Entzweiung*). Even Plato sensed this need, but still tried to avoid it as a calamity. Generally speaking, the development of spirit is reflected in the spirit or conceptual awareness of a people at a given time. It would be "senseless" to foist constitutional arrangements on a people that diverge from or exceed its level of intellectual maturity. On the other hand, once the spirit of a people has grown or matured, established positive provisions must eventually give way, no matter how time honored their origin: "No power on heaven or on earth can prevail against the right of spirit." In this context, the introduction coined a phrase that succinctly pinpointed Hegel's outlook (while shedding light on a later, more well-known formulation): "What is rational becomes real, and the real becomes rational." The phrase clearly does not mean that every contingent-empirical reality is as such rational. Nor, however, is it the intent of the phrase to oppose abstractly rational maxims to the real world (which as such would be divorced from reason). Rather, the point is that reason is itself an unfolding or becoming reality and that reality is the unfolding or becoming of reason.[16]

As indicated, this unfolding of reason occurs in stages, which can be retraced or reconstructed. Taken by itself or in its immediacy, spirit is a set of categories that rest or circulate in their own (noumenal) sphere. However, spirit seeks to externalize itself and thus to "become" or unfold in the world, which requires its transition through human self-consciousness. By entering or passing through human consciousness, spiritual life—unified in its inception—gives rise to diverse individual initiatives and hence to the opposition between particularity and universality. Generally speaking, the process of philosophical reflection ushers in the division between subject and object, between (inner) thought and external reality. This division announced itself in late antiquity but reached its distinct contours in the modern age, starting with Cartesian rationalism. Concentrated inwardness blossomed forth at this point, promoting the growth of individual freedom: "When this concentration took the shape of division, when (old-style) public life disintegrated setting individuals free, great enlightened thinkers came onto the scene," cultivating philosophy as a distinct intellectual discipline.

Separated from the world, philosophical reflection became a kind of afterthought, painting life's experience "gray in gray." Yet, division is not the work of philosophy as such nor its final aim but rather a stage in the process of spirit's self-realization (which reflection accompanies and recounts). In its search for self-realization, spirit moves through and beyond division and diremption—in the direction of a reconciliation of the divided realms. Philosophical jurisprudence captures the phases of spirit's movement seen from the angle of free will. Paralleling the general development of spirit, such jurisprudence examines the transformations of free will from the stage of immediacy (abstract right) through the level of diremption (morality) to the point of mediated sublation (ethical life). In Hegel's words: "To find spirit in the concrete

fabric of reality, to grasp the reconciliation of spirit with the world—
this is our [the philosopher's] kind of worship."

Philosophy of Right: Preface

While he was presenting his lecture course at the university, Hegel
at the same time was preparing a text of the course for publication. The
manuscript was completed in June 1820 and was published later in that
year under the title *Outline of the Philosophy of Right* (*Grundlinien der
Philosophie des Rechts*), with the earlier heading figuring as an alternate title. It is primarily this text that is the target of the debate regarding
a presumed change in Hegel's political position. Undeniably, some
formulations in this text seem cautious and circumspect when compared
with his public lectures and with some of his earlier writings. Such
circumspection can readily be attributed to fear of censorship—a fear
that was by no means unwarranted given the increasingly repressive
enforcement of the Carlsbad Decrees. Seeking to safeguard the publication of his book, Hegel (one might say) practiced a kind of *protective
writing,* which still fell considerably short of *esoteric writing* for this
reason: taking into account the overall structure of the argument, the
serious reader could hardly mistake the basic direction of Hegel's
thought.[18] As one should also realize, the book was designed by Hegel
specifically "for use in his lectures"; and students attending the lectures
in 1819-1820 (as well as in later years) could thus readily interpret
written statements in light of oral elaborations.

There is another factor, however, that needs to be taken into account
in gauging Hegel's position. There is evidence to suggest that Hegel
during this time grew increasingly disenchanted with some of the more
extremist and even terrorist strands of the student movement and especially of the fraternities; no doubt, a climactic event in this reassessment
was the murder of Kotzebue by a radical fraternity member (Karl Sand).
In his inaugural address in Berlin, Hegel had indeed appealed to the
élan of German youth and particularly of university students. However,
this appeal was clearly directed at the progressive or reformist elements
of the youth movement—elements that now were in danger of being

outflanked or eclipsed by more reckless slogans. If Hegel's position thus became more conservative, this was prompted by the desire to protect the path of constitutional reform from both reactionary and subjective-utopian tendencies.

Hegel's apprehensions regarding the latter tendencies surfaced with some vehemence in the preface to his book. As on previous occasions, the preface distinguished philosophical jurisprudence from legal positivism or empiricism, from an approach that confines itself to "the immediately given, whether it be upheld by the external-positive authority of the state or by the consensus of public opinion." The real target of critique, however, was a freewheeling intuitionism that, by relying on "the authority of inner feeling and emotion," entirely bypassed the labor of reason. Discarding the shackles of rational-logical rules, this approach allowed "the heart, imagination, and casual intuition to say what they please." The source of this emerging trend, in Hegel's view, resided in enlightened skepticism as well as in Romantic counterenlightenment, with the former curiously paving the way to the latter. Once access to essential reality was barred by skeptical thought—as was the case even in Kant's system—the road was clear for exuberant minds to appropriate the "absolute" by using the shortcut of sentiment and (nonrational) belief. In the words of the preface:

> Recent self-styled philosophy has expressly stated that truth itself cannot be *known,* but that true is only what each individual allows to rise out of his heart, emotion, and inspiration about ethical matters, especially about the state, the government, and the constitution. In this context, how much flattering talk has been dispensed, especially in the direction of the young! And the young certainly have listened willingly enough. The saying 'The Lord giveth to his own in sleep' has been applied to science and philosophy—and hence every sleeper has counted himself among the elect. But, of course, the insights garnered in sleep are themselves only the wares of sleep.

By indulging these exuberant proclivities, Hegel added, philosophy was in danger of discrediting itself in the eyes of many, especially by giving rise to the notion that everyone can master that field without effort or without "further ado." The "more than millenial labor" of reason and intellect and all the trouble of "conceptually guided insight" can seemingly be bypassed "by the simple nostrum of the resort of feeling."[19]

Such resort was becoming increasingly popular in the field of politics or with regard to the state—where its effects were particularly damaging. Bypassing rational inquiry, intuitive-sentimental philosophizing claimed the privilege to transcend all public-institutional arrangements and to erect a speculative counterrealm grounded in private belief. In pursuance of this tendency, the conception was gaining prominence as if freedom of thought and action could prove itself only "through divergence from, and even in hostility to, the publicly recognized sphere," that is, in hostility to the state as a rational concept. Even though rational knowledge of nature was still widely acknowledged, the assumption was spreading that ethical life—the domain of objective spirit—was essentially unknowable, contingent, and hence "God-forsaken," and that (given its intrinsic atheism) the truth of ethical life had to be found *outside* of it, again in feeling or inner conviction.

The chief emblem or trademark of this outlook, in Hegel's account, was its "hatred of law," its contempt for all publicly sanctioned standards. That rightness and ethical life (*Sittlichkeit*) are grasped "through rational thought," he noted, that by virtue of this thought they are invested with "rational form, universality and determinacy" and thus acquire the status of public law—this feature is quite properly regarded as anathema by "a whimsical sentimentalism and a conscience leveling rightness into subjective conviction." Subjective feeling of this kind was liable to erase the distinction between right and wrong, just and unjust, virtue and vice, and all other moral or legal differences. As a consequence, the concept of truth and the laws of ethics likewise "become nothing more than opinions and subjective convictions" and "even the most criminal maxims are placed—as *convictions*—on the same level of dignity as these laws." In this connection, Hegel made specific reference to a "ringleader of this superficiality," namely, the Heidelberg philosopher Jakob Friedrich Fries, who was an ardent supporter of the student fraternities and their activities. In the fall of 1817, Fries had delivered a widely publicized speech at the Wartburg festival organized by the fraternities in which he had reduced public life to a string of sentimental slogans, particularly to "the broth of 'heart, friendship, and enthusiasm.' " In doing so (and through subsequent behavior), Fries also had given aid and comfort to some criminal student activities, including the murder of Kotzebue by an "assassin of conviction."[20]

Hegel's attack on Fries and the fraternities has frequently been criticized in the literature. Given the context of reactionary policies, his attitude has appeared to some observers as either unpatriotic or illiberal (or both). No doubt, the singling out of Fries in a text for university lectures was an uncommon step, one that must have been due to uncommon aggravation. Regardless of whether the naming of the professor was appropriate, Hegel's denunciation of his rhetoric and its effect on the student movement was by no means whimsical or unprovoked. As should be recalled, the Wartburg festival was not merely an innocent student gathering but a meeting fueled by intense chauvinism and xenophobia. Apart from exuberant declamations, the festival was also the site of a book burning (an ugly precedent, particularly in light of events happening more than a century later). Far from being a spokesman of liberal-progressive ideas, Fries was also the author of a violent anti-Semitic pamphlet in which he advocated the suppression of Jewish educational institutions, the prohibition of intermarriage between Christians and Jews, and even the legal provision that Jews should be made to wear a distinctive mark on their clothes. Anti-Semitic sentiments of this kind were widespread among fraternities at the time. On this point, as on many others, I find Avineri's assessment both judicious and accurate when he writes:

> Because the student fraternities, the *Burschenschaften,* which organized the Wartburg festival, were later ruthlessly repressed by the German governments, their actions received a posthumous halo of sanctity in the eyes of latterday liberals. The truth of the matter is that in their ideology and actions these fraternities prefigured the most dangerous and hideous aspects of extreme German nationalism. To present their aim as merely agitation for German unification is simple-minded: they were the most chauvinistic element in German society. They excluded foreigners from their ranks, refused to accept Jewish students as members and participated in the anti-semitic outbursts in Frankfurt in 1819. . . . Finally, one of their members, Karl Sand, murdered the poet Kotzebue whom the students suspected of being a Russian agent.[21]

Countering the sway of intuitionism, Hegel's preface insisted on the importance of rational inquiry and on the conception of law or right (*Recht*) as the public form of rational free will. The distinctive quality of philosophy, he observed, resides in its slow progression "from one topic to another" and in its mode of argumentative demonstration, a mode differing from other scientific methods; adherence to these features alone was able to "rescue philosophy from the shameful decay" into which it had recently lapsed. Proceeding in rational steps, the target or aim of philosophizing is the elucidation of reason itself, more particularly the comprehension of the workings or disclosure of reason in present actuality. For, given its status as essential reality, where else could reason manifest and actualize itself except in real life—and not in a realm of "empty speculation" or of "a beyond supposed to exist God knows where"?

It is at this point of his preface that Hegel inserted the famous (or notorious) phrase to the effect that "what is rational is actual and what is actual is rational," a phrase that becomes intelligible in light of the metaphysical status of both reason and actuality (*Wirklichkeit*). To obviate misunderstanding, the preface elaborated specifically on this metaphysical or ontological character. To the extent that reason or "idea" stands popularly for an abstract fancy or subjective opinion, we read,

> Philosophy rejects this view and shows, on the contrary, that nothing is real except the idea. What is decisive is the effort to apprehend in temporal and transient appearances the substance which is immanent and the eternal (truth) which is present. For reason—which is a synonym for the idea— assumes external existence in its process of actualization, thus taking on an infinite variety of forms, shapes, and appearances. Around its core reason throws a motley crust which consciousness initially inhabits, but which reason must penetrate in order to discover the inward pulse and to find it still beating under the outward husk.

Following the path of reason, philosophy is basically concerned with this inward pulse, while leaving the infinite variety of data to other disciplines; for otherwise it would meddle in matters for which philosophy is "unsuited."[22]

While appropriating elements of traditional (Platonic) metaphysics, the preface was not content with a static essentialism. Once again, Plato's *Republic* was invoked to illustrate the dynamic character of reason or its developmental unfolding in time. In Hegel's account, the *Republic* basically captured the essence or nature of "Greek ethical life," but at a time when that life was already being undermined or disrupted by the "deeper principle" of individual freedom, a principle sensed as an "unfulfilled longing." Although aware of this process, Plato took refuge against it in "external public forms," which were unable to contain the historical advance of "free infinite personhood." Endorsement of this advancing freedom, however, did not mean the surrender of public life and political reflection to subjective whim or arbitrary machinations. The task of philosophical jurisprudence, for Hegel, was "to grasp and portray the essential rationality of the state"— not to construct an imaginary state "as it ought to be." Its goal was to "understand" the state as an ethical universe, rather than to instruct or "lecture" the state as to its abstract possibilities.

This realization counseled a certain modesty on the part of philosophy, and a reluctance to engage in futuristic visions. Like every individual, Hegel noted, the philosopher is "a child of his time"; accordingly, philosophizing means to "apprehend one's time in thought." To assume that any philosophy "can transcend its contemporary world" is just as absurd as to fancy that an individual "can overleap his own age, jump over Rhodes"—which, to be sure, does not halt the advancement of spirit as such. Given its dependence on spirit and its inability to direct or control spirit's movement, philosophy had to be content with registering this movement and deciphering its present meaning. As the afterthought, or "reflective glance," on the world, philosophizing emerges only at the time when actuality has completed its "stage of maturation" and has made itself "ready" (for understanding). Pursuing this insight, the conclusion of the preface invoked the owl of Minerva and its lessons for the *grayness* of theory:

> When philosophy paints its gray in gray, then a shape of life has grown old, and with grayness it cannot be rejuvenated but only understood. The owl of Minerva only spreads its wings with the falling of the dusk.[23]

Introduction: Rightness and Freedom

The general structure of the *Philosophy of Right* is familiar from Hegel's previous lecture courses. However, the text's introduction offers guideposts that clarify further the rationale of the structure as well as the basic thrust of philosophical jurisprudence. In Hegel's account, such jurisprudence is concerned with the "idea of law or right (*Recht*)," where idea means a confluence of rational concept and actualization, of inner essence and concrete existence (or *Dasein*)—a confluence resembling the correlation of soul (or mind) and body. "Concept and its existence," we read, "are two sides of a coin, separate but united, like soul and body." *Existence* denotes the "body" of the concept, a body obedient to the latter as its animating principle; *idea,* however, means "the unity of existence and concept, of soul and body." By focusing on the idea of right, the text provides a "philosophical" type of inquiry, diverging thereby from a number of alternative or competing approaches—some of which have been mentioned before.

One such approach is positivism with its emphasis on positively established legal rules—an emphasis that is said to be not so much antithetical as supplementary to philosophical jurisprudence (which provides grounds for the validity or invalidity of prevailing norms). Another approach, familiar from the preface, is intuitionism, the invocation of "intense feeling, inner conviction and inspiration" as the ultimate source of law and rightness. In addition to these more or less nonphilosophical approaches, the introduction also made extensive reference to another perspective that was gaining prominence in legal circles at the time: the perspective of historicism (promoted by the Historical School of jurisprudence), according to which the rightness and rational cogency of norms can be explained in terms of their historical genesis and background. As Hegel made it clear, at issue is not historical inquiry as such or the insights garnered through historical and cultural comparisons—provided historical explanation is not confused with conceptual explication and the former is not erected into an "absolute standard of justification." Irrespective of the merit of historical research, it was imperative to maintain the distinction between the genesis of norms and their intrinsic validity. No matter how well grounded legal norms may be in historical conditions, it is one thing to describe their "historical emergence" and another thing altogether to demonstrate their "conceptual rightness and rationality." Moreover, taken seriously, historicism ultimately self-destructs. For, given the close nexus of validity and historical background, acknowledgement of the lapse of historical conditions also implies cancellation of the grounds of normative rightness.[24]

Concerned with the idea of right, philosophical jurisprudence is basically a study of freedom or free spirit, more specifically of free will, or of will freely willing itself. As previously indicated, will for Hegel is a complex notion comprising different dimensions or modalities. These modalities include the aspect of immediate indeterminacy (giving rise to purely abstract or negative freedom), the element of concrete-singular determinacy, and the sublation of concreteness and universality. In regard to content, will initially is directed at and drawn toward external objects seen as targets of satisfaction; this is the stage of immediate, or natural, will, a mode governed by "instincts, desires, and inclinations."

Reflection on the act of willing leads to the discovery of the inward source of will, namely, the possibility of "decision" lodged in self-consciousness or singular subjectivity. Discovery of this source, in turn, entails the distinction between inward "infinity" and the finitude of external objects and hence the emergence of free choice—but a choice that is marred by contingency and arbitrariness, due to the continued dependence of will on finite objects. Freedom on this level, in Hegel's account, remains purely formal as well as internally divided or contradictory: "Instead of representing will in its truth, arbitrariness is will in the mode of contradiction." To the extent that legality or a normative system is erected on the basis of this freedom, such a system only provides an external framework coordinating arbitrary preferences; leaving these preferences untouched, such a framework sanctions only individual freedom from public life or the common good, where public life is devoid of intrinsic merit or value.

To proceed to genuine freedom—one transgressing arbitrariness and external constraints—willing has to turn from contingent objects to free spirit, thus making freedom itself its target. At this point, willing gains a self-consciousness that is no longer exclusively tied to private preferences but reconciled with broader, universal aims. Differently phrased, will is elevated from particularism to universality and from the level of abstract rules to the domain of rightness and ethical life. In Hegel's words,

> In having universality for its object, content and aim, will here is free not only in itself but for itself also; it is 'idea' in its truth. . . . Such self-

consciousness which grasps its essence through thought and thereby frees itself from what is contingent and untrue, furnishes the principle of right (*Recht*), morality, and all modes of ethical life.[25]

The sketched modalities of will and their dialectical connections govern the structure and progression of the *Philosophy of Right*. As the introduction emphasizes, dialectics properly conceived is not merely an abstract schema or principle but rather the inner movement of thought and reality—not merely a ploy of subjective fancy but instead the "intrinsic soul" of a subject matter that "organically unfolds its branches and fruits." In terms of its unfolding progression, free will has to be studied first in its immediacy, as an abstract category directed toward contingent objects, which is the level of "abstract or formal right." Next comes the stage of the inward self-reflection of will, the emergence of determinate singularity as opposed to the initial indeterminacy. This is the level of "subjective" right or of free will in its internal "diremption" (*Entzweiung*)—in Hegel's terms, the sphere of "morality." Finally, abstract right and singularity are sublated or reconciled with each other at a point where freedom is both reflective inwardness and actualized reality—the stage of fully developed "ethical life" (*Sittlichkeit*). The latter stage, in turn, is further subdivided or differentiated in a dialectical sequence that leads from immediate or natural ethics, manifest in family life, through the diremption of family bonds in civil society to the embodiment or actualization of freedom in the state—an arena where free individuality is blended with universal rightness.

In an important addendum to the introduction, Hegel further elaborates on the rationale underlying the book's dialectical sequence. After initially being tied to external objects on the level of abstract property rights, he notes, will eventually comes to reflect on itself, thereby uncovering the inward or constitutive source of human freedom. At this point, he writes,

> I am no longer free merely with respect to a given object, but free in the mode of sublated immediacy, that is, free in myself, in my subjectivity. In this sphere the main thing is my reflection, my intention, my purpose— while externality has been relegated to indifference. Yet, goodness which is here posited as universal aim should not remain confined in my inwardness but should actualize itself; for subjective will demands that inward-

ness or inner aim acquire external existence, that goodness be realized in the outer world. Thus, morality as well as formal right are both abstract moments whose truth emerges in ethical life alone. Hence, ethical life is the unity of conceptual will and singular will (or will of the individual subject).[26]

Private Property and Contracts

Given that the focus of the present study is on politics or political philosophy, discussion of the early stages of free will—abstract right and morality—will be relatively brief. As indicated, right (*Recht*) for Hegel means the embodiment of freedom, more specifically of the idea of free will—with idea comprising both the inner concept and its actualization. *Abstract right* accordingly means an indeterminate notion of freedom, a notion lodged in an abstract ego or subjectivity, identical with itself, as it relates to external objects. In line with arguments presented in *Realphilosophie,* this is an initial stage of freedom to the extent that the subject differentiates itself from objects, thereby gaining a generic identity. In Hegel's portrayal, this stage is crucial for the further development of right and for civilized life as such. In a variation on Kant's categorical imperative, he formulates the basic standard operating on this level in these terms: "Be a person (or subject) and respect others as persons (or subjects)."

However, *Philosophy of Right* immediately proceeds beyond this level of formal self-identity by considering the relationship of the subject to external objects—a relationship that, again, is endemic to the very idea of subjectivity, or *personhood.* In Hegel's words, a subject must acquire "an external sphere of freedom in order to exist as idea." Subjectivity and externality, at this point, stand opposed to each other as mutually exclusive in their respective immediacy. Because the subject here is conceived "in its abstractness" as self-identical will, the external sphere likewise must be construed as something "immediately distinct and separate" from the subject. The relationship between subject and external things is a connection of external possession and ownership, that is, a relation of "property" (*Eigentum*). The importance of property, however, resides not in its ability to satisfy needs or desires, but rather in its status as an emblem or embodiment of freedom. By virtue of property, the subject acquires a first sense of rational autonomy: As a propertyowner, "a person exists for the first time as reason."[27]

In this discussion of property, Hegel is clearly informed by the tradition of Western thought from antiquity through Roman law to modern natural-law doctrines. In line with Roman jurisprudence, the subject (abstractly considered) is said to have an unlimited "right to everything" (*ius ad omnia*), that is, an "absolute right" to acquire external objects by making them the target of human will. This right is predicated on the radical distinction between subjectivity and externality, between free will and things devoid of will—with the former enjoying a higher level of dignity. As Hegel writes, only will is "infinite and absolute vis-à-vis all other things," while these things are "merely relative." Hence to appropriate something means basically "to manifest the preeminence of my will over the object" and thus to demonstrate that the latter is not absolute or an "end in itself." This manifestation involves a process whereby an object is given a purpose "not directly its own"; by appropriating something "I infuse it with a soul other than its own, namely, with my soul." This outlook concurs with philosophical idealism, which regards things as dependent on idea or free spirit (a dependence ignored by empirical realism).

Again in conformity with traditional jurisprudence, the *Philosophy of Right* distinguishes between physical *possession* and actual *property*, but the distinction is now rephrased in terms of natural will versus real, or free, will. Whereas natural need and desire are the motives governing possession, the "true and right element" in property is that will here becomes "for the first time free and actual will." Genuine will, however, is the free will of a self-identical subject—which entails that property is essentially "private property" (*Privateigentum*) while communal property is inherently dissoluble. Borrowing a leaf from Aristotle, Hegel at this point launches into a polemic against Plato's *Republic* with its stress on communal ownership as well as against all religious and utopian visions of undifferentiated community:

> The general principle underlying Plato's *Republic* violates the right of personhood by robbing it of the right to own private property. The idea of a pious or fraternal and even compulsory brotherhood of men founded

on a community of goods and the prohibition of private property may readily suggest itself to a disposition which mistakes the true nature of free spirit and of right and fails to grasp it in its constitutive elements.[28]

For Hegel (as for traditional jurisprudence and natural-law theory), property is preceded by an act of acquisition or "appropriation" (*Besitzergreifung*), which necessarily complements the internal intent of ownership. According to *Philosophy of Right*, such acquisition can take the form of physical occupancy, of an investment of formative labor, or else of simple designation through a marker (*Zeichen*). Among these modes, investment of labor is the most important—while occupancy remains temporary, labor functions itself as a lasting marker or sign.

In Hegel's language, to impose form on a thing through labor is the acquisition "most congruent with the idea," since it involves a "union of subject and object"—although it may vary "with the qualitative character of objects and the diversity of subjective aims." In a passage reminiscent of Locke, the text refers especially to acquisition of land and natural objects: "Examples are the tilling of the soil, the cultivation of plants, the taming and feeding of animals, the preservation of game, as well as contrivances for utilizing raw materials or the forces of nature." In such acts of cultivation or formation, one should note, acquisition extends not only to natural fruits or products but also to the land or ground itself yielding these goods: "If I take possession of a field and plough it, it is not only the furrow which is my property, but the rest as well, the ploughed earth"; for I want to own the "whole matter," which consequently does not remain *res nullius* (or "owner-less"). Even though the land or ground may not itself be affected by the shape or furrows imposed on it, still these furrows are a sign or marker of private property extending to the soil. Because property is an outgrowth of free will and because will comprises the land, there is hence "nothing left to be taken into possession by someone else."[29]

In the relation between will and external goods the accent—from the perspective of right—is clearly on the former. Seen as an embodiment of free will, the merit of property resides in the owner's freedom of disposition, not in the quantity of owned things: "What and how much I own, therefore, is indifferent from the vantage of right." To this extent, freedom (of will) takes absolute precedence over equality—if the latter term refers to equality of goods or possessions. On the level of abstract right, equality can only mean equality of the will to own property or equality of opportunity, not a symmetry regarding income or the quantitative distribution of goods.

In Hegel's words, equality denotes first of all that "abstract identity" of reason, which reflection and "intellectual mediocrity" initially seize on when confronting the relation of unity and difference. On this level, we find the "equality of abstract subjects as such," a coincidence which leaves untouched the field of concrete possession, that "seedbed of inequality." As Hegel readily grants, human beings are indeed equal, but only in their capacity as free subjects or in regard to their generic right to own property of some kind. This capacity, however, allows no inference regarding actual possessions. In light of these premises, the text denounces as untenable and misguided demands for an equality of external goods and, more generally, for a leveling of all differences between individuals in real life. Such demand

> for an equal division of land and of other available resources is an empty and superficial postulate—one rendered all the more shallow by the fact that concrete differences arise not only from the contingency of external nature but also from the whole compass of human spirit in its infinite particularity and diversity and its organically developed rationality.

To the extent that inequalities derive from external nature, Hegel adds, it is pointless to speak of an "injustice of nature" in regard to the distribution of goods, because nature as such is not free (or endowed with free will) and hence is "neither just nor unjust." Moreover, even if accepted as a goal, equalization of goods appears unfeasible, for given the diversity of individual diligence such equality "would very soon again be destroyed. But what *cannot* be done, one should also not attempt to do."[30]

As must be emphasized, acceptance of empirical inequalities does not extend to or sanction inequalities of freedom. In terms of the *Philosophy of Right,* freedom is an attribute not of nature (or physical existence) but of human spirit and self-consciousness—a consciousness that, in turn, does not exist "naturally" but emerges only in the laborious transition from natural to free will. In this connection, the text offers some intriguing comments on the issue of slavery and, more generally, on lordship and bondage. For Hegel, the assumption that some humans are "by nature" slaves or destined for bondage is entirely spurious because the assumption neglects spirit or consciousness. The alleged justification of slavery, he writes, and all historical vindications of the justice of slavery and unmitigated lordship, depend "on regarding man as a natural being or physical entity (governed by arbitrariness)—which is wholly unsuited to the concept of man." On the other hand, the assertion of the absolute *injustice* of slavery and bondage insists properly on the "concept of man as spirit and inherently free consciousness." But this claim is still limited or one-sided by insisting on a freedom granted "by nature" or by the concept (of man) in its abstract immediacy, instead of seeing freedom as an achievement of spirit. In Hegel's account, both assertions regarding slavery are flawed, but the first is more seriously defective than the second:

> That side of the antinomy which asserts the concept of freedom has the advantage of containing the essential starting-point, though only the starting point for the discovery of truth, while the other side—fixated on pre-conceptual physical existence—misses the claims of rationality and rightness altogether. Right and jurisprudence begin from the standpoint of free will; hence they are already in advance of a position which regards man as a natural being or as an abstract concept amenable to slavery.

To proceed beyond abstract assertions, the text counsels (again) the path of dialectics, a path which—via the "struggle for recognition" between master and slave—leads from natural to free consciousness or will and ultimately to the sphere of ethical life (in the state).[31]

The motif of mutual recognition applies not only to slavery or bondage but to property relations in general. As pointed out in *Realphilosophie,* acquisition of property through labor is a first step in the formation of individual freedom. But such freedom needs to be exerted not only over objects but also vis-à-vis other freedoms or agents of free will. To qualify as private property, an object must be recognized as "mine" by other individuals; such recognition alone transforms physical possession into property in the full sense. The most prominent expression of recognition is the contractual bond. According to the *Philosophy of*

Right, the relation of "will to will" is the "genuine ground" of the embodiment of freedom. The arrangement whereby property is held not merely by means of "subjective will," but in virtue also of "another person's will" and hence through "participation in a common will," is the distinctive domain of contract.

In Hegelian terminology, contract is a relationship operating on the level of "objective spirit"; for this reason, it is said to imply and presuppose "from the start the element of recognition." As a process of mediation, contractual recognition involves a convergence or mutual agreement of wills—though *not* in the mode of genuine unity or universality but only in that of an intersection of separate wills (whose convergence resides in the value of the external good). As Hegel notes, in contract there are two distinct wills exerted by two distinct subjects or proprietors, thus *arbitrariness* still enters the negotiation. For this reason, not every human relationship can be subsumed under the contractual category. For example, marriage cannot and should not be construed as a mere contractual bond (Kant's contrary opinion notwithstanding). Similarly, public life in the state exceeds contractual arrangements—regardless whether the agreement is viewed as a contract of each citizen with all others or a contract of all with the government and the monarch. The intrusion of contractual (and more broadly private-law) considerations into public affairs, we read, has been "productive of the greatest confusion in both constitutional law and public life," particularly in "recent times."[32]

As a correlation of wills, contractual agreement includes both the acquisition of goods (through purchase, loan, or other means) and their abandonment or surrender (through sale, gifts, and the like). As Hegel emphasizes, surrender or "alienation" (*Entäusserung*) of goods applies only to things that are external, or alien, that is, extrinsic to the core of subjectivity or free will. On the other hand, everything that touches personhood, free will, and the "essence of self-consciousness" is by its very nature an "inalienable" good and the right to such a good is "imprescriptible" (*unverjährbar*). Hence, an individual can as owner dispose of animals, plants, and all other things, provided they are "temporal, finite, mortal, and subject to nature alone." Yet, such an individual cannot surrender his or her intrinsic freedom—and where such a surrender has been negotiated, the agreement is (like all unethical contracts) null and void or revocable through an act of will. In the words of the text:

> The right to inalienable goods is imprescriptible, for the act whereby I take hold of my personhood and basic essence and thus establish myself as a legally, morally and religiously competent agent, withdraws these goods from that externality which alone makes possible the surrender of something into another's possession. By revoking this externality I also cancel the temporal conditions and all other reasons which might be drawn from my prior consent or submission to such a surrender. This return into myself whereby I reaffirm myself as idea and as a legal and moral person, annuls the previous situation and the wrong which I and the other have done to personhood and to reason itself, namely, by treating infinite self-consciousness as something external.

Given the close connection of personhood with "life" as the arena of self-actualization, human life too cannot be willfully surrendered or abandoned by an individual—although such life may on occasion be claimed by a higher agency, such as the state as the embodiment of ethical life.[33]

Morality: Subjective Welfare and Conscience

Given the separateness of wills in contractual arrangements, individual right on this level also makes room for individual "wrong" (*Unrecht*). The *Philosophy of Right* devotes a section to the modalities of such wrongdoing (and also to their correction through restitution and punishment). Generally speaking, will on the level of abstract right is directed at external goods—and subsidiarily at other wills likewise concerned with goods. The next step is the individual's reflection on the source of will in self-consciousness or subjectivity. Such reflection whereby the target of will shifts from goods to inwardness itself brings into view the arena of *morality,* or moral life (*Moralität*). By virtue of this shift, free will transcends the generic indeterminacy characteristic of abstract right and acquires determinate shape in the mode of singular individuality or subjectivity. While abstract right consists basically of a system of rules, the accent in morality focuses on motivation, purpose, and intentionality. In terms of the text, morality denotes the standpoint of free will insofar as the latter is infinite "not only as such (or by definition) but *for itself*" (or inwardly); freedom here means subjectively willed freedom and rightness here designates the "right of subjective will." The step to inwardness, for Hegel, involves basically a movement of maturation and inner emancipation—a movement congruent with the aspirations of modern enlightenment. As he writes,

> Morality deals with man's particular interest and its high worth resides in the fact that man knows himself as absolutely self-determining. Uncivilized man allows himself to be governed by brute force and natural impulses; children likewise have no moral will and are governed in their actions by their parents. Educated (*gebildet*) man, however, develops an inner life and places his own will into everything he does.[34]

The turn to inwardness, however, does not by itself coincide with the actualization of will; inner intentions do not readily mesh with outward conditions. On the level of morality, subjective will stands opposed to objective reality (like noumenal categories stand to the phenomenal world). Given this opposition, subjective will faces the world with a set of moral demands, that is, with postulates located on the level of "ought" (as distinguished from "what is"). Consequently, in view of the recalcitrance of reality, morality necessarily involves a state of conflict, division, or diremption, a division that is inherent in the inner-outer dichotomy. In Hegel's words, "self-determination on the plane of morality must be viewed as pure restlessness and activity which cannot reach the level of 'what is' "; in the moral sphere, "will still relates (externally) to reality in itself and its position is consequently that of strict difference."

In relating to external reality, moral will also relates to other human wills whose motivations must be taken into account. In the context of abstract right, will only concurs with other wills with respect to an object, but morality must seek a concurrence of inner intentions. This difference also is reflected in the outward manifestation of will. Whereas abstract right finds the embodiment of will in external property, moral life is embodied in activity, specifically in subjective and moral action that is intentionally directed at other wills. According to the *Philosophy of Right,* moral will can be studied basically from three angles: from the angle of subjective purpose or intentionality, from that of subjective welfare or happiness (*Wohl*) as the particular goal of action, and from the vantage of the more general objective that may be termed the *good,* or goodness, of will (and that conjures up *evil* as its correlate).[35]

Hegel's discussion of the three dimensions of morality are marked by immense subtlety—of which only the barest glimpse can be offered here. The aspect of purpose or intentionality is closely linked with the issue of subjective responsibility or accountability for an action. In legal terminology, the issue is one of "imputation," revolving around the degree to which an action and its consequences can be imputed to an individual as corresponding to his or her intentions. Such imputation is important primarily in modern legal relations, whereas ancient penal codes were "relatively less concerned" about the matter. The modern cultivation of inwardness, however, necessarily entails concern with subjective accountability. Will, Hegel comments, has a right "to recognize as its action, and to accept responsibility only for those aspects of a deed of which it was conscious in its aim and which were contained in its purpose"; a deed can be imputed only to "a consciously responsible will."

The focus on subjective intention, however, carries with it a major dilemma: the problem of unintended consequences. By inserting itself into the web of external circumstances, every action unleashes a chain of effects that can only partially be foreseen or deliberately chosen. In the language of contemporary ethics, subjective morality at this stage remains *intentionalist* rather than *consequentialist* in outlook; in Weberian terminology, it opts for an ethics of *conviction* over an ethics of *responsibility.* As between intended and unintended consequences, moral will claims the right "to accept responsibility only for the former because they alone were part of its purpose." In Hegel's own view, one should add, this right of morality is also its limitation, because it still relies on a rigid division of inner and outer domains, of subjective choice and external necessity. The maxim "Ignore the consequences of your actions" as well as the opposite maxim "Judge actions by their consequences and make these the yardstick of right and good" are in his account equally principles of purely abstract reasoning.[36]

Moral will is intentionally directed at an aim which, in the first instance, is a particular aim, namely, that of individual welfare or happiness. In Hegel's presentation, this goal has its own (relative) legitimacy, although it is by no means the highest human goal or fully congruent with the idea of freedom. The notion of subjective freedom, he notes, implies attention to the particularity or singularity of the agent, and there is even a right of subjectivity to find some satisfaction in its actions. To the extent that this particularity is respected, actions carry subjective meaning and reflect the agent's individual self-interest. The specific content of welfare or happiness at this point is diverse and hence remains still infected with contingency and private preference. To this extent, moral will is still joined with natural will, although the latter is now reflectively screened or sublimated. Again, the focus on particularity and the value attached to individual happiness are basically trademarks of modernity—as compared with the emphasis of earlier times on role functions and social duties. In the words of the text:

> The right of the particular subject to find individual satisfaction or (differently put) the right of subjective freedom constitutes the central turning point in the difference between antiquity and modern times. In its infinity this right was announced by Christianity and has since become the general effective principle of a new form of civilization. Among the primary shapes of this principle are personal love, romanticism, the quest for eternal individual salvation, but also morality and individual conscience.

While recognizing their legitimacy, Hegel does not unreservedly extol private welfare or satisfaction (thereby implicitly rejecting utilitarian assumptions). Even in its reflective mode, private welfare in his view has a confining or self-indulgent quality stifling the fuller development of freedom. With terms like welfare, he writes, we enter into a "tranquil, nearly private-bourgeois domain" of concerns, while losing sight of the "best in man." Given their indefinite and shallow character, there is "a special tediousness in words like welfare and happiness." Compared with public welfare or the "common weal," both abstract right and subjective will are at best subordinate considerations.[37]

As in the case of private property, moral will in aiming at a particular satisfaction is also necessarily directed at other moral wills and their aims. From this correlation there arises the notion of a general or common will and ultimately the vision of the good or goodness (*das Gute*) as the highest goal toward which individual will can be directed. In Hegel's words, the good is "determinate idea seen as the unity of the concept of will and particular individual will." Goodness denotes "the essence of will in its substantiality and universality," that is, free will as reflected "in and through thought." As one should note, goodness does not yet mean a fully actualized mode of ethical life, but rather a postulate or demand addressed at, and shouldered by, particular will. To this extent, goodness confronts the individual as a moral "duty" (*Pflicht*) or obligation—an aspect that has been properly and admirably accentuated by Kantian philosophy. From this vantage, we read,

> duty shall be done for its own or for duty's sake, and when I fulfill my duty I realize my own true essence: for, in doing my duty, I constitute myself as free. It is the merit and lofty distinction of Kant's moral philosophy to have underscored this meaning of duty.

Appreciation of this merit, however, is instantly qualified by important reservations, deriving chiefly from the pure formalism of obligation. Regarding its content, the standard of duty remains formal and empty—beyond the instruction to do whatever duty commands. In logical terms, the performance of duty for duty's sake is nothing but a restatement of the logical rule of noncontradiction (A cannot be non-A) and hence basically tautological. Although adding a further ingredient, the stipulation of *universalization*—of the universal sway of the imperative (of duty)—does not by itself exceed the rule of noncontradiction and formal identity, a rule that can be filled with the most varied content. "The maxim that there should be no property," Hegel notes, "contains by itself as little contradiction as the rule that this or that people, this or that family should not exist or that mankind as a whole should not be." For contradiction can arise only through conflict with a "determinate content" which is presupposed as a firm starting point.[38]

As a postulate or general goal, goodness appeals to an inner discriminating sense anchored in subjectivity, namely, to "conscience" (*Gewissen*). Such appeal to conscience has been steadily cultivated and refined in modernity—a refinement that Hegel duly acknowledges. Conscience, he writes,

> is this deepest inward solitude with oneself where every external restriction has disappeared—this complete withdrawal into oneself. As conscience, man is no longer shackled by the aims of particularity; in attaining

that position he has risen to higher ground, the ground of the modern world which for the first time has attained this consciousness, this veritable descent into oneself. Earlier, more sensuous periods remained tied to something externally given, provided either by religion or law.

As an inner forum, conscience is not itself endowed with substantive yardsticks—although it inevitably claims the right to judge or evaluate all yardsticks. Given its discriminating capacity, conscience is the ultimate refuge of free will and moral decision—a decision which can given rise to good or evil consequences. According to Hegel, the origin of "evil" (*das Böse*) resides in the "mystery of freedom," more specifically in the struggle between natural and genuinely free will. In the mode of subjective will, he notes, conscience is always "on the verge of lapsing into evil"; it is in inner willing and deciding that both moral goodness and evil have their "common root." For, purged of substantive criteria, inwardness of will always has a dual capacity or potential. It can either embrace genuine freedom and universality or else elevate "caprice and private particularity" over universality and act accordingly, which is the emblem of evil. The origin of evil, from this vantage point, resides neither in nature (including human naturalness) as such nor in the inwardness of willing, but rather in the directedness or orientation of inner will—in the sense that inwardness can choose private whim and separateness over the demands of goodness. Evil, or rather the possibility of good and evil, thus arises from the diremption of natural existence and subjectivity, which is the distinctive mark of mankind—although diremption itself is not the goal but only a threshold for sublation in higher unity. Differently phrased, diremption is the necessary condition for the possibility of evil, which itself is not a necessary consequence: "It is in the nature of evil that man can will it but need not."[39]

Ethical Life: Family

On the level of morality, goodness confronts subjective will as a postulate or demand addressed at inner conscience; objective standard and inward intention are correlated only in the mode of diremption, that is, the mode of conflictual opposition. This diremption is overcome on the plane of ethical life (*Sittlichkeit*) where objective goodness becomes the concrete aim and content of will. In terms of the text, *ethical life* means the "concrete coincidence of goodness and subjective will"; it relies on subjective intention and conviction, but on one animated by *actualized rightness*. By welding together inward will and objective goodness ethical life cancels or sublates diremption, thereby fulfilling the task of *reconciliation*. With this step, a new form of freedom also comes into view, namely, actualized freedom where free will takes itself as its concrete content. Ethical life, we read, is "the idea of freedom"—the "living goodness" that finds "in self-reflection its conscious will and through action its concrete reality."

The actuality of freedom is rooted in the aspect that goodness, although an objective standard, is not an alien or heteronomous yardstick (or an abstract "ought") but one congruent with the innermost human essence or genuine self-consciousness. As in the case of morality, objective goodness is still a human duty, or obligation (*Pflicht*), but a duty that liberates rather than constrains. This liberation occurs on different levels and in different guises: by emancipating will from its dependence on natural impulses; from its subjection to abstract postulates; and even from the prison house of solipsistic existence. When instantiated in individual human behavior, goodness takes the form of "virtue" (*Tugend*)—whose most general trademark is "rectitude" (*Rechtschaffenheit*) to the extent that the latter denotes adequacy of behavior to the duties obtaining in a given situation. To qualify as virtue, however, such adequacy of behavior must be not only sporadic or occasional but also the outgrowth of a continuous disposition reflecting a steadiness of character. Once virtue achieves this kind of steadiness, ethical life turns into "custom" (*Sitte*) or habitual practice where ethical conduct appears as second nature taking the place of "purely natural will."[40]

As concretely actualized freedom, ethical life is embodied or finds expression in different kinds of contexts, from the more intimate to the more distant or universal. Hegel's dialectics reappears here with its movement from immediacy through division to sublation. On the level of immediacy, ethical life develops in the context of the "family," described as "natural ethical spirit." Moving beyond the confines of the family, individuals enter the context of "civil society"—but they do so as "autonomous individuals" connected with other individuals only through bonds of "formal generality" (which Hegel also terms the "external state"). The division of interests prevailing at this stage finally gives way to the context of public life or the "state" where ethics achieves "substantive universality."

In his discussion of this dialectic, Avineri presents the stages of ethical life as "three alternative modes of interhuman relationship," for which he uses the labels "particular altruism" (family), "universal egoism" (civil society), and "universal altruism" (state). Although suggestive, these labels are potentially misleading to the extent that they substitute psychological categories for Hegel's ontological account—a danger that Avineri himself seeks to obviate. Once this danger is properly noted, his discussion remains (as always) instructive. In the family, he writes, "I relate to other human beings with a view of *their,* rather than my, interests in mind"; activities performed for the sake of family members are "other-oriented, 'altruistic' in the analytical (not moralistic) sense" that they are undertaken not for selfish reasons but "for the benefit of someone else with whom the actor is connected through ties which are called 'family ties.' " In civil society, by contrast, "I treat everybody as a means to my own ends," and I even use "the felt need of the other as a means to satisfy my own ends" in pursuit of what is called "enlightened self-interest." This egoism is transcended in the state, which signals "a mode of relating to a universe of human beings not out of self-interest but out of solidarity, out of the will to live with other human beings in a community."[41]

In Hegel's own presentation, family life is held together by a natural bond, that of love or affection, which, however, transcends natural will by its unifying spiritual power. For this reason, the bond is described as ethical spirit in its mode of natural immediacy. In the words of the *Philosophy of Right,* family life "as the immediate substantiality of spirit is characterized by unifying feeling or love" in such a manner that the self finds its individuality "in this unity," considering itself no longer as separate subject but as "family member." In this connection, love (*Liebe*) means basically "consciousness of my unity with another," that is, an awareness that I exist no longer in "selfish isolation" but that I gain myself "through surrender of my separateness" and through a self-understanding that is predicated on "the unity of myself with the other and the other with myself." Reminiscent of some of Hegel's early writings, the text here launches into an eloquent and elaborate portrayal of the phenomenon of love, now couched in terms of ethical spirit. For Hegel, love is marked by two aspects, or moments, that seemingly stand in conflict. The first moment is that of surrender, the aspect that "I do not wish to be an independent person for myself" and that, if I were, "I would feel defective and incomplete." The second aspect is that of renewed self-discovery, the fact that "I find myself in another person," that "I count for something in the other just as the other counts in me." In view of these disparate tendencies, love accomplishes a miraculous feat—that of engendering unity in difference:

> Love, therefore, is the most tremendous contradiction which reasoning alone cannot resolve. For, there is nothing more stubborn than this centeredness of self-consciousness which is negated and yet claimed as an affirmative possession. Love is both the production and the resolution of this contradiction; as the latter it signals ethical unity.[42]

Family life is grounded in marriage or matrimony, finds concrete embodiment in family property, and attains completion in the procreation and education of children. The relationship of marriage partners is both a natural or physical and an ethical-spiritual bond, with the two aspects sustaining each other. Hegel in this context criticizes a number of misconstruals of this bond. One such misconception places the essence in sexual union. No less misguided or "crude" is the view that sees marriage simply as a civil contract—a view still maintained by Kant—whereby the bond is degraded to an arrangement for "mutual contractual usage." Likewise to be rejected is a sentimental approach that reduces love to the ebb and flow of romantic feeling—a conception that misses the steadiness of ethical life.

For Hegel, marriage—although animated by love—is prompted neither by purely subjective whim nor by external command, but by an ethically and spiritually guided affection. In earlier epochs and in cultures where "the female sex enjoys little respect," parents have arranged and continue to arrange marriages without consulting the young couple. And the young raise no objection since at that point "the particularity of feeling still makes no claims for itself." In modern times, however, subjective feeling, the state of being in love, is considered the decisive factor—a view that can easily degenerate into sentimentalism. As a spiritual union, marriage is concluded in a civil or religious ceremony which places on the union the mark of culture and language as the emblem of spirit. Where such a ceremony is dispensed with as mere externality, marriage for Hegel is denuded of its ethical quality and reduced again either to a physical nexus or emotionalism. Not a product of subjective whim, the marital bond once established is also not subject to capricious dissolution by the partners—except in special circumstances carefully (and sparingly) stipulated by public law.[43]

Regarding the character of the spouses or marriage partners, the *Philosophy of Right* contains a number of intriguing observations—some of which no doubt reflected cultural preconceptions of the time (and hence are alien or unappealing to contemporary readers). For Hegel, the place of woman was clearly in the home and her role was closely confined to the private sphere of family life. Man or the male partner, by contrast, was a member both of the family and of the larger civil society and the state or public community. As a result, the male partner cannot remain tied to the home but has to undergo the divisiveness and diremption of society, with the aim of gaining his full spiritual destiny in the state (as the sublation of diremption).

The difference of membership between the two sexes also explains their different ethical orientation. For the woman, ethical life is concentrated in the family and hence still deeply suffused with natural sensuality and concrete-local piety. For the male, on the other hand, ethics is an arena of moral-spiritual contest and of an intense struggle for recognition in the public domain. As Hegel states, commenting on male-female relations, woman in the act of sexual surrender also "surrenders her honor," something that is not equally true of man who has "another field of ethical activity" outside the family. Man or the male partner, in fact, finds "his real substantive life in the state, in science and the like, as well as in labor and in the struggle with the external world and with himself," a struggle that entails that man achieves selfhood or autonomous self-unity "only through diremption." This struggle subsides in the intuitive-sensual unity of family life where woman finds her substantive destiny and ethical fulfillment. According to the text, the contrast between male and female ethics is illustrated in Sophocles' *Antigone* through the conflict between familial law and state law:

> In one of the most sublime portrayals—in Sophocles' *Antigone*—familial piety is presented principally as the law of woman, as the law of sensual-subjective substantiality, of an inwardness which has not yet achieved complete actuality—hence as the law of the ancient gods, the gods of the 'underworld,' as the timeless law of which no one knows the origin, a law which is placed into sharp contrast to the public law, the law of the state—a contrast which captures the highest ethical and highest tragical opposition, and also the opposition between femininity and masculinity itself.[44]

As a legal institution (and hence a manifestation of freedom), family life is actualized in external goods, that is, in family property or "capital" (*Vermögen*). While, in the context of abstract right, property is an appendage of separate individuality, family capital has the character of a shared and thus properly ethical (*sittlich*) possession: "The arbitrariness and selfishness of the particular needs of a single individual are transformed here into something ethical, into labor and care for a common possession." Legally represented by the husband as head of the family, family capital is not the property of a larger clan or lineage (on the male and female side) but specifically of the married couple and their offspring. While in previous ages legal codes often privileged lineage or kinship relations, modern legislation tends to vest property rights in the "nuclear family" (thereby honoring the higher dignity of ethical love over blood relationships). Family life is completed and crowned by the presence of children in whom love—as the inner soul of marriage—emerges itself as a visible object. In Hegel's words, the parents now "love the children as their love, as the embodiment of their own substance."

While family capital symbolizes family unity only through the medium of external goods, such unity is embodied in the children on a spiritual plane "where the parents are loved and show love in return." As participants in a loving union, children are not servants nor the property of parents, but rather free agents—although their freedom still needs to travel the long road from natural to genuinely free will. The main right of children is to be properly nourished and educated out of family property. Education here is particularly important, for what humans are meant to be is not "given to them by instinct" but must be acquired through training. The aim of education is first of all to instill ethical sense into immediate feeling and sensibility. But next, education must guide children slowly out of "natural immediacy" to the level of "autonomy and free individuality," and thus enable them to participate in society at large beyond the confines of their parents' home. Both aspects of education are important, but autonomy cannot properly be pursued without the nurturing of sensibility, which in infancy is primarily the mother's task:

> The child must have lived with its parents encircled by their love and trust; in this manner, reason dawns on the child as its innermost subjective endowment. Particularly in the early years, education by the mother is crucial, for ethics must be implanted in the child as feeling or sensibility.[45]

Civil Society: System of Needs and Labor

While in the bosom of the family, individuals enjoy the benefits of ethical cohesion nurtured by love. This cohesion is left behind once adults enter the broader context of society that is constituted by a multitude of families and single individuals. In Hegel's account, this is the level of "civil society" (*bürgerliche Gesellschaft*) and, in ethical terms, the "stage of difference" or diremption where the accent is placed on individual particularity and the diversity of human interests that are held together only by an abstract framework of formal rules. Civil society, we read, comprises two aspects or dimensions: the particular individual seen as "a bundle of needs and a mixture of caprice and physical necessity," and the relationship among individuals established on the level of "formal universality." Because ethical standards here do not directly penetrate into individual behavior but are only distantly reflected therein (while still forming the deeper backdrop of social existence), Hegel describes civil society also as the "stage of appearance" or as the "appearing world (*Erscheinungswelt*) of ethical life."

Given the accent on particularity and the diversity of interests, ethics is radically dispersed or sedimented in the multiplicity of individual concerns and thus seemingly stripped of a unifying bond; civil society to this extent can be defined as the "system of ethical life lost in its extremities." At the same time, individual pursuits remain linked through a web of reciprocal dependence that, in turn, is governed by a system of formal rules—which Hegel also terms an "external state" or the "state based on need and abstract reasoning" (*Not-und Verstandesstaat*). Basically, civil society is a complex intermeshing of particular interests and formal rules, with the presumption generally operating in favor of individual preferences and goals. In the words of the text: Because particularity remains inevitably conditioned by formal universality, the sphere of civil society is the "terrain of mediation" where there is "free play for every idiosyncrasy, every talent, every accident of birth and fortune," and where "the waves of every passion continually gush forth" regulated only by reason "glinting through them."[46]

In its attention to individual particularity, civil society develops an important element of the idea of freedom and ethical life—although this development remains partial and in need of further sublation. In Hegel's view, this attention is the crucial mark of modernity as distinguished both from Greek antiquity and non-Western societies. "The creation of civil society," he asserts, "is the achievement of the modern world which for the first time gives their proper due to all elements of the idea (of freedom)." Although emphasis on particularity entails divisiveness and diremption, the latter is a necessary step in the process of ethical maturation. Spirit, we read,

attains its actuality only by undergoing division or diremption, by imposing on itself—in the midst of natural needs and external necessity—this
inner limit and finitude and by proceeding, through the labor of education
(*Bildung*), to overcome this limit and thus to attain objective reality. The
end of reason is neither natural simplicity nor the unleashing of pleasures
fostered by civilization but rather the laborious effort to subdue naturalness . . . and particular immediacy in which spirit is buried and to acquire
the rationality of which particular existence is capable, namely, the
rational form of universality.

This role of individual particularity in ethical maturation was not fully appreciated in antiquity, and particularly in Plato's *Republic*. Instead, as already indicated in earlier contexts, the unfolding of particularity emerged in the ancient world as a signal of "impending ethical decay" and ultimately as "the cause of that world's downfall." Grounded on patriarchal or religious principles and generally on greater "ethical simplicity," the states of antiquity could not withstand "diremption and the unfolding of reflective self-consciousness" and hence succumbed to this process as soon as it arose. Although Plato's *Republic* portrayed the substance of ethical life "in its ideal beauty and truth," he could not cope with the emerging diversity except by erecting a substantively unified state that downgraded private property and family life. Latent already in the context of Greek city-states, the notion of individual autonomy only gained recognition in the postclassical age, to be later resumed and fully developed in modernity:

> The principle of autonomous, infinite individual personality, or of subjective freedom, could not come into its own in the substantive shape (of the *Republic*). This principle first dawned in inward form in Christianity and in external form, linked with abstract universality, in the Roman world; it is historically later than the Greek world.[47]

Although an advance over classical simplicity, modern individualism in Hegel's view is Janus-faced and not an unmixed blessing. On the one hand, by emphasizing individual initiative, modern society makes room for the display of subjective freedom that is a key ingredient in developed ethical life. On the other hand, emancipation of subjective freedom also unleashes a stream of needs, desires, and predilections—a stream that is potentially infinite and hence incapable of being fully satisfied. On one side, individual particularity belongs essentially to the process of ethical maturation; on the other, this process can also be the harbinger of moral depravity and corruption. "In these contrasts and their complex intertwining," Hegel writes, "civil society affords a spectacle of extravagance and want as well as of the physical and ethical degeneration common to both."

In cultivating individual interests and tastes, modern society encourages the expansion of knowledge and ideas, and hence an enormous broadening of the range of reflective self-consciousness. However, with growing sophistication and the broadening of horizons comes also the expansion and multiplication of desires, which, in contrast to animal instincts, are not confined in a closed circle but are basically measure-less. Lack of measure in regard to desires has as a corollary the possible emergence of "want and destitution likewise beyond measure," a condition of disarray that can only be mitigated or corrected by governmental intervention. This spectacle of want and disparity has sometimes been erected into a general indictment of modern society, especially in comparison with presumably simpler or more natural modes of life. The lecture course of 1819-1820 speaks of the "alienation (*Entfremdung*) of ethical life," adding that the "sight of multiple misery" often presented by society has prompted "noble souls like Rousseau" to launch "invectives against civil society itself"—invectives which are one-sided, however, by ignoring the dialectical character of ethical life.[48]

In the *Philosophy of Right*, civil society is discussed from a number of angles, though mainly in light of the following three: human needs and their satisfaction through labor; private or civil law and jurisprudence; and social welfare and group pluralism. Regarding the first dimension, the text stresses particularly the interlocking character of needs and their satisfaction—a nexus, or system, that is all the more surprising given the enormous variety of desires and preferences. Inspired by the pioneers of modern economic theory, Hegel in this context pays tribute to the discipline of political economy—as a science that again is "endemic to modernity" or modern social conditions. As illustrated in the writings of Smith and Ricardo, Hegel argues, the development of this discipline demonstrates in a fascinating way how rational inquiry is able "to extract from the endless mass of details which initially confronts it the simple principles governing the subject matter and hence its inherent rationality." At a first glance, the activities in modern society give the impression of utter chaos and confusion. The amazing thing, however, is to see how "this medley of arbitrariness" generates out of itself general patterns and rules and how "seemingly disparate and nonrational elements" are held together by a "spontaneous necessity." To uncover this kind of necessity is the objective of modern political economy—a science that is "a credit to thought" because it manages to find "laws for a mass of accidents." It is an "interesting spectacle," Hegel adds,

> to observe how all relationships here are reciprocal, how particular spheres are grouped together, and how they influence others while being helped or hindered by them in turn. Most remarkable is the mutual interlacing of activities, which at first seems unbelievable because everything appears governed by individual whim—an interlacing which has a parallel in the system of planets which initially displays to the eye only irregular movements but whose laws can nonetheless be ascertained.[49]

On the level of civil society, human needs are not simply natural instincts or impulses but rather reflected or culturally conditioned needs—a circumstance that reveals again the dialectics of ethical maturation, the complex advance from nature to spirit. By comparison with animal life, human life in society is accordingly both more stimulating and diversified and more demanding. "The need of shelter and clothing," Hegel writes, "the necessity of eating cooked rather than raw food (which destroys its natural immediacy) entail that man has less comfort than an animal—and, as spiritual creature, he ought to have less." This ascendancy of spirit over animal nature is completely at odds with the notion of a "state of nature" in which humans supposedly lived in blissful harmony with their surroundings by satisfying only "simple natural needs." In Hegel's account, this notion is a false view because natural needs and their satisfaction signal a condition of nonspirit or of a "spirit buried in nature" and hence a state of "savagery and unfreedom," whereas freedom resides in conscious reflection and its "difference from nature."

As objects of conscious reflection, needs in civil society are no longer spontaneous but reflectively interpreted needs just as their satisfaction has cultural connotations; in the end, it is "no longer need as such which must be satisfied but opinion." Moreover, due to the interlocking character of social activities and modes of satisfaction, needs are not so much or not only generated by individual agents themselves but also by society at large, and especially by other agents whose interests are served by the generation or cultivation of needs: "Hence need is triggered not so much by those who sense it immediately as rather by those who hope to make a profit by its creation."[50]

The chief means of satisfying needs in society is labor (*Arbeit*). In conformity with the great diversity of needs and preferences, labor likewise is increasingly diversified and specialized, particularly in modernizing-industrializing societies. Moreover, due to the close interdependence of needs, labor tends to form an interlocking system in which work satisfies no longer the laborer's own needs but those of other members of society. Economic production in this manner comes under the sway of the "division of labor," a division that has the result of rendering the individual's labor simpler, or less complex, while simultaneously increasing the individual's skill in his or her particular job and also the level of his or her output. The most important effect of the division, however, resides in its strengthening of the formal network of relationships connecting the diverse facets of society. In Hegel's words, advances in skill and methods of production

> solidify and underscore the necessity of the interdependence and reciprocal relation among individuals in the satisfaction of their needs. Further, the abstract refinement of productivity tends to make labor more and more mechanical—until finally man is able to step aside and install machines in his place.

Diversity of skills and of specialized occupations is matched in civil society by disparities of social status and economic fortune. As the text points out, differences in talent, diligence, and luck all conspire to produce in society an inequality of property or private capital (*Vermögen*), an inequality that is likely to grow with the advancement of industry. As on the level of abstract right, such diversity of external goods cannot be abolished in society without at the same time abolishing subjective freedom and hence the possibility of ethical life. Turning against a time-honored natural-law doctrine, *Philosophy of Right* asserts that "men are made unequal by nature where inequality is in its element." This condition is compounded in society by the ethical "right of particularity," which adds to natural diversity an "inequality of skill and resources, and even of moral and intellectual formation (*Bildung*)." To oppose to this right the postulate of equality means to lapse into a mode of "empty reasoning" that considers such an abstract demand as "concrete rationality."[51]

Social Welfare and Group Pluralism

Although the arena of subjective freedom and particularity, social life in Hegel's account is not completely abandoned to the sway of individual caprice and diversity with their (likely) corollaries of inequality and exploitation. The *Philosophy of Right* discusses a number of devices and arrangements that mitigate (without completely subduing) the turbulence of civil society. One such device is civil law and jurisprudence with their guarantees of equal justice or equality before the law. Again, the notion of equal justice is preeminently a modern acquisition, reflecting the progress from natural immediacy to reflective consciousness. "To have a conception of right (*Recht*)," Hegel writes, "man must be trained to think instead of being imprisoned in sensation"; thinking, however, means to grasp objects under "universal categories" and to let one's will be guided by "universal rules."

Given this linkage with thought or reflection, modern jurisprudence necessarily endorses the principle of equality before the law for which each individual is treated as a "universal being," or as an instance of the species. It is part of education, of thinking as the ability to "subsume singulars under universals," Hegel insists, that the individual comes to be seen as "universal person" on a plane where "all are identical." At this point, a man counts as human "because of his humanity, and not because he is a Jew, a Catholic, Protestant, German or Italian." To operate properly, equal justice requires the presence of a known and duly promulgated law (or system of laws) that is general in character and applies equally to all members of society. The *Philosophy of Right* in this context heaps lavish praise on lawgivers or legislators, especially those who have left behind a "well-ordered and clear-cut legal code," referring to them as the "greatest benefactors of their peoples" and performers of a "great act of justice." More specifically, Hegel's text supports ongoing efforts of legal codification as preferable to the hodgepodge of feudal regulations and the vagaries of the common-law tradition. Regarding the inequities of the common-law tradition, one only needs to consult "the practice of English jurisprudence." Insistence on general laws, of course, does not rule out adaptation to concrete circumstances or the later addition of further laws—all of which does not impair the need for a "compact law book."[52]

Rational legislation and equal justice, however, are only limited correctives to the reign of difference and caprice endemic to civil society. In addition to legal remedies, the text examines a number of social provisions designed to safeguard at least rudiments of common interest in the midst of private interests. Among these are rules regulating the conduct of business and commerce, requirements of mandatory education, and provisions for sanitation, health care and social welfare. Between the extremes of complete individual freedom and extensive government intervention, Hegel here steers a middle course that seeks to give "both sides their due" and that mediates individual self-interest with the general social matrix enabling the pursuit of such interest.

Most important in this context—and most difficult to resolve—is the issue of social welfare, that is, the provision for a general level of subsistence as an antidote to the spreading of poverty or indigence (*Armut*). Basically, the problem is how to ensure such a subsistence level without at the same time undermining the subjective will of recipients, their sense of subjective worth and responsibility. Hegel's discussion of the issue is sensitive and nuanced, and his description of the effects of poverty—especially in English factory towns—is gripping. As he notes, poverty is a multiheaded monster that affects not only physical subsistence but also educational opportunities, legal rights, and even religious or spiritual welfare. In the words of the lectures of 1819-1820:

> Poverty in civil society is a condition which is in every respect unhappy and forsaken. It is not only external misery which the poor have to endure; that misery is compounded by moral degradation. The poor lack in large part the consolation of religion: frequently they cannot go to church because they do not have proper clothes or because they have to work on Sundays. . . . Moreover, the poor often have trouble finding legal assistance. Their health care is equally desparate: even if provision is made for real illness, they lack the means to sustain ordinary health.[53]

The chief remedies for social indigence are private philanthropy and public assistance, with the two types ideally supplementing each other. The singular or particular aspects of individual misery place a premium on remedial action that is personal in character and attentive to special needs. Here is the task of philanthropy which, mindful of the particular circumstances of a case, proceeds from motives of "love and sympathy."

According to the text, this is the field suitable for charity and the place "where morality finds plenty to do despite available public programs." Yet philanthropy cannot entirely take the place of public assistance, as this would place the burden on private altruism alone. Individuals, in Hegel's view, have a right to demand subsistence from civil society and the latter is "responsible for feeding its members." Thus the casual practice of charity and alms giving needs to be supplemented by public programs and institutions, such as poorhouses, hospitals, and the like.

While recognizing public responsibility in this domain, Hegel is skeptical or pessimistic about the ability of society to eradicate or significantly alleviate misery, especially under conditions of progressive industrialization. As illustrated in the case of England (the most advanced country in this respect), industrialization means a growing division or gulf between rich and poor. "When civil society is in a state of unimpeded development," Hegel notes, "it experiences a growing expansion of population and industry." This expansion, in turn, yields a steady "amassing of wealth" on the side of business and industry, which is accompanied, on the other side, by the increasing "dependence and misery of the working class"—a misery compounded by the truncation of "other liberties" and of the ability to reap the "moral benefits" of society. When physical indigence and moral deprivation reach large proportions and affect a large mass of people, personal misery gives way to the emergence of a "rabble of paupers," which forms the opposite pole to "disproportionate wealth concentrated in a few hands." As Hegel emphasizes, it is not poverty as such that creates pauperism and the rabble but rather the mental disposition linked with poverty, the "inner indignation against the rich and against society"—an indignation fueled by the lack not just of livelihood but of basic rights.[54]

Under the impact of industrialization and economic development, society thus is polarized and nearly torn apart. In one of the most sober and somber passages of the *Philosophy of Right,* Hegel remarks that the question of how to deal with poverty is "one of the most tormenting problems beleaguering modern society." Although reflecting a social obligation, the remedies provided by society through public assistance are all intrinsically flawed. To the extent that assistance is offered directly in the form of food and shelter, the poor are secured in their subsistence but without having to work for it—something that violates "the principle of civil society and the sense of individual autonomy and self-respect." On the other hand, if assistance is offered in the form of public employment or public work projects, the increased labor pool is bound to increase the volume of production—something that aggravates the economic predicament by fostering overproduction coupled with inflation and the decline of purchasing power. "It hence becomes apparent," Hegel notes, "that despite an excess of wealth civil society is not rich enough, that is, its own resources are insufficient, to check excessive poverty and the creation of a penurious rabble."

Despairing of a domestic remedy for economic polarization, the *Philosophy of Right* at this point turns attention to overseas expansion and colonization—an enterprise promising an outlet both for over-population and overproduction. In Hegel's account, industrial society is peculiarly linked with the sea and seafaring—just as family life is tied to the "earth," to "firm land and soil." As he writes, "all great, progressive-developing nations strive to the sea." Overseas colonies provide a new home and livelihood for poor and unemployed masses while at the same time opening up new markets for domestic overpro-duction. Civil society for these reasons is "driven to found colonies." Colonization of far-off lands, incidentally, does not necessarily imply political domination. On the contrary, as the history of English and Spanish colonies demonstrates, "colonial independence proves to be of the greatest benefit to the mother country."[55]

While leaving the matter of public assistance unresolved (and perhaps insoluble), the *Philosophy of Right* discusses a number of other devices designed to counteract social polarization as well as the perils of individual isolation and destitution. The central means of social integration is the complex, interlocking network of social estates and private associations. Defined in a nonascriptive sense, social estates are the natural outgrowth of the diversity of occupations that, in turn, is a result of the social division of labor. In terms of the text, the overall system of needs characterizing civil society subdivides quite naturally into a number of subsystems marked by distinct modes of labor, satisfaction, and educational training— that is, into a cluster of "estates" (*Stände*). Apart from their economic or occupational role, the central significance of estates resides in their integra-tive function—their tendency to infuse centrifugal social relations with a quasi-familial spirit of ethical union. In Hegel's words:

> If the family is the first pillar of the state, the estates are the second. This
> is all the more important as private individuals—although self-seeking—
> are also constrained to direct their attention to others. Here is then the root
> whereby self-interest is tied to the universal or the state—whose care it
> must be that this nexus remain firm and solid.

While promoting social cohesion, estates in Hegel's account are not
"closed" groupings in the sense of being based on birth or constraint.
Rather, membership in estates is determined by individual choice—
although this choice is guided by economic and other considerations. As
he writes, individual membership is influenced by temper, birth, and other
circumstances, but the "essential and finally decisive factor is subjective
opinion and arbitrary will," which in this domain claim their "legitimate
right." It is in this respect for particularity that Hegel finds (again) a crucial
distinction between modernity and antiquity and also between Occident
and Orient. Society in antiquity and in the Orient, he notes, is also
subdivided into estates, but only along objective-functional lines. Thus
membership is either decided by public authority (as in Plato's *Republic*)
or the result of birth (as in the Indian caste system). Exiled from the
social order, subjective particularity hence can only surface as a "hostile force" or as a source of "corruption and utter degradation."[56]

The cluster of estates discussed in *Philosophy of Right* is familiar
from earlier writings, especially from the *Jenaer Realphilosophie*. In
line with the dialectical schema, three types of estates are distinguished:
the immediate, or *substantial;* the reflective, or *formal;* and the *universal* type (in which substance and reflection are sublated). The first type
is the agricultural estate whose capital resides in the "natural products
of the cultivated soil"; ethical disposition here is directly tied to family
or kinship relations and manifests itself in the virtue of trust. According
to Hegel, family and agriculture have rightly been described as the
"beginning and original foundation" of political communities. In the
process of modernization, however, the solidity of this grounding is
transformed, especially to the extent that agriculture itself is mecha-
nized or industrialized: "In our day, agronomy proceeds along rational
lines, like a factory, and thus assumes the character of an industry which
is contrary to its naturalness."

The second type is the commercial estate (*Gewerbe*), which can be
further subdivided into the three branches of artisans, manufacturers,

and merchants or businessmen. By contrast to dependence on nature, this estate is devoted to the deliberate reshaping of natural goods through labor and through commercial interaction in the broader system of needs. On Hegel's account, this estate is the chief carrier of modern civil society and, as such, imbued with the spirit of subjective particularity and self-interest, which is a synonym for individual free will. In the domain of commerce and business, we read, the individual is "thrown back on himself" and this sense of selfhood is closely tied to the demand for an "ordered condition of rights." Unsurprisingly, the taste for orderly freedom "first arose chiefly in the cities," which were centers of trade and commerce.

The third type finally is the universal estate or class of civil servants whose task is care for the common good, or for the universal interests of society. Given that the energies of this estate are completely absorbed by this task, needs of individual members must be covered either out of private capital or else out of public funds provided by the state. As in *Realphilosophie,* no mention is made here of the working class or the estate of industrial labor—although, in discussing economic polarization, Hegel speaks specifically of the laboring class or the "class tied to labor" and marked by dependence and destitution.[57]

Beyond the occupational structure of estates, the *Philosophy of Right* also refers to a welter of private or civil associations that Hegel calls "corporations" (*Korporationen*). Like estates, corporations have basically an integrative function by countering individual isolation and destitution through a spirit of ethical cooperation and partnership. Together with family and estates, corporate associations constitute a crucial "ethical pillar" or foundation of the political community—although, in contrast to the family, they fully respect the principle of individual particularity. Akin to estates but of more limited scope, corporate bodies are not closed entities but depend on individual talent and preference. In Hegel's words, a properly functioning corporation is "not a closed guild" but rather a means to integrate "independent branches of business" into an ethical context. The main task of such bodies, however, is to serve as an antidote to social atomization, a danger that looms large in modern industrial societies and that even tends to undercut the significance of political franchise. Under modern political conditions, we read,

citizens have only a restricted share in the public affairs of the state; yet
it is essential to provide ethical creatures with the opportunity for public
or universal activity above and beyond their private business. This universal or general purpose which modern states do not always furnish, is
granted to individuals in the corporation.

eg Bowling
clubs?)
(Rotary?)

In this concern for some social or public engagement, the *Philosophy
of Right* anticipates arguments of later perceptive commentators on the
frailties of liberal institutions, even or especially when liberalism is
joined with political democracy. As Avineri notes, a chief drawback of
traditional liberal democracy has been "its hostility to any intermediate
groupings standing between the individual and the state. Like Tocqueville
a decade or two later, Hegel wants to redress the balance."[58]

Although in principle germane to civil society as a whole, corporate
associations in Hegel's account play their chief role in the middle class
or estate, that of commerce and business. The agrarian estate finds its
ethical grounding in family and kinship; civil service is devoted to
affairs of the state; but commerce thrives peculiarly in the elements of
diversity and particularity—thus placing a premium on cooperative
partnership. Although the scope of a given corporation is restricted to
a special branch of trade or business, cooperative partnership gives to
members a sense or experience of general or universal aims. Selfish
purpose, the text states, "while directed toward its particular self-
interest, apprehends and evinces itself here at the same time as something universal." By participating in trade or business associations,
individuals also gain effective recognition (*Anerkennung*) both from
their peers and from society at large—a recognition crucial for their
sense of personal freedom and self-worth. Membership thus furnishes
the individual with "status honor" (*Standesehre*), which is a powerful
corrective to tendencies of social alienation and isolation. In Hegel's
estimation, marriage and status honor are the "two axes" around which
the centrifugal tendencies of modern society revolve.

As one should note again, these tendencies are not by themselves
objectionable or defective, as they are part of the process of ethical
maturation that passes through particularity and diremption. While
engendering separateness and possible alienation, modern civil society
also fosters self-reflection and personal freedom—without which modern public life is inconceivable. Whereas agriculture and the country-

side promote the virtues of family life, town and cities are "the seat of bourgeois commerce" and thereby also the seat of "growing reflection and individual selfhood." To this extent, town and country—seen as "ideal types"—are "the two dimensions whose true ground and culmination is the state."[59]

The State as Embodiment of Reason

The crowning dimension in the *Philosophy of Right*—and the apex of the realm of objective spirit—is the state seen as the actualization of freedom and as the embodiment of fully developed ethical life. On this level, the ethical unity characterizing family life is recovered, though now mediated through the reflectiveness and individual differentiation present in civil society. While, in its mode of immediacy, will is directed at external goods, and while, on the plane of morality, reflection discovers the inner source of willing, ethical will now is directed at freedom itself—no longer in a purely internal but in an actualized sense. As Hegel explains, the state is "the actuality of the ethical idea"; it is "ethical spirit now revealed as self-transparent, substantive will." Given the nexus of ethics and freedom, the state can also be called the actuality of free will achieved through a "universalized self-consciousness," that is, "reason as such" as the unity of universality and particularity.

Hegel's statements along these lines have frequently been criticized as manifestations of an extreme kind of *statism* and even authoritarianism, although the emphasis on the mediation of unity and diversity, of identity and difference should give grounds to pause. Suspicions of statism are aggravated or intensified by some additional comments on the topic that if read out of context (as they frequently are) seem to justify even accusations of impiety if not idolatry. The state, we read at one point, is by itself "the ethical whole, the actualization of freedom," and it is an "absolute end of reason" that freedom should be thus actualized. For the state is nothing but "spirit acting in the world and realizing itself there consciously." While, in nature, spirit operates only in its "otherness" or as a "slumbering spirit," the state is a conscious reality which "knows itself as really existent." Seen as actualization of spirit (which is not only a human but an absolute or divine spirit), the existence of the state is part of "divine providence in the world" (*Gang Gottes in der Welt*)—a notorious phrase. Its grounding is "the power of reason actualizing itself as will."[60]

A proper assessment of Hegel's statements, in my view, clearly requires attention to their philosophical and historical context as well as to the critical edge demarcating them from alternative conceptions. As it happens, this critical edge is explicitly articulated in the lectures of 1819-1820. Two main conceptions are singled out there for criticism: one stressing the divine institution of public authority and the state, the other locating their origin in private will or preference. The first view was favored by the reactionary temper of the time, especially by European monarchies banded together in a *holy alliance* designed to protect the divine right of kings against revolutionary upheavals; the second view derived from the natural-law tradition and continued to reverberate in liberal utilitarianism. "One hears it said on the one side," Hegel comments,

> that the state derives from divine authority, that governments are instituted by God. On the other side one claims that the state is a product of human caprice. Both views are one-sided, because the idea of the state comprises in itself both principles.

The notion, Hegel proceeds, that kings and governments are instituted by God is plausible and legitimate insofar as the state is indeed the embodiment of *objective* spirit, a spirit that is something divine. Hence, seen as manifestation of reason or spirit, the state is properly part of divine providence. The notion becomes false or obnoxious, however, if reason is radically opposed to faith, and divine power to human institutions—as has happened in "recent times" in some quarters where the divine has been "expelled" into a realm "beyond," leaving human reality denuded and forsaken.

Here, then, is the clear edge of Hegel's position: the conception of the state as embodiment of reason or spirit militates against divine right extolled as an article of nonrational belief. The state, he insists, is "divinely authorized not as something non-rational but as something rational"; for what is elevated above reason would be merely nonrational, or irrational. The claim regarding divine institution has often been misrepresented as signaling the imposition of a "destiny beyond reason or rational cognition"; but this would only inaugurate a "system of passive obedience." In a sense, the opposite view (stressing human origins) is only the other side of the coin: by centerstaging arbitrary will the view again robs the state of universal rationality, reducing it instead to an instrument of private caprice.[61]

The critical edge against alternative conceptions is resumed in the *Philosophy of Right,* though with slightly different accents. Close attention is again given to the derivation of the state from private will or preference. Where individual self-interest is stipulated as the highest aim and final yardstick, Hegel writes, there the state is "confused with civil society" and its purpose is located in "the security and protection of private property and personal freedom." Accordingly, membership in the state is seen as "purely optional or contingent," something that violates humanity's universal rational calling, the principle that individuals are properly individuated only in the context of ethical life. The focus on self-interest is closely connected with contractarianism or the view of the contractual origin of the state. In this respect, the text pays critical tribute to Rousseau. In comparison with his predecessors, Rousseau's merit or achievement resided in his concentration on a principle "grounded in thought" or reason, namely, on "will" as foundation of the state. Yet by construing will only as particular will and by conceiving the "general will" not in terms of universal reason but merely as a "commonality" or convergence of wills, Rousseau's argument in the end led to a contractual state deriving its legitimacy "from individual will and opinion and from capriciously given consent."

A different, but equally misguided conception is one accentuating the factual positivity and empirical power of the state. The starting point in this case is again the aggregation of individuals. In contrast to contractarianism, however, the focus is not on constructive rational analysis but instead on "empirical details with their purely accidental characteristics such as strength and weakness, wealth and poverty, and the like." The chief reference in the text here is to Ludwig von Haller, a conservative jurist who recently had published a treatise devoted to the "restoration of political science" along positivist and historicist lines. In Hegel's account, the treatise was remarkable chiefly for its empiricist myopia, its determination to ignore the universal rationality of the state and generally "to banish thought from the comprehension of its essential nature." In bypassing rational criteria in favor of empirical contingencies, Haller's work had made it a point to denounce the rule of law and legal codification as being in conflict with historical customs and with the "naturally grown" web of social distinctions, inequalities and hierarchies. Among such distinctions the treatise extolled, in particular, differences of power, defending in this respect a kind of social Darwinism by stating that "it is the eternal, unalterable ordinance of God that the mightier rules, must rule, and always will rule." One can clearly see, Hegel comments dryly, "in which sense 'might' is taken here: it is not the might of justice and ethics, but only the irrational power of brute force."[62]

In opposing empiricist construals, Hegel is not unaware of the empirical dimension of the state and also of the possibility of corruption and deformity. His critical point is directed chiefly against an intellectual confusion with its attendant practical consequences: the confusion of mistaking contingent, empirical factors for the essence of the *idea* of the state. As a philosophical treatise or inquiry, the *Philosophy of Right* is concerned first and foremost with the idea, that is, with the actuality of free will and objective reason. "In considering the nature of the state," the text states, "we must not fix our eyes on particular states or particular institutions, but instead must focus on the idea itself." Particular states are liable to deviate from the idea in numerous ways, which is due to history and a host of natural and social circumstances; yet, particularly in developed modern conditions, states also are bound to exhibit the essential features endemic to their nature. Since, however, it is easier to criticize manifest defects than to grasp a philosophical idea, there is a widespread tendency to cling exclusively to empirical and contingent traits, which often enough mar or disfigure the essential design. The state, Hegel observes,

> is no ideal work of art; it stands in the world and so in the sphere of caprice, chance and error. Hence bad behavior can disfigure it in multiple ways. Yet, the ugliest man, or a criminal, or an invalid, or a cripple, still remains a living human being. The affirmative element—life—persists despite such defects; and it is this affirmative factor which is here our theme.[63]

Comparable to individual maturation and education (*Bildung*), states likewise undergo a process of development or maturation in the course of history, which is not merely a succession of random events but the steady unfolding of reason in public life. Immature or undeveloped states, in Hegel's account, are those communities in which the rational idea is still "veiled" and where the concrete characteristics have not yet fully emerged into their own. The classical state or *polis*, again, serves to illustrate this undeveloped condition because—submerged in a substantive bond—there individual particularity had not yet been "released and emancipated" and ultimately reconciled with the universal purpose of the whole. In the Platonic *Republic,* in particular, subjective freedom "counted for nothing," because individuals had their duties assigned to them by guardians. The same limitation, even in aggravated form, prevailed in Oriental or Asiatic states where functions were determined by birth and where individuals were not granted any "inwardness and personal right."

By contrast with this heteronomy or external constraint, individuals in modernity demand to be respected in their *inner life* and to be able to nurture their "own opinions, preferences, and individual conscience." The nature of the modern state thus implies that the universal or common good be bound up with "the complete freedom of particularity and the happiness of individual members." Accordingly, there is here a convergence or interlacing of perspectives with the result that public unity is maintained while individuality experiences "full and lively development." This convergence, or interpenetration, of universal and particular aspects also entails a close connection between right and duty, in the sense that the individual's obligation to the substantive or common good is at the same time the emblem of personal freedom and of the rights attached to this freedom. To this extent, public life marks an advance over both abstract right and subjective morality, and the nexus of right and duty must be seen "as one of the crucial features and as source of the inner strength" of modern states. In the words of a well-known and often-cited passage:

> The principle of modern states has this prodigious strength and depth of allowing the principle of subjectivity to develop to the extreme of personal singularity and independence while at the same time guiding the latter back into substantive unity, and thus maintaining this unity in and through subjectivity itself.[64]

As embodiment of rational spirit, the state relates not only to private will but also to perspectives or institutions concerned with spirituality or with the spiritual aim of life—of which religion is the foremost exemplar. A long paragraph—one of the longest and most elaborate in the text—deals with the relation between church and state or, more broadly, between religious belief and the state as rational idea. Hegel's argument on the topic is intriguing and unusual in that it advocates neither a rigid separation nor a complete fusion of the two domains but rather something like a differentiated unity or a unity with difference.

Historically, the main backdrop for Hegel's argument is again a certain religious conservatism or fundamentalism that—loosely along Augustinian lines—asserted either the strict subordination of the state to religion or else the irrelevance of the former in comparison with faith. As indicated before, a central thesis advanced in this context was that of the *foundational* role of religion as source of public legitimacy. Responding to this thesis, Hegel notes again its basic ambivalence—its appeal either to the objective spirit operative in the state or else to a radical fideism relying solely on religious belief outside the bounds of (public) reason. Taken in the latter sense, as preferred by fundamentalists, the thesis involved a thorough denigration of the state and its reduction to an instrument of caprice and repression. In Hegel's words, the mere "world-liness" of the state here serves to rob the affairs of the state of any "essential and serious concern" and to downgrade these affairs as entirely a matter of "random caprice" governed solely by "passions and lawless domination."

Having thus downgraded public life, fideism was bound to emerge victoriously, but its triumph was not innocent. As Hegel points out, fideism of this kind can have noxious political consequences. It must first of all "seem suspicious," he writes, that pure faith is extolled chiefly in times of "public calamity, disorder and oppression" when religion serves as "compensation" for public injustice. In treating public affairs as merely worldly and insignificant, fideism in these conditions tends to counsel pliant submission to ruling powers. As history teaches—whose lessons should "not be forgotten"—religion at times can sponsor "the hardest bondage under the fetters of superstition and even a degradation of humans below the level of animals." Faith at this point becomes an emblem of unfreedom and servile obedience—in violation of the spirit of Christianity, which is a "religion of freedom."[65]

In its relation to politics and the state, however, fideist fundamentalism can engender different and even conflicting consequences or postures. One such posture is inward retreat into a private faith contemptuous of public affairs. Yet, inwardness can also serve as a springboard for a religious activism bent on imposing private beliefs on the world in a direct and unmediated fashion. As Hegel's text notes, the guiding motto in this case tends to be "No law is binding on the just; be pious and do as you please." Pursued with fundamentalist zeal and intensity, this motto is the hallmark of religious fanaticism, a posture that, like fanaticism in politics, discards all governmental and legal institutions as "barriers cramping the inner life of the heart" and that banishes private property, marriage ties, and the rules of civil society as "unworthy of love and the spontaneity of feeling."

Hegel's objections to this outlook are basically the same as those leveled against an abstract essentialism and subjective moralism that, disdainful of the labor of reflective thought and action, proceed to impose summary verdicts on concrete reality. Piously assured of the possession of truth, fundamentalist believers rush to an apocalyptic dénouement, or demolition, of human affairs, instead of undergoing the labor of educating themselves in the rational *cognition of truth* and in the understanding of objective right and duty. In the political context of the Restoration period, fundamentalism of this kind surfaced only occasionally in radical (even terrorist) actions. More prevalent was the attitude of inward retreat coupled with the denunciation or depreciation of worldly politics. In Hegel's words:

It is not strength but weakness which has turned religiosity in our days into a polemical kind of piety, regardless of whether this turn is prompted by real need or simply by unsatisfied vanity. Instead of subduing one's opinions through the labor of study and of raising one's (natural) will through discipline to the level of free obedience, the line of least resistance is to renounce knowledge of objective truth, to cultivate a feeling of dour humility flattering to self-conceit, and to claim to possess in godliness everything needed to penetrate to the heart of law and government.[66]

While critical of fundamentalism, the *Philosophy of Right* is by no means opposed to religiosity or to religious inwardness as such. On the contrary, properly construed (and without its polemical edge), religious feeling of this kind is seen as the ideal supplement of the state viewed as actualized reason. The object of religion, Hegel insists, is "absolute truth," and hence it can claim "the highest of dispositions"; in the midst of the flux and mutability of human conditions, religion grants to humanity a "sense of permanence" and also of "complete freedom and fulfillment." Focused inwardly on God or the divine as the absolute source of all being, religiosity carries with it (quite properly) the demand that everything be viewed and justified with reference to this source.

At issue, however, is the precise meaning of this demand. While providing indeed the source and grounding of all being, Hegel adds, religion at the same time furnishes "*only* a grounding," stopping short of its actualization and determinate development—which is precisely the domain of the state. Religion involves a relationship to the absolute couched "in the mode of feeling, imagination, and faith"; whatever falls outside its "living center" is seen as merely accidental and transient appearance. The state, by contrast, is spirit assuming concrete shape and a definite structure in the world; moreover, it is a rational spirit that relies basically on rational insight and knowledge instead of intuition or belief. In religion, the content of truth is given without being amenable to conceptual grasp; in revealed religion, the content is based on authority, while individual testimony and acknowledgment take the form of faith and feeling. As against this stress on inner conviction, the state is guided by reason that replaces intuitive feeling by determinate thought. As a corollary of this focus on rationality, the state also takes the form of a legal structure or a sphere of public law replete with a specified set of individual rights and duties—where the latter are not simply dependent on feeling. Seen in this light, religion and state complement each other, but do not coincide. "Just as the state," we read, "in raising religious demands would violate the right of inwardness, so the church in acting and imposing punishments like a state degenerates into a tyrannical religion."[67]

The relationship between state and religion is somewhat more complicated where the latter is organized as a church, or a distinct community of believers. As a concrete structure standing in the world, a church necessarily gets involved in property relations and other legal matters that regularly are the province of the state. For Hegel, the general rule governing the relationship is "simple." Given its own rootedness in (divine) spirit, the state has to protect and support the activities of churches and generally to encourage a sense of religiosity, irrespective of the particular content of religious belief (which is "not the state's business"). The state's protection and tolerant support extends from ritual and worship to the doctrines or teachings of churches, although here matters become entangled because teachings are an overt manifestation of spirit, which is also the hallmark of the state (as embodiment of objective spirit). Hence it is in the domain of teaching that church and state meet most directly and intimately—and may clash in radical opposition.

Hegel refers in this context to the traditional (Augustinian) doctrine of the two realms or two cities where spirit is entirely reserved for the "heavenly city" represented by the church. The difference of the two domains, he writes,

> may be exacerbated by the church into radical antagonism, namely through the claim that—in enshrining the absolute content of religion— the church also exerts monopoly over spirit and over ethical life as such. By portraying itself as the kingdom of God or at least as its highway and vestibule, the church here degrades the state to a mere mechanism for the attainment of non-spiritual, external aims, that is, to a purely mundane or worldly realm marked by transient finitude. Seen in this light, the church appears as an end in itself and the state as a mere means.

In this conception (favored again by fundamentalists), the state is a structure established simply for the protection of life and property and for the containment of harmful behavior. Differently phrased, the state is an arrangement for the satisfaction of elementary needs, whereas higher spiritual aspirations are reserved for inner religiosity. As Hegel comments, such a construal may be appropriate for conditions of "barbarism" and complete political corruption, in which higher spiritual life may indeed find its only refuge in the church and where the state has degenerated into a "purely worldly regiment" based on "brute force, caprice, and passion." History provides examples of such conditions; however, it is far "too shallow and myopic" a stratagem to present these situations as congruent with the idea (of the state).[68]

Recognition of the rationality and spiritual quality of the state also implies rejection of the church's exclusive monopoly in spiritual matters. In the field of church doctrine, this rejection entails a certain curtailment of religious teachings to the extent they directly undermine public life—as may happen in cases of sectarian fanaticism. Faced with blatantly obnoxious or destructive opinions, Hegel observes, the state has to protect "objective truth and the principles of ethical life"—just as, when confronted with a church claiming absolute authority over minds, the state has to vindicate the right of self-consciousness to engage in inquiry and rational reflection regarding the nature of truth. For the rest, Hegel's text counsels utmost tolerance, a tolerance predicated not on indifference but on genuine respect for religious belief. Respectful tolerance of this kind is an emblem of a properly constituted public order, that is, of a state seen as the manifestation of rational freedom. A properly developed state, Hegel notes, can be "all the more liberal" in this domain, by overlooking, for instance, details of religious practices and even by tolerating sects that refuse to recognize "direct duties toward the state" on religious grounds, such as Quakers and Anabaptists (although "a lot depends here on numbers").

Hegel in this context strongly defends the extension of civil rights to religious and ethnic minorities. With specific reference to the Jewish community, he writes that "to exclude Jews from civil rights means to confirm the isolation with which they have been reproached," a result for which the state would be "blamable and reproachable because, through this refusal, it would have misunderstood its own basic principle." Tolerance of religious beliefs underscores both the affinity and the basic difference between church and state. While linked on the level of spirit and true principles, the difference between these institutions is demonstrated by the coexistence of diverse religious communities within the borders of the rational (though not merely worldly or secular) state. For the state to unfold as rational actuality, Hegel affirms, it had to differentiate itself from the authority of faith. But this distinction, in turn, could only emerge once the church itself was internally differentiated or divided, that is, with the rise of particular churches and sects comprised by the universality of the state. Hence, he concludes, so far from the division of the church being a "misfortune" for public life, it is "only as a result of that disunion that the state has been able to reach its appointed end as self-conscious rationality and ethical life."[69]

Constitutional Government and Separation of Powers

The *Philosophy of Right* explores the operation of the state under several rubrics, although chiefly these: constitutional government (pertaining to the domestic side of public life), international politics (involving external relations between states), and world history (as the manifestation of divine providence governing the fortunes and misfortunes of states). The relationship between the three dimensions is again dialectical in that the first deals with the structure of the state as such or by itself, the second with the mode of separation and division, and the last with the sublation of these elements in the ongoing movement of spirit.

Under the rubric of constitutional government, the text considers first of all the issue of governmental powers and their mutual correlation or separation. As in the case of the church-state nexus, Hegel advocates here a modified *separation of powers* principle that one might call holistic separation, or separation with unity. As he writes, a constitution is rationally structured insofar as the state "inwardly differentiates its activity in accordance with the nature of the concept," which means in such a manner "that each of the [state's separate] powers constitutes in itself the totality by containing the others effectively in itself" and thus allowing the constitution to operate as an integral whole. Separation in the sense of differentiation does not imply segregation or radical division, something that is incompatible with the cohesion of ethical life. As Hegel recognizes, the idea of separation of powers reflects a crucial aspect of rationality, namely, the element of determinate negation, of difference, and hence of actualized reason. This aspect, however, is vitiated where it is exaggerated into segregation and complete reciprocal autonomy. At this point, the relationship between the powers turns into a purely negative mode of mutual restriction: "The attitude of each power toward the others becomes hostile and apprehensive, as if the others were evil forces, and the goal becomes one of mutual opposition."[70]

The danger of governmental division is strongly underscored in the text—an emphasis prompted in large measure by the experience of the French Revolution and its turbulent aftermath. Where governmental powers oppose each other as autonomous entities, we read, the situation is clearly a recipe for strife or civil war, a strife leading "either to the destruction of the whole or else to the restoration of unity by force." Several passages in the *Philosophy of Right* read as if they had been triggered by some arguments in the *Federalist Papers,* especially by those accentuating the need for mutual limitation over the aspect of mutual cooperation. Generally speaking, in Hegel's view, public life—as embodiment of reason—cannot properly be grasped and is necessarily distorted by a one-sided focus on wrongdoing and possible usurpation. "To take the merely negative as starting point," he writes,

> to foreground ill-will and the attendant distrust and then—proceeding on this premise—to construct dikes whose effectiveness simply necessitates further counter-dikes, this outlook is characteristic of purely negative reasoning, while its inner sentiment reflects the view of the rabble.

Given the close linkage of reason and ethical life, one-sided preoccupation with distrust and wrongdoing is demoralizing and hence detrimental to, or incongruent with, a public edifice sustained by civic spirit. As Hegel insists, the powers of the state must indeed be distinguished but not in a mutually exclusive way; rather, "each of them must constitute itself as a whole and embrace the others in itself." The basic point, he reiterates, is that—since the powers combined are meant to form a unity—their actual operation must reflect and coalesce into a holistic fabric. Differently put, their actualized existence must "satisfy the concept as a whole."[71]

A state in which powers are properly distinguished and correlated is a constitutional form of government, which, in turn, can take different shapes among which Hegel prefers constitutional monarchy. As he asserts, the development of the state into constitutional monarchy is "an achievement of the modern age where the substantive 'idea' has gained infinite form." The accent in this formulation is not on the specific monarchical shape as on constitutionalism as such, seen as the differentiated articulation of powers. The principle of modernity generally, he adds, is "freedom of subjectivity," which implies that "all essential factors present in the totality of spirit are developed and given their due."

Constitutionalism of this kind is the result of a long historical evolution and was lacking in ancient or premodern times. Thus the traditional classification of governments into monarchy, aristocracy, and democracy—a scheme found in Aristotle—was still constitutionally undeveloped because it relied on the "undivided, substantive unity" of government and hence had not yet advanced to "internal differentiation" of powers and to the spiritual "depth" and "concrete rationality" associated with this distinction. In terms of traditional categories, modern constitutional monarchy—and constitutional government in general—might be described as a mixed type of regime in the sense that it comprises rule by *one,* by *the few* and by *the many* (the Aristotelian criteria of classification). In Hegel's view, however, the notion of mixture and of numerical combination is inadequate and superficial, because it does not penetrate to the essence of constitutionalism. From the vantage of the modern idea of the state, the three traditional types of regimes—monarchy, aristocracy and democracy—are all equally irrelevant and indifferent, because they remain inadequate to the unfolding of reason and thus fail to grant to reason its right and actuality. For the same reason, it is also quite idle to inquire which of these traditional regimes is the "most excellent," or most preferable, as they all are now relics of history. What is crucial is not this or that particular shape but rather constitutional government as such, which is the result not of arbitrary human fabrication but of a long process of maturation, of the "labor of centuries" molding and transforming social and public life.[72]

Regarding governmental powers, the *Philosophy of Right* diverges from the customary separation of executive, legislative, and judicial branches of government. In view of its chief preoccupation with conflicts of private interest, the judicial branch is treated in the text mainly under the heading of civil society rather than that of the state. In line with his preference for constitutional monarchy, Hegel distinguishes between three powers or branches whose correlation is again dialectical in character: "legislative power" (*gesetzgebende Gewalt*), which establishes general or universal public rules; "ministerial power" (*Regierungsgewalt*), whose task it is to apply general rules to particular situations or cases; and "royal power" (*fürstliche Gewalt*), which sublates the other powers into a unified but individuated shape. The assumption behind this distinction is roughly that of a cabinet system of government in which cabinet ministers take care of most of the business of government—by implementing laws, administering policies, and introducing legislation in the assembly—while receiving ultimate legitimation of their actions from the monarch seen as representative of the unity and sovereignty of the state. Because many aspects of Hegel's argument are today only of historical significance, discussion will be limited here to some key features of the governmental powers of constitutional monarchy as outlined in the *Philosophy of Right.*

The linchpin of the latter regime is obviously royal power, translated also as "the crown." In conformity with the differentiated unity of powers, royal authority is said to comprise the "three moments of the whole," namely, the universality of constitutional and legal rules, the application of rules to concrete situations (effected through ministerial consultation), and the element of ultimate decision and public self-determination. As one should note, constitutional monarchy for Hegel is not merely a matter of preference but a corollary of his underlying metaphysics (of absolute idealism). The guiding thread of this metaphysics (as indicated before) is the steady unfolding and actualization of spirit in the mode of consciousness or subjectivity. On the level of public life, this means that the state too must be actualized or individuated as a subject, which happens in the person of the monarch. According to the *Philosophy of Right,* royal power manifests the subjectivity or individuality of the state, its existence in the mode of oneness. Subjectivity, however, has actuality only in the *subject,* personality only in the *person;* the decisive element, therefore, is not just individuality in general, but "a single individual: the monarch."[73]

The treatment of royal power in the *Philosophy of Right* has given rise to considerable debate regarding Hegel's political outlook. In particular, it has served to buttress the thesis (advanced by Ilting and others) of Hegel's "change of political position" after the Carlsbad Decrees. Undeniably, royalty, or the crown, is the apex of the constitutional system in the *Philosophy of Right,* but not in the sense of a glorification of royal absolutism (and even less of a eulogy for the Prussian monarchy). Comparison of the *Philosophy of Right* with the texts of the lecture courses reveals only slight differences of accent that do not disturb the overall constitutional conception. In this respect, Henrich is entirely correct (in my view) when he writes that Hegel's notion of the state "derives directly from his metaphysical conception and not from an orientation or option of a political kind."

Consistent with this view, essentially the crown for Hegel is the embodiment of the state, which, in turn, is the actualization of freedom or free will—where free will is a synonym for reason and by no means equivalent to arbitrary caprice. Hence, the monarch in his treatment is the preserver or protector of the constitutional order as actualized reason—and not an absolute sovereign of a Hobbesian kind (guided by sheer will). In a famous passage, Hegel portrays the state as a "grand architectonic structure," as a "hieroglyph of reason" manifest in governmental institutions and ultimately in the monarch. The monarch, he writes, represents the sovereign will of the state and, more concretely, the "I will" of the crown. But, he adds, this does not mean that the monarch may act "capriciously." Rather, he is "bound by the concrete content of ministerial advice" and, in a stable constitution, has usually "no more to do than sign his name," although this name "is important." According to another famous passage, the monarch "only has to say 'yes' and dot the 'i,' " because at the apex of the regime "personal whim and idiosyncrasy" are insignificant. In a well-ordered constitution, the central feature is the rule of law—to which the monarch only has to add "the subjective 'I will.' " Nonetheless, this addition is not marginal but the emblem of modernity (or modern subjectivity): "This 'I will' constitutes the great difference between the ancient and the modern world, and in the great edifice of the state it must find its appropriate place."[74]

Sovereignty or sovereign power in the *Philosophy of Right* means basically rational self-determination or the autonomy of public reason from private self-interest (as well as from external compulsion). Tied up with rational universality, sovereignty in this sense is again an acquisition of modernity and cannot retrospectively be applied to premodern conditions. Medieval feudalism, in particular, was devoid of universal rules because of its blend of public and private functions and its array of intermediary powers. In Hegel's words, although externally independent, feudal kingdoms in domestic affairs "lacked not only royal sovereignty but sovereignty of the state as such." Given its translation as supreme power, the term *sovereignty* is often associated in the common view with lawlessness or random caprice, which runs counter to the very essence of modern statehood. The term's comprehensive sweep, Hegel comments, readily gives rise to the "widespread misunderstanding" that sovereignty denotes "sheer might and empty caprice" and that hence it is "equivalent to despotism." Yet, he counters, this view is entirely mistaken, for despotism designates a "state of lawlessness where particular will as such—be it of a monarch or a mob—counts as, or takes the place of law."

By contrast, sovereignty in a "lawful, constitutional state" simply means the "moment of ideality" linking together the diverse spheres and functions; in this sense it might be called the *soul,* or *animating principle* of the state, comprising in itself "all differences." As the animating spirit of a lawful, constitutional state, sovereignty in Hegel's account is not simply an exceptional or extraordinary power, a force that disrupts or supersedes the functioning of the rule of law. His account, in this respect, is sharply at odds with some recent construals that treat sovereignty as a mode of rupture and willful disruption of ordinary lawfulness. According to the lectures of 1819-1820, sovereignty persists in normal and abnormal times, in peaceful and emergency conditions. In times of peace when everything takes its "orderly, rational path," we read, sovereignty has little to do or to "meddle." Things are different in more troubled situations when laws are silent or inadequate or when there are external threats to the state. At such junctures, sovereignty—as the "innermost unity and identity"—has the task of "standing before the rupture" (*vor dem Riss zu stehen*), that is, it acts as healing or unifying bond instead of aggravating the rupture of particular spheres and interests.[75]

The *Philosophy of Right* elaborates in detail on the functions of the crown, which cannot be pursued here. Suffice it to say that the text attributes to the monarch a symbolic function of representing the state as a whole, the function or power of appointing ministers, the conduct of foreign relations, and the right of pardoning criminals. For the sake of constitutional order and the steadiness of the rule of law, the text also expresses a preference for hereditary monarchy over an elective type. The second branch of constitutional government is the "ministerial power" or governmental power in the narrow sense. Regularly appointed by the monarch, ministers and other governmental officials are selected on the basis of their aptitude and demonstrated qualifications—although no citizen should be barred from acquiring and demonstrating these qualifications. In this respect, the modern state in Hegel's account supports the principle of the "career open to talent" or of the equal opportunity of entering public service. Members of this governmental branch and their subordinates form what Hegel has previously called the "universal class" or the estate of civil servants, which is marked by the strict subordination of private self-interest to public interest or the common good. Public service, Hegel writes, requires individuals to sacrifice or forego the satisfaction of "selfish and capricious subjective ends"—a sacrifice through which they acquire the right to participate in the "dutiful discharge of public functions."

This linkage of right and duty manifests here the nexus of universal and particular interests that generally constitutes "the concept and inner stability of the state." As Hegel explains, an important aspect of ministerial power and public administration is the proper balance between central direction and local or regional initiatives. In this respect, the *Philosophy of Right* voices a strong critique of the French practice of bureaucratic centralization, a practice inaugurated by the Revolution and continued by Napoleon and his successors. While benefiting from the efficiency and dispatch of centralized power, Hegel comments, "France lacks corporations and local communes," that is, institutions "where particular and universal interests meet." While in feudal contexts local autonomy was perhaps extreme, remedy cannot be found in a simple reversal; for one can "confidently assert that the proper strength of states lies in local communes (*Gemeinden*)." For some time now, he adds,

> one has tended to organize and govern from above and all effort has been devoted to this enterprise, while the infrastructure or the mass of the population has been left more or less unorganized. And yet it is of the utmost importance that the latter be organically structured, because only in this manner can it gain political power instead of being merely a heap or an aggregate of isolated atoms. Legitimate authority derives only from the organic formation of the particular spheres of the state.[76]

The third branch of constitutional government is the legislature, or "legislative power," which is precisely the place where the infrastructure of society gains political significance—in an organically structured way. In discussing this branch, the *Philosophy of Right* returns to the theme of estates, which, as indicated, perform a crucial integrative function in society by preparing it for public life. Estates provide a bridge between subjective will and public will, between the self-interest governing society and the general interest of the state. The distinctive role of estates, Hegel argues, resides in the fact that "the subjective element of freedom—namely, private judgment and individual will as trademarks of civil society—are brought here into integral relationship to the state." By virtue of this relationship, the state enters the "subjective consciousness of the people," just as the latter is prepared or enabled to "participate in the state." Operating as a corrective both to despotic government and to civil divisiveness and alienation, the estates have the character of a "mediating organ," that is, an organ placed in the middle between royal and ministerial power, on the one hand, and the people at large, on the other. For this reason, members of estates are required to possess both a political sense, or civic disposition, and a sense for the interests of individuals and particular groups.

Mediation of this kind is a central feature of all organically designed structures and hence of constitutionalism as such. In fact, constitutional government is "essentially a system of mediation." As on previous occasions, Hegel at this point launches into a polemic against individual representation based on individually exercised voting rights (one person one vote)—a principle that he views as a recipe for individual alienation and for the divorce between private and public life. The focus on estates and their role in the legislative branch, he writes, runs counter to "another prevalent idea," namely, the notion that members of society should participate in this function "as *individuals,* either by electing representatives or delegates or else by directly casting their vote" (without representation). However,

> this atomistic and abstract point of view vanishes already at the level of the family, as well as that of civil society, where individuals are in evidence only as members of a general group. The state, finally, is basically an organization each of whose members is in itself a group of this kind, and hence no one of its elements should appear as an unorganized multitude. The 'many' seen as individuals—what is often meant by 'the people'—are indeed a gathering, but only in the mode of an aggregate or formless mass.[77]

In the *Philosophy of Right,* the legislative branch is divided into two chambers designed to represent the two remaining estates of civil society (apart from the universal class of civil servants). The first, or upper, chamber is reserved for the *substantive* or agrarian estate, the estate governed by the natural ethics of trust and familial loyalty and economically grounded in the possession of land. Details are somewhat hazy in the text, but it seems that the estate was broadly conceived by Hegel as comprising both the landed nobility and the peasantry, and that membership in the chamber was meant to be ascriptive and thus based on birth (rather than election). The second chamber is set aside for the "dynamic element" of civil society, the estate of commerce and business.

Due both to the size and the inherent mobility of this second estate, membership in the chamber here is not ascriptive but assigned to duly selected delegates or representatives. Yet, care is again taken to counteract in the election process the randomness of individual caprice. Hegel proposes some kind of proportional scheme whereby the major fields or branches of business and commerce are allocated an appropriate share in the seats of the chamber. Once elected, members are expected to behave not as delegates of a specific interest restricted by a binding mandate, which would undercut the freedom of debate and will-formation in the chamber. Members' relation to their electors, Hegel notes, is "not that of agents with a commission or specific instructions"—particularly in view of the fact that the chamber is "meant to be a living body in which all delegates deliberate in common and reciprocally instruct and persuade each other." Instead of functioning as restricted agents, delegates in the chamber serve more like trustees or people entrusted with deliberate judgment—and again, trustees not of a narrowly circumscribed interest but of a broad sphere of civil society. If deputies are regarded as "representatives," we read, this makes good sense provided they are representatives not of "individuals or an aggregate of individuals" but rather of "one of the essential spheres of society and its large-scale interests." Representation, from this angle, denotes no longer the mere "substitution of one person for another" but rather the circumstance that a social interest is "actually present in its representative" just as the representative stands in for an "objective element" of social life.[78]

A further aspect regarding legislative power deserves mentioning, namely, the provision for the "publicity" (*Öffentlichkeit*) of debates in the chambers. The openness of the legislative forum is seen as a source of instruction and guidance for ministers and civil servants; more important, it exerts a major educational impact by instructing and shaping public opinion and hence by enhancing the political maturity of the people. In Hegel's words, the publicity of debates has the broader significance of offering to public opinion the example of "careful deliberations" and thus of providing "insight" into the condition of the state and public affairs. In this manner, people are enabled "to form a rational judgment" of their own. According to another passage, assembly debates, open to the public, are a "great educational spectacle for citizens," one in which people learn "the true character of their interests." Contrary to the assumption that interests are quite well known and only articulated in the chambers, the reverse sequence holds true in Hegel's account: It is only in the assemblies and in public service that "those virtues, talents, and aptitudes are developed which then serve as exemplars for the public."

While attentive to the importance of public opinion, the *Philosophy of Right* carefully weighs its ambivalent status, that is, its openness to public insight and its simultaneous proneness to narrow parochialism and prejudice. Enlightened or educated public opinion is particularly significant in modern states where "the principle of subjective freedom is accorded its importance and value." Public affairs now can no longer be predicated "on force, and only to a small extent on habit and custom" but must be guided by "insight and reason." To this extent, public opinion is the repository of the "substantive principles of justice" and of the "true meaning" of constitution, legislation and public affairs, namely, in the form of "common sense" seen as pervasive ethical disposition cloaked in the guise of prejudice or prejudgment. At the same time, however, public opinion can also betray this disposition and lapse into idiosyncratic myopia or sectarian frenzy. Exhibiting an inextricable blend of "truth and endless error," public opinion in Hegel's view hence deserves to be "as much respected as despised"—the latter for its parochial myopia, and the former because of its essential direction that "more or less dimly shines through" its concrete-parochial expression.[79]

International Politics

A corollary of the individuality of statehood is the individual uniqueness of modern states. Individuality, however, is achieved through differentiation and determinate negation, that is, through the distinction of self from nonself, of identity from otherness, which, on the level of statehood, means the separation of states and their reciprocal autonomy from each other. The state from this vantage, we read, is "endowed with individuality" that, in turn, is embodied in the monarch "as actual, immediate individual." In its relation to other states, this individuality appears as an "exclusive distinctness" giving rise to contacts of "mutually independent units." Achieved through determinate negation, distinctness seems to inaugurate only a negative relation to otherness and thus to constitute a purely external attribute; in fact, however, it denotes the state's "most intrinsic quality" by pointing to its "actual infinity as the ideality of everything finite in it."

Given the separation and independence of states, international (or interstate) politics occurs in a kind of *state of nature* where relations are governed by the will of individual agents. The most important correlation among agents is of a contractual sort and enshrined in international treaties. However, performance of treaties is based on sovereign will and not on "a universal will holding sway" over states. Hence, international politics shows a fluctuation of compliance with, and violation of, treaty obligations. The situation is even more unstable in regard to international law seen as a set of "universal norms supposedly binding on states." Here again respect and disrespect alternate, depending on considerations of public interest. Matters would not be very different in a "league of nations"—such as had been proposed by Kant for the purpose of securing "perpetual peace"—because support for the league would require the consent of member states, a consent resting "on moral, religious or other grounds and in any case on particular sovereign prerogative" and hence always "infected with contingency."[80]

Due to the separate autonomy of states, international politics bears a resemblance to the relation between individuals in civil society, especially when the latter is seen as a mere aggregate of atomistic agents.

The similarity resides in the abstractness or "ought" character of moral rules (a feature earlier discussed under the heading of "morality"). The difference between the two cases, however, is twofold. For one thing, states are not private agents but public entities, and more important, even in loosely integrated societies, individual behavior is still governed by enforceable legal sanctions, something that is lacking in the international arena. As Hegel writes, the situation of private individuals is such that they are "under the jurisdiction of a court which implements what is objectively right and lawful." Although relations between states "ought to be lawful" in a similar way, the problem is the absence of a higher agency of enforcement.

Given this lack of a superior power or institution that determines "what is right and lawful" and implements this decision "even against states," international relations are liable to remain on the level of an *ought,* or abstractly moral rules. As autonomous entities states are prone to stipulate rules among themselves while simultaneously placing themselves above these stipulations. According to the *Philosophy of Right,* the problem of autonomy persists even in the case of a league of nations attempting to act as a superior enforcement agency. Hegel returns at this point to Kant's proposal, noting that the holy alliance of European monarchs was precisely an endeavor to institutionalize this idea. The trouble with such an alliance, in his view, is that either it remains dependent on member states, and hence lacks enforcement power, or else it does acquire such power but at the price of succumbing to the dialectic of political agency: as a superior agent, the alliance gains autonomous identity again through determinate negation and differentiation from otherness, that is, by inaugurating a new friend-foe dichotomy:

> The state is an individual and individuality essentially implies negation. Hence even if a number of states coalesce into a united family, this federation or alliance must, as individuality, engender an opposite—and thus must create an enemy.[81]

Like his treatment of the state, Hegel's discussion of international politics has spawned considerable controversy, with critics attacking his presumed glorification of "reason of state" (*raison d'état*) and even of international conflict or war. Undeniably, there are passages in the *Philosophy of Right* that are jarring to contemporary sensibilities, especially passages referring to the ethical benefits of war and to the importance of courage and of individual sacrifice for public aims. Repeatedly Hegel speaks of the purging and invigorating effects of warfare, particularly in times when the moral fabric of a country has become ossified or stagnant, as was the case in the old German empire before Napoleon. War in such situations demonstrates the power of "negativity" in the midst of mundane life, shaking people out of their complacency through its stern *memento mori*. The text also speaks of the value of self-sacrifice, noting that "true courage in civilized nations means readiness for self-sacrifice in the service of the state" and that the crucial thing here is not "personal mettle" but "integrating oneself into the common (public) order." There are also passages that appear quaint or naive in light of later experiences of total warfare. In this category belong statements about the increasing mechanization of warfare and its presumed humanizing effects. The "principle of the modern world," we read at one point, has given courage a "higher form" by making its manifestation "seem more mechanical" and not the action of "particular individuals"; hence warfare is no longer individual combat but the collision of larger entities. An instance of this development is the "invention of fire-arms," which has changed personal bravery into a "more abstract form." This supposedly entails that modern wars are "waged more humanely" and that "person is not set over against person in hatred."

Reviewing these and a host of related passages, Avineri correctly insists on the need to read them both in their philosophical and their historical context. Once this is done, he says, warfare in Hegel's text is "no more than what a disease is to a body"; in any event, war is "not the health of a state—in it a state's health is put to the test." As he adds judiciously, cautioning against anachronistic misconstruals:

> Hegel's view is obviously at odds with any ideological interpretation of war. It certainly cannot fit into any nationalistic, or totalitarian, ideology which naturally would tend to glorify and romanticize both the conduct of the war itself and its results.[82]

Apart from the need to contextualize Hegel's comments, there are also internal features of the text that point beyond a simple realism in the sense of a mere acceptance of international conflict. One such feature is the aspect of mutual recognition between states. Just as in the case of private individuals, states are unable to attain genuine freedom or to actualize free will without this freedom being recognized as such by other states. Hence, while distrustful of abstractly moral rules and also of a superimposed world league or alliance, Hegel placed his confidence in the reciprocal "struggle for recognition" as the only viable way to achieve a shared ethical life and a durable bond of international comity. In his words: "Just as little as the individual can be a real person without rapport with other persons, the state cannot exert actual individuality without relating to other states." The legitimate authority of a state derives in part from its internal constitutional arrangements. To a significant degree, however, this legitimacy must be complemented and buttressed by the "recognition granted by other states," a recognition that needs to be safeguarded by the proviso that "where a state is to be recognized by others, it shall likewise recognize them, that is, respect their autonomy."

In the process of mutual recognition, states undergo a formative learning experience regarding their respective institutions and customs, an experience that counteracts their mutual isolation and prejudices. The bond forged through the struggle for recognition persists even in times of war—in the sense that conflicts do not become wars of annihilation but remain temporary interludes that are always geared toward, and are conducted in such a manner as to permit, the eventual restoration of peace. "By virtue of the mutual recognition of states," Hegel writes,

> there remains even in war—that condition of lawlessness, brute force, and chance—a bond whereby states count as autonomously existing for each other (or in reciprocity). Hence in war, war itself is marked as something transitory which ought to cease. This implies the provision of the *jus gentium* that war should preserve the possibility of peace—for example, that envoys must be respected and, in general, that war not be waged against domestic institutions, against the tranquility of family and private life, or against individuals in their private capacity.

Where these conditions are observed, states can over time learn to respect each other and live together peaceably in a family of nations, a community forged not so much by abstract maxims as by common experiences and by shared cultural and ethical dispositions. In this manner, he adds, the European nations "form a family in accordance with the general principles underlying their laws, their customs, and their education (*Bildung*)." Thus international conduct is gradually transformed in a context "where otherwise the mutual infliction of harm is paramount."[83]

World History

Although independent or autonomous in their mutual relations, states in international politics are not entirely left to their own devices. Their fortunes and misfortunes or their rise and fall not only depend on their initiative but are guided by a higher providential power, which Hegel calls *universal,* or *world,* spirit. The concluding section of the *Philosophy of Right* is devoted to the working of this spirit as it manifests itself in the course of world history.

In their particularity, or viewed as particular individualities, Hegel writes, states or nations (*Volksgeister*) are basically "limited" agents. Their fortunes and reciprocal actions belong to the "phenomenal (or appearing) dialectic of finite spirits"—a dialectic out of which the "universal or world spirit" forges its own realm to preside over these fortunes in the process of world history understood as a "world tribunal" (*Weltgericht*). World history acts as such a tribunal in the sense that the worth of states or nations is judged or weighed in terms of a long-range historical perspective. Yet, the historical process is not simply a blind destiny or fate that befalls states or nations randomly or capriciously. Rather, it denotes the progressive unfolding of spirit or the idea of freedom—and hence is amenable to rational insight and reconstruction. According to the text:

> World history is not the verdict of sheer might, that is, of the abstract and irrational necessity of a blind destiny. Instead, since spirit is basically reason and the latter implies knowledge, world history is the necessary development—necessary by virtue of the concept of freedom—of the various moments of reason and thus of the self-consciousness and freedom

of spirit; differently put: it is the unfolding exegesis and actualization of
universal spirit.

Given the nexus of spirit and human reason and the spirit's self-
realization through the medium of consciousness, the *Philosophy of
Right* endorses the notion of a rational-historical teleology and of a
progressive maturation of humankind. Hegel thus sharply denounces
the view of history as a heap of random events or as a "shallow play of
contingent and 'merely-human' strivings and passions." The important
question of the "perfectibility and education of mankind," Hegel notes,
is pertinent here. Those asserting this perfectibility "have indeed di-
vined something of the nature of spirit whose governing maxim is
'know thyself' (*gnothi seauton*) and which, by grasping itself, ascends
to a higher level than its original being."[84]

From the vantage of world history as the steady unfolding of spirit,
individual states or nations are like actors playing a part or role in a
larger drama that ultimately exceeds their control. Basically, states or
nations are destined to contribute to the development of spirit and the
maturation of mankind, but they do so at a given stage or phase of that
development. While legitimately preoccupied with their historical task,
they are at the same time the "unconscious agents and organs of that
inner movement where their particular shapes vanish" and where spirit
already "prepares and works out its transition to the next higher stage." In
Hegel's presentation, some states or nations in their outlook correspond to
or embody directly a given stage or phase of spirit's development; where
this matching fit occurs, a nation becomes dominant in that period of world
history—and "its historical hour strikes only once." As long as this moment
or hour lasts, the nation embodying the particular stage "secures its
good fortune and fame and its deeds are brought to fruition."

Historically more advanced states or nations are liable to treat representatives of an earlier stage as inferior or as "barbarians," as has
happened in the relation of agricultural versus hunting and gathering or
nomadic nations or of modern states versus feudal or patrimonial
countries. In the course of spirit's historical maturation, the *Philosophy
of Right* distinguishes mainly four phases whose succession is dialectical.
Considered abstractly, the first stage is spirit in its substantive immediacy
where singularity remains submerged in unity; in the second phase, sub-

stance is raised to the level of reflection and knowledge, thereby giving to unity a living form, or the form of "beautiful ethical individuality"; the third stage brings a further deepening of self-reflection to the point of abstract universality and hence of the conflict between inwardness and external objectivity; in the fourth stage, this conflict or contradiction is finally sublated in the sense that inwardness is reconciled with objective reality, thereby gaining its rational truth.[85]

Extrapolating from this dialectical process to the level of world history, Hegel (somewhat boldly) identifies the four stages with four successive "world-historical realms," namely, the Oriental, Greek, Roman, and Germanic realms. In this scheme, the Oriental realm represents the epoch of simple naturalness and holistic immediacy where all distinctions are still indiscriminately fused and blended. In Hegel's words:

> This first realm is marked by an undifferentiated, substantive world-view predicated on a patriarchal natural wholeness—a world-view where worldly government takes the form of theocracy, where the ruler is also high priest or a god, where constitution and legislation are fused with religion while religious and moral norms or customs function simultaneously as public and legal rules. In the splendor of this wholeness individual personality perishes without rights, while external nature is directly divined or treated as a divine ornament and actual history as a mode of poetry.

In lieu of a rational differentiation of particular elements or spheres, the Oriental realm develops cumbersome distinctions of status and hierarchical position backed up by religious ritual and mythical beliefs. The prevailing simplicity of manners is thus supplemented or counterbalanced by "unwieldy, diffuse and superstitious ceremonies," by the vagaries of "personalized power," and by a division of estates taking the "solid shape of ascriptive castes." On the whole, the picture of Oriental society portrayed in the *Philosophy of Right* is primitive and unflattering and clearly meant as an antipode to modern rationality. A mixture of natural flux and ritualistic ossification, the Oriental state is said to gain dynamic momentum only in external relations where it turns into "elemental fury and devastation." For the rest, internal-domestic quietude is only "the calm of private life and of the lapse into lethargy and feebleness."[86]

In contrast with the mysterious diffuseness of Oriental society, the Greek realm emerges into the clarity of rational self-knowledge. While still relying, like Oriental society, on the substantive unity of finitude and infinity, Greece proceeds, through the labor of differentiating spirit, onto the plane of rational individuality and hence into the "daylight of knowledge," a daylight tempered and transfigured "into beauty and into free and unclouded ethical life." With this development, the principle of personal individuality dawns in Western civilization, a distinctness still untainted by any self-enclosure but maintained in its ideal unity and universality. The aspect of substantive unity, however, was also the drawback of Greek antiquity. Individuality at this point still denoted the individuality of the *polis* or political community and did not yet denote the subjectivity of autonomous self-consciousness. Moreover, no room was yet made for the pursuit and satisfaction of particular needs (an area consigned to the toil of slaves).

The emergence or unleashing of individual self-consciousness occurred only in the Roman realm or empire, and with a vengeance, namely, by driving a wedge between private and public life. To this extent, the Roman epoch corresponds to the domain of morality, where private individual interests are held together only by abstractly universal rules—and politically by absolutist (imperial) power. In the Roman realm, Hegel observes, differentiation is "carried to the point of an infinite sundering of ethical life into the extremes of private personal self-consciousness, on the one hand, and abstract universality, on the other." While individuals are atomized and equalized as private persons with formal rights, the only public bond remaining in the end was the sway of a "grandiose and insatiable caprice." The seeds for this decay were planted already in republican times in the rigid division between patricians and plebeians, with the rule of the patricians progressively degenerating into "cold, self-seeking domination" and the restiveness of the plebeians into the "corruption of the rabble." The final outcome of the drama was "universal misfortune and the destruction of ethical life."[87]

In the *Philosophy of Right* the path leading to the concluding epoch of the Germanic realm is a complex and arduous process, punctuated by a number of distinct episodes. The division between inwardness and externality, between absolute (transcendental) yearning and corrupt worldliness had to be experienced first of all as a radical diremption and as a source of infinite grief and suffering—a grief that is epitomized in Judaism and Hebrew faith. In Hegel's terms, "the loss of spirit and its world gives rise to infinite suffering—for whose articulation a people, the Jewish people, was held in readiness"; struck with grief, spirit is here plunged into the extreme of its absolute negativity. Yet negativity is not the terminal goal but only a stepping-stone or turning point on the road to reconciliation—the reconciliation of spirit and world, of God and man, of immanence and transcendence.

On a religious plane, this reconciliation was announced by Christianity, while the elaboration of its political implications was bequeathed as a task to Germanic (or Nordic) peoples. At this turning point, we read, spirit grasps "the infinite positivity of its own inwardness, that is, the principle of the unity of divine and human nature, and hence the reconciliation of objective truth and freedom as the truth and freedom appearing in consciousness and subjectivity"—a sublation whose implementation was entrusted to "the Nordic principle of Germanic peoples." This implementation, however, is not readily achieved. Initially, reconciliation remains confined to the religious sphere, to the inward feelings of faith, love, and hope, while political life continues to be embroiled in barbarian crudeness and the lust for power. This situation gives rise to the juxtaposition of two realms, the spiritual realm of faith and the worldly (or terrestrial) realm of political domination. Inwardness of spirit, the text continues, unfolds its content first of all in the form of a "mundane realm," which—although animated by sentiments of comradeship—is still a realm of "raw caprice and barbarous manners." As such it is set over against a "world beyond, an intellectual realm" whose content is indeed the truth of spirit, although a truth "still unthought and hence wrapped in barbarous imagery."[88]

In subsequent centuries (during the Middle Ages), the juxtaposition of the two realms developed into an intense struggle for supremacy. In the course of this struggle the spiritual realm—represented by the medieval church—was increasingly secularized or transformed into just another worldly power, while the political realm was progressively rationalized or elevated to the level of rational lawfulness and objective spirit. In the stern conflict of the two realms, Hegel notes, the spiritual realm "lowered the abode of its heaven to the level of earthly power and ordinary worldliness," while the worldly realm elevated its existence to the plane of "rational knowing and being," that is, to the rationality of right and law. The conflict was sublated by the Reformation and ensuing centuries (of Enlightenment) whereby faith was again spiritualized in the same measure as rational yardsticks were progressively implemented in the public structure of the state. With these developments, the original conflict or opposition vanishes or is deprived of significance. The *Philosophy of Right* concludes with an apotheosis of modernity or the achievements of the modern age:

> The present world has discarded its barbarity and unrighteous caprice, just as truth has abandoned its radical transcendence and arbitrary force. In this manner, genuine reconciliation has become objective, a reconciliation which discloses the state as the image and actuality of reason. On this level, self-consciousness finds the organically developed actuality of its substantive knowing and willing, just as it finds in religion the feeling and imagination of its own truth as ideal essence. In rational inquiry, finally, consciousness pursues the free cognition and comprehension of this truth in its mutually complementary manifestations, namely, in the state, in nature, and in the ideal world (of art, religion, and philosophy).[89]

Epilogue: The English Reform Bill

As indicated in its subtitle, the *Philosophy of Right* was meant as a text "for use in [Hegel's] lectures," that is, as a study aid for students attending lecture courses on the topic in which Hegel would amplify and elaborate in various ways on the text. In this manner, the book served as a college manual throughout Hegel's years in Berlin—although he soon delegated the actual lecturing to some of his students. Hegel himself taught the lecture course during the winter semesters of 1821-1822, 1822-1823, and 1824-1825 (with slightly varying titles). Starting in 1822, the concluding section on world history was dropped from the presentation, because Hegel was at that time developing a separate, comprehensive lecture course on the philosophy of history.

Beginning with the winter semester of 1825-1826, the lectures on *Philosophy of Right* were entrusted to Eduard Gans, one of Hegel's close disciples, who proceeded to put the stamp of his own political preferences on the course. Thus, in commenting on constitutional government, Gans tended to privilege the principle of republicanism over constitutional monarchy—an interpretation that shifted the accents of Hegel's conception (although, as one may recall, Hegel himself subordinated the question of monarchy versus republic or democracy to the issue of constitutionalism as such). The gathering revolutionary unrest during the later part of that decade sufficiently alarmed governmental authorities in Berlin to remonstrate with Hegel over the excessively liberal slant of his student and to urge him to resume the task of lecturing. In the wake of the July Revolution of 1830 Hegel expressed, indeed, a willingness to shoulder the task and accordingly announced the course under his own name for the winter of 1830-1831; illness, however, prevented him from implementing this intent, and again a student, Michelet, was called in as a substitute. The announcement was repeated for the following year and Hegel opened his lecture course in October of 1831—one of the last public functions of his life, which was cut short after the first few lectures.[90]

During his last years Hegel was busy fleshing out and completing the sprawling edifice of his encyclopedic system, concentrating particularly on its crowning apex, the history of philosophy and the philosophy of religion. Preoccupation with this task did not prevent him, however, from remaining attentive to social or political events of the time—as is evident both from his letters and various occasional pieces or essays. The last important work in that domain was a long essay on the English Reform Bill, published (in incomplete form) during the fall of 1831 in an official Prussian journal.

The Reform Bill—actually a first version of it—had been introduced in March of that year and immediately became the target of intense parliamentary and popular debate, a conflict so heated that passage did not occur until mid-1832 (and only after new elections and a royal threat to "pack" the upper chamber). The basic objective of the bill was to restructure the electoral system in England, mainly by extending the franchise to middle-income groups and by abolishing the so-called rotten boroughs (the assignment of parliamentary seats to fictive or uninhabited districts). Written before the bill's passage, Hegel's essay was meant as a contribution to the ongoing debate and as an attempt to clarify some basic issues. Given the critical tenor of many passages, the essay has been taken by many interpreters as (further) evidence of a conservative bent or of a reluctance to embrace liberal reforms. Couched in these ideological terms, that interpretation (in my view) entirely misses the point. Although critical of many features of the Reform Bill, Hegel's comments—far from opposing the spirit of re-form—castigate the lukewarmness or half-heartedness expressed in the bill's implementation of that spirit. Seen in this light, the essay is fully congruent with Hegel's conception of modern politics as outlined in the *Philosophy of Right* and other writings. Instructively focused on a concrete example or empirical case study (as it is called today), the essay's arguments provide further vindication for the notion of the modern state as embodiment of reason or rational free will.

Hegel's support for the principle of modernizing reform, as applied to the English context, is evident in the opening pages of the essay. The central goal of the Reform Bill pending before Parliament, he notes, is "to bring justice and fairness into the allotment of the parts played by the different classes and divisions of society in the election of members of Parliament" and to do so "by substituting a greater symmetry for the most bizarre and haphazard anomalies and inequalities prevailing at present." For Hegel, the abuses and defects pervading English political life were glaring and incontestable. The proposed bill, he adds, starts from the "undisputed fact" that the basis determining the allocation of parliamentary seats to counties and boroughs had been "completely altered in the course of time" and that, as a result, this allocation was now "completely at variance" with the original rationale and contradictory to "everything that seems right and fair to elementary common sense." Allocation or reallocation of seats, however, was not merely a matter of numbers or quantitative arrangements, but touched at "the very heart and vital principle of the constitution and condition of Great Britain."

Given the close linkage of the traditional allocation with vested interests and inveterate privileges, attempts at reform were bound to be an uphill struggle by no means assured of a successful outcome. Faced with the formidable array of entrenched prerogatives, proponents of the bill could rely only on the hope "that a new sense of justice had mastered the obstinacy of privilege in those favored by these prerogatives." This hope could gain some fuel from disturbing events in France and, more broadly, from the general historical lesson that the mingling of the franchise with "private interest and corrupt monetary advantage" is at all times the "harbinger of the eventual loss of political freedom and of the ruin of the constitution and the state itself." To this extent, the English bill was a welcome herald of both moral and political reformation and recuperation. In Hegel's words:

> It must be recognized as a good sign of the reawakening of a moral temper in England that one of the sentiments which the need of reform brings with it is the antipathy to the [prevailing] political depravity. Likewise, one must acknowledge that the right way to pursue improvements and to counteract corruption and its entanglements is not merely through reliance on moral ideas, admonitions, and individual cooperation but through institutional change.[91]

A chief merit of the Reform Bill, in Hegel's view, was its opposition to the feudal disarray of vested rights, that is, its attack on the positivity of traditional customs and practices in favor of modern rationality or rational principles of government. Familiar from the earlier essays on the German Constitution and on the Württemberg Estates, this theme of positivity versus reason need only briefly be reviewed here. As Hegel observed, the attack on vested rights implied a challenge to a feature peculiar to English common law and jurisprudence. Namely, it questioned "the character of 'positivity' prevalent in English institutions of public and private law" in the sense of their complete dependence on historical and political accidents. Problematical in itself, the latter dependence was particularly incongruent with modern rationalization and enlightened political progress. "At no time more than today," the essay continues, has public attention been alerted to the difference between rights that are "merely positive in their material content" and rights that are "inherently right and rational"; and nowhere is this distinction more important or urgent than in the English setting.

According to Hegel, the celebrated rights and liberties of the English constitution were all "granted by or extracted from kings and Parliament on special occasions." But the entire "disconnected aggregate" of positive provisions had not yet undergone the development and recasting "carried out in the civilized states of the Continent." A major progressive element lacking in England was a rational-philosophical jurisprudence yielding statutory laws or statute books whereby universal principles could be applied to particular situations and their complexities, just as concrete instances could be subsumed under simplified rules. Another, still more crucial deficiency was the absence of enlightened princes or monarchs willing to take as lodestar of their policies such principles as "the well-being of the state, the happiness of their subjects and the general welfare"—and above all "the sense of an absolute justice" overarching and overruling "merely positive privileges." Due to these deficiencies, in the development of legal institutions England lagged remarkably behind "other civilized states in Europe," mainly because governing power was wielded by people possessed of "so many privileges incompatible with rational constitutional law and true legislation." As a consequence, a "broad field for reform" was open in England, comprising the most important domains of social and public life; and the necessity of change was "beginning to be felt."[92]

While endorsing and underscoring the need for reform, Hegel's essay was not satisfied, however, with the manner and direction of change as envisaged in the Reform Bill. As indicated, the bill sought to remedy prevailing abuses through a restructuring of the electoral system, largely by extending the franchise to some previously excluded groups. One of the complaints lodged by Hegel against this remedy is again familiar from his earlier writings. Hegel's critique takes to task a purely numerical and individualistic treatment of the franchise and the atomistic-alienating consequences of such treatment. As the essay states, an important point stressed by sponsors and opponents of the bill alike was that in Parliament "the various great interests of the nation should be represented"; the precise question was how this representation would be affected by the bill. According to Hegel, the bill paid homage to the "modern principle" that requires that "only the abstract will of individuals as such should be represented"—although it did so in an ambivalent way, namely, by circumscribing the franchise with property qualifications (thus approximating it again to a privilege). In this respect, the bill was in effect a mixture of "old privileges and the general principle of the equal suffrage of all citizens."

Taken in an unalloyed form—the form propagated by radical utilitarians—the general principle of equal suffrage was liable to engender not only reform but the disruption and unraveling of the English constitutional fabric (and of sound constitutional government per se). Even when this outcome could be avoided—and English common sense was prone to act as a solid barrier—individualized suffrage was bound to produce other detrimental consequences, like voter apathy coupled with the isolation and alienation of voters. "Experience proves," Hegel comments, "that the exercise of the voting right is not so attractive as to arouse strong claims and associated public movements"; on the contrary, what tends to surface in the electorate is "great indifference or apathy" in this matter. The reason is chiefly the numerical or quantitative disproportion between the individual vote and the electorate as a whole. The individual, it is true, scarcely realizes "in numbers the triviality of his effectiveness," but nonetheless has a "definite inkling of the quantitative insignificance of his vote," and this numerical aspect is here alone decisive. It is in vain to invoke the "high ideals of freedom, duty, exercise of sovereign rights" as a counterpoise to voter apathy or indolence; for ordinary common sense is "glad to cling to what is effective."[93]

As on previous occasions, Hegel's essay expresses a preference for an organically structured mode of suffrage over individualized voting rights. This preference follows from, or is closely connected with, the aforementioned issue that in Parliament "the various great interests of the nation should be represented." As Hegel recognizes, this principle had indeed been observed in some manner in England in the past, just as it was a basic ingredient of other constitutional monarchies or kingdoms with representative institutions. That the "different great interests of the realm" should be represented in Parliament, we read, is an indigenous feature of English public life, just as it was a central provision in the "older imperial or regional estates in all the European monarchies." The problem is that, in English history, the principle was implemented largely through corruption, bribery, and other devious means. Thus it was hitherto quite customary—through the simple trafficking in parliamentary seats—that "bank directors or directors of the East India Company were insured of places in Parliament," as were the great plantation owners in the West Indies and other businessmen whose affairs, no doubt, "are important for the national interest of England."

The question raised in the essay is whether these methods could not be changed without abandoning the idea of organic representation. In the past, Hegel writes, moral qualms had to give way to public imperatives.

But it is "a constitutional defect to leave to chance what is necessary and to compel people to attain public ends through methods of corruption repugnant to morality." Given the recent rise of commercial and industrial interests, he acknowledges, the traditional organic division of society into estates (nobility, clergy, burghers, and peasants) may no longer match completely the prevailing situation in most states. Yet, he adds,

> this discrepancy could easily be remedied if the earlier basis of constitutional government were understood once more: namely, that the real constituents of public life—in their concrete differences and distinct roles to which government and administration have to be attentive—must be deliberately and expressly recognized and accentuated and be empowered (without this being left to chance) to speak for themselves whenever their interests are discussed or decisions are taken concerning them.

The essay in this context refers approvingly to the constitution Napoleon gave to the kingdom of Italy that divided representation between the estates of the *possidenti, dotti,* and *merchanti.*[94]

A second major complaint voiced in the essay has to do with the limited character of the attempted reform, specifically its focus on electoral procedures to the neglect of underlying social and economic inequities. Hegel's comments on this score amply demonstrate his sense of social justice and his realization that public reason was bound to falter in the absence of equitable social conditions. Although a defender of a liberal *polis* respectful of private property rights, his outlook was far removed from an empty proceduralism. Avineri ably pinpoints this aspect of the essay when he writes:

> The crux of Hegel's argument is that a mere reform of the franchise cannot by itself cure the social problems of English society. Hegel's essay is one of the most scathing indictments of English social conditions to come from a continental writer. Yet his critique is aimed not only at existing conditions in early industrial Britain, but also at liberal attempts to overcome them through a purely electoral reform of Parliament. Behind these attempts Hegel sees the self-interest of the new middle class which identifies reform with its own coming to power.

As Avineri also observes, Hegel's critical comments were not based on shallow hearsay. During preceding years he had avidly collected information about social conditions in England, which then was the leading industrializing country. From newspaper clippings and other sources he sought to ascertain the character of social stratification and the situation of the poorer classes, focusing particularly on the operation of "Poor Laws," the exploitative nature of the so-called Corn Laws, and the inequitable harshness of criminal and police procedures as applied to the underprivileged. The conclusion that Hegel derived from his studies was that social conditions and class relations in England were in a dismal state and in urgent need of a major overhaul, although the latter would, he hoped, occur through enlightened legislation rather than revolutionary agitation. As his comments on the Reform Bill state: "In England the contrast between immense wealth and utterly abject poverty is enormous." Equally great and perhaps greater is the contrast between "aristocratic privileges and the general institutions of English positive law, on the one hand, and the legal provisions developed in the civilized states of the Continent, on the other," provisions that, grounded on universal reason, cannot for long remain "foreign to the British way of thinking."[95]

In his essay, Hegel's critique was backed up by a long bill of particulars that in detail reviewed existing abuses. A major source of these abuses were the so-called manorial rights, which granted to the landed gentry quasi-feudal privileges. "For long past," the essay notes, "these rights subject the agricultural class no longer to outright serfdom; yet they press as heavily on the bulk of that class as serfdom or villeinage did, indeed they reduce it to a worse condition of indigence than that of serfs." Another source of exploitation and social inequity were ecclesiastical tithes, that is, mandatory contributions to the established church—a prerogative that, together with manorial rights and game laws, had progressively been abolished on the Continent without fanfare or "spoliation," thereby laying the groundwork for "increased welfare and essential freedom." In England, traditional justifications for tithes were likewise fading or under attack but without affecting the institution itself; stripped of religious or theological grounds, tithes there were increasingly transformed into "a sort of private property revenue" for the clergy (especially the church hierarchy).

The situation was particularly grievous in Ireland where tithes were exacted from the Catholic population for the benefit of the Anglican establishment. Beyond imposing these taxes, moreover, the English had confiscated Catholic churches, leaving the Irish to fend for themselves. As Hegel disgustedly observes (putting aside his own Protestant leanings): "Even the Turks have generally left alone the churches of Christian, Armenian, and Jewish subjects"; but the English have "taken all the churches away from their conquered Catholic population." Hence the Irish, whose "poverty and misery" is a "standing theme in Parliament," are compelled to pay their own priest and construct a place of service "out of the few pence they have left," while simultaneously paying tithes to Anglican clergymen (even in areas with few Anglicans). This injustice was compounded by economic injury, particularly the extreme oppressiveness of manorial rights in Ireland. There the land owners (or manor lords) had so completely appropriated the soil and abrogated any obligation to the Irish peasants that the latter were pushed into a condition so wretched "that it is not easy to find a parallel in small or poor and even backward regions of Continental countries." A crucial problem was the absence of a reasonable agrarian reform promoting a more equitable distribution of land ownership. "The moment of transition from feudal tenure to property," Hegel writes,

> has slipped by without giving the peasant class the chance to own land. A chance of achieving this might have been afforded by altering rights of inheritance, introducing an equal distribution of patrimony among children, allowing confiscation and sale of property for the payment of debts, and in general altering the legal character of land ownership. . . . But English legislation about property in these and other respects is too far removed from the freedom enjoyed in these matters on the Continent.[96]

Although severely critical in its tenor, Hegel's essay should not simply be read as an anti-English document, which would run counter to many Anglophile statements scattered throughout his writings (especially his appreciation of English common sense). Like his comments on royal power and the structure of estates, his critique of social conditions in England should be seen as an outgrowth not of partisan or parochial sentiments but of a general philosophical or metaphysical conception. As will be recalled, Hegel had leveled similar strictures against his native Württemberg and against the situation in Germany under the old imperial constitution. In a sense, with his essay on the

Reform Bill, Hegel's thinking came full circle by recapturing or resuming the élan of his first political tract: the indictment of the oligarchical abuses present in the Bernese administration of the Pays de Vaud.

Between the two writings, to be sure, there was a long span of both personal maturation and social-historical evolution. While the youthful piece attacked a traditional feudal regime, the last published essay grappled with the social-economic malaise of a rapidly industrializing and modernizing country—whose problems were likely to afflict other industrial nations in the future. Although a staunch defender of modernity and modernization, Hegel to the very end maintained the vision of a modern *polis*, that is, of a society not completely rent by class division and private greed but nurtured and sustained by a sense of justice and a shared fabric of *Sittlichkeit*. The hallmark of modernity and the modern *polis*, for Hegel, was the unfolding and exercise of human freedom, but the latter was not synonymous with caprice or willful machination. Faithful to classical teachings and to the notion of absolute spirit, his work to the last upheld the concordance of individual and society, and of the human and the divine. Shortly before his death, Hegel lectured on his *Philosophy of Right*. His last recorded words from these lectures were: "Freedom is the innermost core and the foundation on which rises the entire edifice of the spiritual world."[97]

Notes

1. Shlomo Avineri, *Hegel's Theory of the Modern State* (Cambridge: Cambridge University Press, 1972), 116. As he adds, "The old feudal system of serfdom was abolished, the cities were granted municipal self-government, the army was transformed through universal conscription, an enlightened and forward-looking bureaucracy took the place of the old military caste, and Berlin appeared to be replacing Jena or Heidelberg as the capital of German letters."

2. G. W. F. Hegel, *Berliner Schriften, 1818-1831*, ed. Johannes Hoffmeister (Hamburg: Meiner, 1956), 3-8. For an English version see G. W. F. Hegel, *Encyclopedia of Philosophy*, trans. Gustav E. Mueller (New York: Philosophical Library, 1959), 57-60. I have altered the translation slightly for purposes of clarity.

3. G. W. F. Hegel, "Verhandlungen in der Versammlung der Landstände des Königreichs Württemberg im Jahre 1815 und 1816," in *Politische Schriften* (Frankfurt-Main: Suhrkamp, 1966), 142-143, 146. For an English version see G. W. F. Hegel, *Hegel's Political Writings,*

trans. T. M. Knox (Oxford, UK: Clarendon, 1964), 247-249, 251-252. In the above and subsequent citations I have altered the translation slightly for purposes of clarity.

4. Hegel, *Politische Schriften*, 174-175, 186; *Hegel's Political Writings*, 273-274, 282-283.

5. Hegel, *Politische Schriften*, 182-183; *Hegel's Political Writings*, 280-281.

6. Hegel, *Politische Schriften*, 184-185; *Hegel's Political Writings*, 281-282. Among public rights, the charter specifically sanctioned equality before the law, equal access to public office, limited freedom of religion (for three Christian confessions), and freedom of occupation and of emigration.

7. Hegel, *Politische Schriften*, 152-154, 156; *Hegel's Political Writings*, 256-257, 259.

8. Hegel, *Politische Schriften*, 160-161; *Hegel's Political Writings*, 262-264. Regarding the reduction of citizenship to isolated acts of balloting, the essay contained statements that seem eminently prescient in view of later developments in the United States: The right to vote is "exhausted by a single act, an act occurring only once in several years. Given the large number of voters, the individual may regard as very insignificant the influence of his own vote—all the more so as the deputy whom he helps to elect is in turn only one member of a numerous assembly where only a small number can ever gain much importance and where, in any case, the contribution made by one vote out of many is unimpressive. On psychological grounds one might expect that the interest of citizens would impel them to seek the franchise most eagerly and to regard it as an important distinction; one might also expect them to push to exercise this right and to use it with great circumspection and without ulterior motive. Yet, experience has shown that the excessive gap between the importance of the effect which is supposed to ensue and the extremely small influence which the individual seems to exert, soon produces the result that voters become indifferent to their right" (Hegel, *Politische Schriften*, 162; *Hegel's Political Writings*, 264).

9. G. W. F. Hegel, *Vorlesungen über Naturrecht und Staatswissenschaft (Heidelberg 1817/18)*, ed. C. Becker et al. (Hamburg: Meiner, 1983), 5, 10. Here and in the following, one should note the complex character of the German term *Recht*, which can mean "law, right, and rightness."

10. Hegel, *Vorlesungen über Naturrecht*, 6-7.

11. Hegel, *Vorlesungen über Naturrecht*, 9, 11-13.

12. G. W. F. Hegel, *Vorlesungen über Rechtsphilosophie, 1818-1831*, ed. Karl-Heinz Ilting (Stuttgart: Frommann-Holzboog, 1973), 231. Carl Gustav Homeyer later became one of the leading jurists in Germany. For the text of the Wannenmann notes see Hegel, *Vorlesungen über Naturrecht*, 269-280.

13. Hegel, *Vorlesungen über Rechtsphilosophie*, 231-233.

14. G. W. F. Hegel, *Philosophie des Rechts (Die Vorlesung von 1819-1820)*, ed. Dieter Henrich (Frankfurt-Main: Suhrkamp, 1983), 28. In support of his thesis of a change of political position, Ilting marshals various kinds of evidence that are not always telling or persuasive. Among other things, he juxtaposes a passage from the Württemberg Estates celebrating the French Revolution and a passage from the *Philosophy of Right* criticizing the theory of social contract—forgetting that the same critique of contractarianism was formulated in the Württemberg Estates as well as in earlier writings. See Karl-Heinz Ilting, "Introduction," in G. W. F. Hegel, *Vorlesungen über Rechtsphilosophie, 1818-1831*, (Stuttgart: Fromman-Holzboog, 1973), 25, 34.

15. Hegel, *Philosophie des Rechts*, 47, 49-50.

16. Hegel, *Philosophie des Rechts*, 48, 50-51.

17. Hegel, *Philosophie des Rechts,* 49-52, 54-55, 333.

18. Regarding esoteric writing, cf. Leo Strauss, *Persecution and the Art of Writing* (Glencoe: Free Press, 1952). For Hegel, philosophy could not possibly be an esoteric discipline given the necessary transparency of its arguments.

19. G. W. F. Hegel, *Grundlinien der Philosophie des Rechts* (Frankfurt-Main: Suhrkamp, 1976), 12, 14, 17-19; G. W. F. Hegel, *Hegel's Philosophy of Right,* trans. T. M. Knox (Oxford, UK: Oxford University Press, 1967), 2-3, 5-6. In the above and subsequent citations I have sometimes changed the translation for purposes of clarity.

20. Hegel, *Grundlinien,* 15-16, 18-20, 23; *Hegel's Philosophy of Right,* 4-7, 9.

21. Avineri, *Hegel's Theory of the Modern State,* 119-120. As Avineri also notes, Hegel may have had an influence on the decision of the Heidelberg fraternity to admit Jews, the only fraternity to do so; see in this context Shlomo Avineri, "A Note on Hegel's Views on Jewish Emancipation," *Jewish Social History,* 25 (1963): 145-151. Pöggeler reports in a similar vein that Hegel in Heidelberg supported, and directed the dissertation of, a law student (Carové) who was active in opposing the practice of duelling and in promoting the admission of Jews into the local fraternity. Cf. Otto Pöggeler, "Introduction," in G. W. F. Hegel, *Vorlesungen über Naturrecht und Staatswissenschaft (Heidelberg 1817/18),* ed. C. Becker et al. (Hamburg: Meiner, 1983), xxvii.

22. Hegel, *Grundlinien,* 12, 24-25; *Hegel's Philosophy of Right,* 1-2, 10-11.

23. Hegel, *Grundlinien,* 24, 26-28; *Hegel's Philosophy of Right,* 10-13. Regarding the relation between philosophy and reality cf. also this important passage: "To recognize reason as the rose in the cross of the present and thereby to enjoy the present, this is the rational insight which offers reconciliation with actuality—a reconciliation which philosophy affords to those in whom there has once arisen an inner voice bidding them to understand" (Hegel, *Grundlinien,* 26-27; *Hegel's Philosophy of Right,* 12).

24. Hegel, *Grundlinien,* par. 1-3, pp. 29-30, 32, 35-37; *Hegel's Philosophy of Right,* 14-17, 225. The chief spokesman of the Historical School criticized in the introduction was Gustav Hugo. In my presentation I do not differentiate between the main text of the *Philosophy of Right* and the "additions," which Hegel's student Eduard Gans inserted on the basis of Hegel's oral elaborations.

25. Hegel, *Grundlinien,* par. 4-7, 11-15, 21, pp. 46-55, 62-66, 71-72; *Hegel's Philosophy of Right,* 20-23, 25-27, 29-30. The critique of formal legalism—with its emphasis on external constraints imposed on arbitrary preferences—is directed chiefly at Kant's moral philosophy.

26. Hegel, *Grundlinien,* par. 31-33, pp. 84-91; *Hegel's Philosophy of Right,* 34-36, 234.

27. Hegel, *Grundlinien,* par. 34-36, 41, pp. 92-95, 102; *Hegel's Philosophy of Right,* 37, 40, 235-236. In the above, I do not entirely follow Hegel's terminology, especially his use of *person* for the carrier of abstract right, which conflicts too sharply with more recent usage (influenced by personalist philosophy).

28. Hegel, *Grundlinien,* par. 44-46, 106-108; *Hegel's Philosophy of Right,* 41-43. In Hegel's view, exceptions from the rule of private property may be granted by the government or the state, which also may revoke such exceptions. Referring to recent postrevolutionary events, he illustrates this point by saying, "Many states, for example, have dissolved the monasteries, and rightly so—for in the last analysis no community has a right to property in the same way as a subject has" (Hegel, *Grundlinien,* par. 46, p. 110; *Hegel's Philosophy of Right,* 236).

29. Hegel, *Grundlinien,* par. 51-56, pp. 114-121; *Hegel's Philosophy of Right,* 45-47, 238.

30. Hegel, *Grundlinien,* par. 49, pp. 112-114; *Hegel's Philosophy of Right,* 44, 237. While denouncing equality of possessions, Hegel is not unconcerned about extreme

inequalities of wealth and the maintenance of basic subsistence levels; this concern, however, has its place not on the plane of abstract right but on that of ethical life (particularly civil society and the state).

31. Hegel, *Grundlinien*, par. 57, pp. 122-126; *Hegel's Philosophy of Right*, 57-58. By locating the issue of slavery and bondage not in nature but in will, Hegel is necessarily led to a dialectical struggle of wills involving the emergence of right from its initial denial:

> If a man is a slave, his own will is also responsible for his slavery, just as it is its will which is responsible if a people is subjugated. Hence the wrong of slavery lies at the door not only of enslavers or conquerors but of the slaves and conquered themselves. Slavery occurs in man's transition from natural-ness to a genuinely ethical condition; it occurs in a world where a wrong is still right. (*Grundlinien*, 126; *Hegel's Philosophy of Right*, 239)

32. Hegel, *Grundlinien*, par. 71-72, 75, pp. 152-155, 157-159; *Hegel's Philosophy of Right*, 57-59, 242.

33. Hegel, *Grundlinien*, par. 65-66, 70, pp. 140-144, 151-152; *Hegel's Philosophy of Right*, 52-53, 57, 241-242.

34. Hegel, *Grundlinien*, par. 105-107, pp. 203-206; *Hegel's Philosophy of Right*, 75-76, 248.

35. Hegel, *Grundlinien*, par. 108-114, pp. 206-213; *Hegel's Philosophy of Right*, 76-79, 248-249.

36. Hegel, *Grundlinien*, par. 115-118, pp. 215-218; *Hegel's Philosophy of Right*, 79-80, 250. For the Weberian distinction, see Max Weber, "Politics as a Vocation," in *From Max Weber: Essays in Sociology*, trans. and ed. H. H. Gerth and C. Wright Mills (New York: Oxford University Press, 1958), 118-128.

37. Hegel, *Grundlinien*, par. 121-126, pp. 228-237; *Hegel's Philosophy of Right*, 82-85.

38. Hegel, *Grundlinien*, par. 129-135, pp. 243-245, 250-254; *Hegel's Philosophy of Right*, 86-90, 253. As Hegel adds,

> While we laid emphasis on the elevated character of Kantian philosophy because of the connection of duty and reason, still we must notice here as its defect the lack of any concrete articulation. The rule "Act so that the maxim of your action can become a universal principle" would be admirable if we already had determinate principles of conduct. . . . Here, however, such a principle is not yet available; and the rule of non-contradiction yields nothing, since where there is nothing, there can be no contradiction either. (*Grundlinien*, 253-254; *Hegel's Philosophy of Right*, 253-254)

39. Hegel, *Grundlinien*, par. 136-139, pp. 254-265; *Hegel's Philosophy of Right*, 90-93, 254-256. While emphasizing the rise of inwardness in modernity, Hegel grants that a certain tension between conscience and officially sanctioned rules is a persistent theme in history:

> As one of the commoner features of history (exemplified in Socrates, the Stoics, and others), the tendency to turn inward and to seek and determine from within what is right and good appears in epochs when, what counts as

right and good in social reality and custom, no longer satisfies the better insight of people; when this insight is betrayed by existing reality and no longer reflected in prevailing duties, then man must find the last harmony in a merely ideal inwardness. . . . It is only in such times when reality is hollow, spiritless and unstable that the individual may be allowed to seek refuge from actuality in inner life. (*Grundlinien,* par. 138, pp. 259-260; *Hegel's Philosophy of Right,* 92, 255)

40. Hegel, *Grundlinien,* par. 141-151, pp. 286-301; *Hegel's Philosophy of Right,* 103-108, 259-260. For Hegel, custom (*Sitte*) is the cultural equivalent to the natural laws operating in external nature. Yet, contrary to the laws of nature, the rules of custom and ethical life do not operate automatically but presuppose educational formation (*Bildung*). As he writes,

Education is the art of making men ethical: it starts from man's naturalness and points the way to a rebirth whereby his first instinctive nature is transformed into a second, intelligent nature, rendering the latter habitual. At that point, the conflict between natural and subjective will disappears, the struggle of the subject (with itself) subsides. (*Grundlinien,* 302; *Hegel's Philosophy of Right,* 260)

41. Hegel, *Grundlinien,* par. 158, pp. 306; *Hegel's Philosophy of Right,* 110; Avineri, *Hegel's Theory of the Modern State,* 133-134.

42. Hegel, *Grundlinien,* par. 158, pp. 307-308; *Hegel's Philosophy of Right,* 110, 261-262.

43. Hegel, *Grundlinien,* par. 160-164, pp. 309-317; *Hegel's Philosophy of Right,* 111-114, 262-263. As Hegel writes:

Since marriage has feeling for one of its moments, it is not an absolute bond but vacillating and potentially dissoluble. Legislators, however, must make its dissolution as difficult as possible and uphold the right of ethical life against caprice. (*Grundlinien,* 315; *Hegel's Philosophy of Right,* 263)

The polemic against sentimentalism is chiefly directed against Friedrich von Schlegel, a Romantic poet who had depicted inner feeling as the sole criterion of marriage.

44. Hegel, *Grundlinien,* par. 164-166, pp. 317-319; *Hegel's Philosophy of Right,* 114-115, 263. Intriguing comments of this kind are unfortunately interspersed with undoubtedly sexist remarks, which mar this section of the text. Notorious is the following passage:

Women are capable of education, but they are not made for activities which demand a universal faculty such as the more advanced sciences, philosophy, and certain forms of artistic production. Women may have happy ideas, taste, and elegance, but they cannot attain to the ideal. The difference between men and women is like that between animals and plants: men correspond to animals, while women correspond to plants because their development is more placid and governed more by the rather vague unity of feeling. (*Grundlinien,* 319-320; *Hegel's Philosophy of Right,* 263)

45. Hegel, *Grundlinien*, par. 170-175, pp. 323-329; *Hegel's Philosophy of Right*, 116-118, 264-265. Hegel adds,

> It is noteworthy that on the whole children love their parents less than their parents love them. The reason for this is that they are gradually increasing in maturity and autonomy and so are leaving their parents behind—who, on the other hand, have in their children the objective embodiment of their union. (*Grundlinien*, 329; *Hegel's Philosophy of Right*, 265)

46. Hegel, *Grundlinien*, par. 181-184, pp. 338-340; *Hegel's Philosophy of Right*, 122-123, 266-267. For an instructive discussion of Hegel's conception of civil society, see Manfred Riedel, *Studien zu Hegels Rechtsphilosophie* (Frankfurt-Main: Suhrkamp, 1969), esp. 135-166; cf. also Manfred Riedel, *Between Tradition and Revolution: The Hegelian Transformation of Political Philosophy*, trans. Walter Wright (New York: Cambridge University Press, 1984).

47. Hegel, *Grundlinien*, par. 182, 185-187, pp. 339, 341-344; *Hegel's Philosophy of Right*, 123-125, 266. The critique of natural simplicity seems to be directed chiefly against Rousseau's notion of the *bon sauvage*.

48. Hegel, *Grundlinien*, par. 185, pp. 341-343; *Hegel's Philosophy of Right*, 123, 267; Hegel, *Philosophie des Rechts*, 149.

49. Hegel, *Grundlinien*, par. 189, pp. 346-347 ; *Hegel's Philosophy of Right*, 126-127, 268.

50. Hegel, *Grundlinien*, par. 190-194, pp. 347-350; *Hegel's Philosophy of Right*, 127-128, 268-269.

51. Hegel, *Grundlinien*, par. 196-200, pp. 351-354; *Hegel's Philosophy of Right*, 128-130.

52. Hegel, *Grundlinien*, par. 209-216, pp. 360-369; *Hegel's Philosophy of Right*, 134-138, 271-273.

53. Hegel, *Grundlinien*, par. 235-241, pp. 384-388; *Hegel's Philosophy of Right*, 147-149, 276-277; Hegel, *Philosophie des Rechts*, 194-195.

54. Hegel, *Grundlinien*, par. 244-248, pp. 387-390; *Hegel's Philosophy of Right*, 148-150, 277. As the lectures of 1819-1820 state, regarding the source of indignation:

> The poor feel excluded and despised and hence a sense of inner indignation. They have a consciousness of themselves as infinitely free, and thus there arises the demand of a congruence of their external existence with this consciousness. . . . Self-consciousness is here driven to the extreme where it has no rights, where freedom has no existence. In this state, inner indignation is inevitable. (*Philosophie des Rechts*, 155)

55. Hegel, *Grundlinien*, par. 244-248, pp. 390-393; *Hegel's Philosophy of Right*, 150-152, 278. The lecture course of 1819-1820 speaks of seafaring as "the poetry of commerce," because it encourages a kind of "courage" that transcends immediate commercial interest. Overseas commerce also promotes the conception of the "unity or universality of mankind," thereby erasing the separateness and "difference of nations, their customs and cultures." Regarding colonization, Spanish, Portuguese, and Dutch colonizers still went overseas with the notion of the inferiority of foreign peoples. Proceeding from the "concept

of man" (as universal), only the English managed to place "the entire world in a universal relationship" (see Hegel, *Philosophie des Rechts,* 200-201).

56. Hegel, *Grundlinien,* par. 201, 206, pp. 354-355, 358; *Hegel's Philosophy of Right,* 130-133, 270.

57. Hegel, *Grundlinien,* par. 202-205, 207, 243, pp. 355-357, 359, 389; *Hegel's Philosophy of Right,* 131-133, 149-150, 270-271. Hegel seems to distinguish sharply between the clustering of society in estates (which is functional and integrative) and economic class division (which is polarizing and destructive in its effects).

58. Hegel, *Grundlinien,* par. 249, 255, pp. 393, 396-397; *Hegel's Philosophy of Right,* 152, 154, 278; Avineri, *Hegel's Theory of the Modern State,* 164-165.

59. Hegel, *Grundlinien,* par. 250-254, 256, pp. 393-397; *Hegel's Philosophy of Right,* 152-155. The term *ideal types* is borrowed, of course, from Weber; Hegel speaks of *ideal moments.*

60. Hegel, *Grundlinien,* par. 257-258, pp. 398-403; *Hegel's Philosophy of Right,* 155-156, 279. The phrase *Es ist der Gang Gottes in der Welt, dass der Staat ist* has been variously translated, even as "The state is the march of God in the world." For judicious comments on the phrase and its translations see Avineri, *Hegel's Theory of the Modern State,* 176-177. Avineri concurs with this translation, first proposed by Kaufmann: "It is the way of God in (or with) the world that there should be the state." See Walter Kaufmann, ed., *Hegel's Political Philosophy* (New York: Atherton Press, 1970), 4.

61. Hegel, *Philosophie des Rechts,* 211-212. Regarding the assumption of human origins, Hegel criticizes the reliance both on a (nonrational) "instinct of solidarity" and on deliberate human will (or a conjunction of wills in a social contract). In addition to the two main conceptions, the lecture course also opposes patriarchal traditions and the stress on personal charisma:

> Since rational insight marks the form of spirit in the state, the idea of the patriarchal (or patrimonial) state is excluded; for in the latter, public life is guided by feelings, customs and divine oracles. Likewise, it cannot be left up to an individual in the state to agitate the people through enthusiasm. (*Philosophie des Rechts,* 209)

In Weberian terminology, the Hegelian state is differentiated both from purely traditional and affective modes of behavior as well as from traditional and charismatic types of authority.

62. Hegel, *Grundlinien,* par. 258, pp. 399-404; *Hegel's Philosophy of Right,* 156-159. As Avineri correctly observes, the criticism of Rousseau may be somewhat unfair given the explicit distinction between *volonté générale* and *volonté des tous* (*Hegel's Theory of the Modern State,* 184).

63. Hegel, *Grundlinien,* par. 258 (addition), p. 404; *Hegel's Philosophy of Right,* 279. As Hegel adds at a later point: "A bad state is one which merely exists [instead of being actualized reason]; a sick body exists too, but it has no genuine reality. A bad state, to be sure, is merely worldly and finite, but the rational state is inherently infinite" (*Grundlinien,* par. 270, p. 429; *Hegel's Philosophy of Right,* 283).

64. Hegel, *Grundlinien,* par. 260-262, pp. 406-410; *Hegel's Philosophy of Right,* 160-162, 280. Hegel in this context pays tribute to Montesquieu for having developed the "philosophical notion of always treating the part in its relation to the whole."

65. Hegel, *Grundlinien,* par. 270, pp. 415-416, 430; *Hegel's Philosophy of Right,* 164-165, 284.

66. Hegel, *Grundlinien,* par. 270, pp. 418-420; *Hegel's Philosophy of Right,* 167-168.

67. Hegel, *Grundlinien,* par. 270, pp. 417-418, 424-425, 430; *Hegel's Philosophy of Right,* 165-166, 171, 284. Due to their shared reliance on rationality, Hegel finds a close linkage between the state and modern science, commenting explicitly on the fate of Giordano Bruno and Galileo at the hands of religious authorities.

68. Hegel, *Grundlinien,* par. 270, pp. 420, 423-424; *Hegel's Philosophy of Right,* 168, 170-171.

69. Hegel, *Grundlinien,* par. 270, pp. 420-421, 427-428; *Hegel's Philosophy of Right,* 168-169, 173-174. As Hegel adds, church division was the "best piece of good fortune" to befall both church and state for the sake of their respective integrity and autonomy.

70. Hegel, *Grundlinien,* par. 272, pp. 432-433; *Hegel's Philosophy of Right,* 174-175.

71. Hegel, *Grundlinien,* par. 272, pp. 434-435; *Hegel's Philosophy of Right,* 175, 286. Cf. in this context esp. *Federalist Papers* nos. 10, 47-48, 51 in *The Federalist Papers,* ed. Clinton Rossiter (New York: New American Library Penguin, 1961), 77-84, 300-313, 320-325.

72. Hegel insists particularly on the noninstrumental character of the constitution:

> Above all, it is absolutely essential that the constitution should not be regarded as something made or fabricated, even though it originates in time. It must rather be treated as something existing in and by itself, as something divine and permanent which transcends the sphere of fabrication.

Hegel, *Grundlinien,* par. 273-274, pp. 435-440; *Hegel's Philosophy of Right,* 177-179, 286-287.

73. Hegel, *Grundlinien,* par. 275, 279, pp. 441, 444-445; *Hegel's Philosophy of Right,* 179, 181. As Hegel adds, "The personality of the state is actual only as one person: the monarch." The metaphysical aspect is still more neatly underscored in the lectures of 1819-1820: A crucial feature of royal power is "identity or sovereignty," which

> is actual as subjectivity. In the highest form, subjectivity exists as an I (ego). The ego is pure self-identity sublating particularity. This identity is only a formal moment which requires for its truth also objectivity. . . . Subjectivity becomes necessarily individuality (of spirit). State sovereignty hence has its existence in a subject or individual, and this is the monarch. (Hegel, *Philosophie des Rechts,* 239-240)

74. Hegel, *Grundlinien,* par. 279-280, pp. 449-451; *Hegel's Philosophy of Right,* 288-289; Hegel, *Philosophie des Rechts,* 26.

75. Hegel, *Grundlinien,* par. 275, 278, pp. 441-444; *Hegel's Philosophy of Right,* 179-181, 287-288. Given his metaphysical emphasis on subjectivity, Hegel has little sympathy for the notion of popular sovereignty, or sovereignty of the people; for, apart from the monarch and the determinate articulation or differentiation of the whole, the *people* denotes for him only a "formless mass which is no longer a state" (*Grundlinien,* par. 279, p. 447; *Hegel's Philosophy of Right,* 183). For a view of sovereignty as exceptional power or as power to decide in exceptional cases, cf. esp. Carl Schmitt, *The Concept of the Political,* trans. George Schwab (New Brunswick, N.J.: Rutgers University Press, 1976).

76. Hegel, *Grundlinien,* par. 287-294, pp. 457-462; *Hegel's Philosophy of Right,* 188-192, 290-291. Regarding French government, of course, we know at least through Tocqueville that centralization was already the work of the *ancien regime;* see Alexis de

Tocqueville, *The Old Regime and the French Revolution,* trans. Stuart Gilbert (Garden City, N.Y.: Anchor Books, 1955), esp. 32-41. .

77. Hegel, *Grundlinien,* par. 301-303, pp. 470-473; *Hegel's Philosophy of Right,* 195-198, 292. As Hegel adds,

> The concrete state is a whole articulated into its particular spheres. The member of the state (citizen) is a member of such a sphere or estate, and only in this objective status is he relevant in the state. The general character of the individual has this dual aspect: to be both a private person and also a reflective consciousness, a will directed at the universal. (*Grundlinien,* par. 308, p. 477; *Hegel's Philosophy of Right,* 200)

In the case of individualized suffrage, Hegel points astutely to the prospect of voter apathy:

> Regarding individual voting rights it may be further remarked that, especially in large states, the result is inevitably electoral indifference toward voting, since a single ballot is of little significance in a multitude. (*Grundlinien,* par. 311, p. 481; *Hegel's Philosophy of Right,* 202-203)

78. Hegel, *Grundlinien,* par. 305-312, pp. 474-481; *Hegel's Philosophy of Right,* 199-203, 293-294.

79. Hegel, *Grundlinien,* par. 314-318, pp. 482-485; *Hegel's Philosophy of Right,* 203-205, 294. Hegel adds a paragraph on freedom of speech and press, which grants broad latitude to this freedom circumscribed only by restrictions placed on libelous and incendiary statements ("a spark falling on a heap of gunpowder is more dangerous than if it falls on hard ground where it vanishes without a trace"—a phrase reminiscent of Justice Holmes's caveat against "shouting 'fire' in a crowded theater"; see *Grundlinien,* par. 319, p. 489; *Hegel's Philosophy of Right,* 207).

80. Hegel, *Grundlinien,* par. 321-323, 332-333, pp. 490-491, 499-500; *Hegel's Philosophy of Right,* 208-209, 213-214.

81. Hegel, *Grundlinien,* par. 324, 330, pp. 493-494, 497-498; *Hegel's Philosophy of Right,* 295-297. The contemporary reader can hardly avoid being struck by the prescient character of these comments.

82. Hegel, *Grundlinien,* par. 324, 327-328, 338, pp. 491-496, 502; *Hegel's Philosophy of Right,* 209-212, 297; Avineri, *Hegel's Theory of the Modern State,* 199, 204. Avineri continues correctly:

> When Hegel envisaged wars as waged on a limited basis, he made the same misjudgment which had led him to underestimate the enormous force of modern nationalism: he totally failed to see the prevalence of modern, total war. (*Hegel's Theory of the Modern State,* 205)

83. Hegel, *Grundlinien,* par. 331, 338-339, pp. 498, 502-503; *Hegel's Philosophy of Right,* 212-213, 215, 297. The same view is further developed in Hegel's lectures on the philosophy of world history where we read:

The trend of the states is toward uniformity. There prevails among them one aim, one tendency which is the cause of wars as well as of friendships and the needs of dynasties. But there also prevails among them another uniformity which parallels the idea of hegemony in Greece, except that now it is the hegemony of spirit.

See G. W. F. Hegel, *Vorlesungen über die Philosophie der Weltgeschichte*, ed. Georg Lasson (Leipzig: Meiner, 1920), 761. I follow the translation offered by Avineri, *Hegel's Theory of the Modern State*, 207.

84. Hegel, *Grundlinien*, par. 340-343, pp. 503-504; *Hegel's Philosophy of Right*, 215-217. The text here refers obliquely to Gotthold Ephraim Lessing's *Erziehung des Menschengeschlechts* (Education of the Human Race), which appeared in 1780.

85. Hegel, *Grundlinien*, par. 344-347, 351-353; *Hegel's Philosophy of Right*, 217-220.

86. Hegel, *Grundlinien*, par. 354-355, p. 509; *Hegel's Philosophy of Right*, 220. In his lectures on the philosophy of history, Hegel subdivided the Oriental realm further into three stages: those of Chinese, Indian, and Persian society. For illuminating comments, see Avineri, *Hegel's Theory of the Modern State*, 224-225.

87. Hegel, *Grundlinien*, par. 356-357, pp. 510-511; *Hegel's Philosophy of Right*, 221-222.

88. Hegel, *Grundlinien*, par. 358-359, pp. 511-512; *Hegel's Philosophy of Right*, 222.

89. Hegel, *Grundlinien*, par. 360, p. 512; *Hegel's Philosophy of Right*, 222-223.

90. See Hegel, *Grundlinien*, pp. 525-527; also Pöggeler, "Introduction," xxx-xxxi.

91. Hegel, *Politische Schriften*, 277-280; *Hegel's Political Writings*, 295-297. In the above and subsequent citations I have altered the translation slightly for purposes of clarity.

92. Hegel, *Politische Schriften*, 282-285; *Hegel's Political Writings*, 299-301.

93. Hegel, *Politische Schriften*, 298-300, 302-306; *Hegel's Political Writings*, 312-313, 315-318. As Hegel adds,

It is no wonder that in England a great number of individuals—perhaps even the majority of them—require to be stimulated by the candidates before they will take what is to them the trifling trouble of voting, and for their trouble, which benefits the candidates, they have to be compensated by them with badges, roasts, beer, and a few guineas. (*Politische Schriften*, 309; *Hegel's Political Writings*, 321)

94. Hegel, *Politische Schriften*, 299-301; *Hegel's Political Writings*, 313-314.

95. Hegel, *Politische Schriften*, 314; *Hegel's Political Writings*, 325;* Avineri, *Hegel's Theory of the Modern State*, 208, 214. Regarding Hegel's study of English conditions see Hegel, *Berliner Schriften*, 718-724.

96. Hegel, *Politische Schriften*, 288-294; *Hegel's Political Writings*, 303-309.

97. The words were reported by David Friedrich Strauss; see Pöggeler, "Introduction," xxxi. Hegel's critique of social inequities sufficiently alarmed Prussian censors that they canceled publication of the last part of his essay on the Reform Bill.

4

Effective History:
Hegel's Heirs and Critics

egel's work marked the culmination of a phase of modern Western history, but not, of course, the end of that history itself. During his own lifetime, developments were afoot that were bent on reshaping dramatically social and political conditions in the West and thereby also the meaning and possibility of an actualization of spirit in time. Foremost among these developments was industrialization whose socially dislocating effects were described so vividly by Hegel in his last published essay (on the Reform Bill).

Spreading from England to the Continent and beyond, the industrial revolution steadily unhinged the traditional moorings of social life by accentuating large-scale production and flexible markets. Impinging first of all on the relation between city and countryside, this process in due course shifted the locus of attention to urban areas and to the intensifying antagonism between capital owners and the industrial working class. Internationally, the economic imperatives of scale demanded a steady expansion of production, which eventually triggered a scramble for colonies or at least for readily available overseas markets. Simultaneously, the same imperatives placed a premium on scientific and technological innovation as a means to increase productive efficiency and to reduce dependence on human labor. Migrating from economics to the political arena similar efficiency considerations soon invaded public institutions, by remolding the state progressively into an instrument of policymaking and social planning (and, more generally, an instrument of power). Standing ajar to these developments, and hence ambivalent in its import, was the ongoing democratization of Western society—a process caught in the crossfire of economic demands and recurrent wares of populism. In the 20th century, all these trends came together in the sequence of two world wars and the cycles of economic upsurge and depression. This sequence cast doubt for the first time on the linkage of modernization and progress and, by implication, on Hegel's conception of modernity as the steady unfolding of reason.

The latter implication, to be sure, was not instantaneous or self-evident but the outcome of reflective interpretation. Generally speaking, the above developments—sketched here in their barest outlines—were only mute occurrences in the absence of theoretical guideposts or frameworks facilitating understanding. A prominent if not leading guidepost was Hegel's social and political philosophy. Although originating in the early part of the last century—and unable or unwilling to "jump over Rhodes"—Hegel's thought has accompanied as a silent witness and commentator all the subsequent transformations of Western life, which in turn have affected the meaning and status of his original work. This journey of a work through time is what Gadamer means by "effective history" (*Wirkungsgeschichte*), that is, the story of the varying repercussions and reinterpretations of an opus through successive generations.

Seen from the vantage of effective history, Hegel's work is not simply a finished artifact, a congealed monument of a past era, but rather a steady companion of ongoing discussions open to new insights and arguments. Approaching him from the distance of nearly 2 centuries, we today cannot help but assess his writings in light of contemporary concerns and preoccupations—that is, from the angle of our prejudgments that, although corrigible, are not simply mistaken. Reflectively pondered and seasoned, our judgments and prejudgments form also part of spirit's continuing actualization and hence are prone to reveal new facets or dimensions in past teachings—without, on this count, subjecting them to interpretive whim. In turn, Hegel's work still responds to our inquiries, thereby providing a benchmark or at least a critical foil for assessing our own experiences and theoretical predilections. In the words of one contemporary philosopher, Derrida, Hegel's discourse "still holds together the language of our era by so many threads"—which does not mean a coincidence or convergence of idioms. [1]

Given the sweep of Hegel's work and the intricacy of historical developments, the story of Hegel's effects or effectiveness is extremely complex and multifaceted. Bypassing a full account (which must be left to another context), I shall limit myself here to a few highlights, that is, to points of interpretive engagement animated by significant philosophical (or ontological) concerns. On these premises, I shall on the whole sidestep or bracket purely polemical forays launched against Hegel and Hegelianism, of which the literature of the last century and of our own is replete.

Such polemical attacks surfaced quickly after Hegel's death and contributed greatly to a climate of opinion that Marx deplored barely a few decades later when he noted that Hegel was treated as a "dead dog." To give a flavor of these attacks, it may suffice to cite briefly the diatribe of Schopenhauer who called Hegel "a flat-headed, insipid, nauseating, illiterate charlatan," someone who had reached "the pinnacle of audacity in scribbling together and dishing up the craziest mystifying nonsense." Extending his attack to Hegelianism in general, Schopenhauer added that the academic influence of Hegel had enabled him to achieve or perpetrate the "intellectual corruption of a whole generation." Hegel's first biographer, Haym, was by no means above such polemics, which did not contribute to his philosophical understanding. Thus, elaborating on the *Philosophy of Right*, Haym managed to portray the text simply as a "scientifically formulated justification of the Carlsbad police system." His grasp of the *Phenomenology of Spirit* was on a similar level. "To say everything," he wrote, "the *Phenomenology* is psychology reduced to confusion and disorder by history, and history deranged by psychology." Unfortunately, Kaufmann—otherwise an able Hegelian scholar—does not trouble to correct Haym's portrayal, but instead compounds it by offering a still more severe verdict. Even the cited statement, he observes, is "too kind: instead of mixing only history and psychology, Hegel offers us what Richard Wagner was later to call a *Gesamtkunstwerk,* leaving out little but music." Where Haym spoke of a "romantic masquerade," Kaufmann prefers to speak of "charades: now a tableau, now a skit, now a brief oration."[2]

Subjective Inwardness: Kierkegaard

On a philosophical plane, one of the first to criticize or challenge Hegel's work was the Danish thinker Kierkegaard. While studying at the University of Copenhagen (in the decade of Hegel's death), Kierkegaard was strongly exposed to Hegel's teachings, which, at this time, still reverberated throughout the European continent. His initial reaction to these teachings was critical if not hostile, an aversion that steadily gathered momentum and intensity during the remainder of his life. Although idiosyncratic in many ways, Kierkegaard's reaction is instructive and significant on a broader scale, because his arguments have served as a precedent and exemplar for many later interpretations or critical initiatives.

At the core of his remonstration was the presumed neglect (on Hegel's part) of concrete human particularity, of the uniqueness of individual experience, in favor of an overarching metaphysical system ready to engulf or swallow up individual details. A major complaint was Hegel's reliance on objective spirit or reason, that is, on the correlation of idea and reality by means of conceptual mediation. Such mediation appeared to Kierkegaard as an abstract metaphysical subterfuge inattentive to the concrete agonies and paradoxes of human existence and to the unbridgeable gulf between inwardness and external world. Part and parcel of this complaint was the conception of the progressive unfolding or actualization of spirit in time, a notion that was dismissed by the Danish thinker as either naively optimistic or else as a sinister accommodation to prevailing states of affairs (or both). In contrast to the universal-rational sweep of Hegel's system, Kierkegaard placed the accent on the difference, or rupture, between thought and concrete practice and on the rationally impenetrable mystery of the deeper sense of human life. In lieu of the close linkage of reason and will and the marginalization of caprice, his writings put a premium on subjective choice or decision—a choice devoid of general guideposts and ultimately grounded in a leap of faith.

The opposition to Hegel surfaced already in one of Kierkegaard's first writings, titled *Either/Or* (1843). Thematizing the conflict between sensual hedonism and strict moralism, this work accentuated the necessity of radical choice and the absence of binding yardsticks (although morality was more strongly predicated on will than hedonism). The opposition was continued and intensified in *Fear and Trembling* (of the same year) where the move from moralism or morality to religious faith was shown to imply a transgression even of moral considerations and a readiness to venture on a radical leap. While still implicit in these writings, the confrontation with Hegel was more openly addressed in *Sickness unto Death* (composed during the ensuing years). Written under the pseudonym "Anti-Climacus," the book in a sense offered a parody but also a serious reformulation of Hegelian thought—a parody mainly of the sweeping rationalism marking that thought and of its successive "climactic" endeavors of rational mediation and synthesis. "Man is spirit," the book opened in a quasi-Hegelian vein, adding:

> But what is spirit? Spirit is the self. But what is the self? The self is a relation which relates itself to its own self. . . . Man is a synthesis of the infinite and the finite, of the temporal and the eternal, of freedom and necessity, in short it is a synthesis. A synthesis is a relation between two factors.

While thus seemingly endorsing a Hegelian motif, Kierkegaard quickly introduced a twist that canceled that endorsement. As he noted, in the relationship between the two factors the relation itself, or the synthesis, is a "third term" that cannot be provided or supplied by the self on its own accord. Awareness of the absence of synthesis leads to "despair" and even to "sickness unto death," experiences triggered by the "disrelationship" or yawning abyss lurking in the heart of self-relation. In his words, despair arises from the very structure of self-relation "in that God who made man a relationship lets it go (as it were) out of His hand." According to *Sickness unto Death,* the lacking synthesis can be obtained not through reason or conceptual mediations but only on the level of faith. As a self-relation and an aspiring synthesis of finitude and infinity, we read, the task of the self is indeed consciously to become itself—"a task which can be performed only by means of a relationship to God."[3]

In still more explicit fashion, anti-Hegelian arguments were articulated and fleshed out in the *Concluding Unscientific Postscript* (of 1846). Published under the pseudonym "Johannes Climacus," the work already in its title signaled a challenge to Hegel's *Science of Logic* and to the latter's attempt to erect an encyclopedic system on logical-ontological grounds. For Kierkegaard, this endeavor amounted to a form of existential escapism and bad faith by allowing the "scientific logician" to abscond into the web of his conceptual formulas. In line with earlier writings, the book again presented the philosophical situation in terms of a radical alternative or choice:

> Two ways, in general, are open for an existing individual: *Either* he can do his utmost to forget that he is an existing individual—whereby he becomes a comical figure, since existence has the remarkable trait of compelling an existing individual to exist whether he wills it or not. . . . *Or* he can concentrate his entire energy upon the fact that he is an existing individual. It is here, in the first instance, that objection must be made to modern philosophy: not that it has a mistaken presupposition, but that it has a comical presupposition, occasioned by its having forgotten, in a sort of world-historical absentmindedness, what it means to be a human being.

In Kierkegaard's account, Hegel was such an absentminded and comical figure who submerged his own life, and particular existence as such, in the grand scheme of his speculative metaphysics.

In neglecting concrete existence, Hegel also failed to tackle the issue of human action, of the agonizing travail of individual decision making. According to the *Concluding Unscientific Postscript,* Hegel was "utte ly and absolutely right in asserting that viewed eternally, *sub specie aeterni,* in the language of abstraction, in pure thought and being, there is no either-or." Counterbalancing this concession, however, Climacus quickly added that Hegel was "equally wrong when, forgetting the abstraction of his thought, he plunged down into the realm of existence to annul the double *aut* with might and main." Such a move was impossible in existence "for in doing so the thinker abrogates existence as well." To live concretely and authentically means to "interpenetrate one's existence with consciousness"—that is, to open oneself fully to the multitude of existential possibilities—and then to make a decision with "passionate enthusiasm" or inward conviction and in full awareness of the radicalness of human freedom and the absence of rational-logical recipes. From this vantage, the real action is "not the external act, but an internal decision in which the individual puts an end to mere possibility and identifies himself with the content of his thought in order to exist in it. This is the action."[4]

As it happens, the focus on action and inward decision was not quite Kierkegaard's final word, because decision still remains plagued by the agony of irrational freedom, an agony that can be healed only (if at all) by the intervention of faith and saving grace. Because faith, however, is a gift that cannot be commandeered, human existence by itself remains mired in paradox and suspended over the abyss of self-relation. This is the reason why Bernstein compares Kierkegaard's basic outlook with the stage of the "unhappy consciousness" as portrayed in the *Phenomenology of Spirit,* that is, with the condition of radical diremption and human self-alienation. In his words, the locus of experience for Kierkegaard is not "the realm of pure thought," but rather the tension between the self as "existing individual" and the self as "conscious thinking being"—and "there can be no mediation, no higher synthesis in which existence and thought are happily reconciled." In adopting this stance, Kierkegaard unwittingly subscribed to a part of Hegel's dialectical phenomenology, although in a manner precluding rational mediation. "A man," Bernstein writes,

> is in constant tension with himself—he can never escape the condition of unhappy consciousness by any of his *own* efforts. His task as a human being is not to 'think' himself out of his condition: such an attempt is pathetic and comic. His task is to *become* an existing human being, and this means to become subjective, not objective, to passionately appropriate and identify himself with the existential possibilities that confront him. In the task of becoming subjective, man is constantly confronted with an either/or. At the very juncture where Hegel indicates the possibility (and the necessity) of reason as mediating the self-divisiveness of the alienated soul, Climacus points to the need for passion, decisiveness, and action.

For Climacus, the need for action and decision could not be side-stepped or overcome through conceptual or rational-philosophical means. In human terms, the agony of radical freedom was not amenable to resolution or sublation, but had to be undergone as a concrete existential dilemma, as evidence of the stark "diremption between existence and consciousness." This, Bernstein notes, is "the profoundest difference between the existential dialectic suggested by Climacus and Hegelian dialectic." As he adds, radical action for Kierkegaard was not a facile recipe or an emblem of human distinctiveness but rather an avenue of suffering and despair, because of its inevitable embroilment in paradox. Hence, to be human here meant to be someone "whose existence is that of an unhappy consciousness that is never *aufgehoben*"—unless salvaged by grace.[5]

Bernstein's assessment can be supplemented and expanded. As described by Kierkegaard, the predicament of self-alienation reflects and captures not only the stage of "unhappy consciousness" in the *Phenomenology of Spirit*, but a central strand in Hegel's entire philosophy, namely, the theme of divisiveness and diremption (*Entzweiung*) seen as the crucial motor of individual and social maturation. As previously indicated, this theme looms large at many junctures of Hegel's work, including the discussion of morality and civil society in the *Philosophy of Right*. In none of these contexts, one should recognize, was human maturation equated with an abstract-mental stratagem or an exercise performed in the realm of pure thought, a view that ignores the close linkage of logic and existential-ontological experience in Hegel's work. In his *Phenomenology,* the maturation of consciousness is expressly described as a "highway of despair" and the reversal of naive-natural awareness as the "calvary" or "golgatha" of human reason. In light of these and similar statements, Hegel's thought cannot fairly be confined to the level of pure speculation, a confinement he persistently sought to rupture through his attacks on philosophical abstractness and cognitive-moral formalism. In Bernstein's judicious words, it is a "false criticism of Hegel" to claim that he "gets lost in the speculative realm of 'pure thought' which lacks 'the concrete filling of life.' "

These comments also relate to other basic categories of Hegelian thought, especially those of consciousness and subjectivity, whose abstract construal entirely misses the inner pathos or passion animating their status in his work. Properly conceived, one might add, these categories further cement the nexus of Kierkegaard's and Hegel's outlook: although anti-Hegelian in motivation, the former's writings invariably invoke consciousness and subjectivity as foundational premises, in a manner broadly congenial with German idealism. In this respect, Sartre seems entirely correct in writing that "Kierkegaard is inseparable from Hegel" and that his "vehement negation of every system can arise only within a cultural field entirely dominated by Hegelianism."[6]

These observations, to be sure, need to be qualified, because Kierkegaard obviously cannot be absorbed into Hegel's system without loss. At least in intent, an intent passionately pursued, his writings sought to escape the latter's encyclopedic embrace, although the escape was frustrated by the philosophical premises he adopted. This aspect is acknowledged by Sartre when he notes that while constituting in one sense "the very peak of idealism" Kierkegaard's outlook in another sense also marks a "progress toward realism," namely, by its insistence on "the primacy of the specifically real over thought, that the real cannot be reduced to thought."[7] What complicated or eroded Kierkegaard's progress was his identification of the specifically real with subjectivity and of human existence with subjective inwardness.

By and large, Kierkegaard shifted or rearranged accents available in modern Western metaphysics, thereby foregrounding theoretical options or possibilities that Hegel himself had pondered repeatedly in his life—and had struggled to overcome. Thus the opposition between reality and thought reopened the gulf (familiar from Kant's critiques) between human consciousness and the thing-in-itself, a gulf the preconceptions of which were relentlessly scrutinized and exposed in the *Phenomenology of Spirit* and the later *Logic*. Likewise, the focus on radical action and decision tended to rupture the linkage of reason and will celebrated in the *Philosophy of Right*, sanctioning instead the primacy of subjective caprice and its juxtaposition to anonymous rules (a correlation characterizing the "external state" or the "state of need and abstract reasoning"). Most important, the divorce of the human and the divine tended to support a religious fundamentalism downgrading reason and objective spirit in favor of a mysterious otherness—an outlook Hegel had bemoaned in a string of writings stretching from "Faith and Knowledge" to his latest reflections on the philosophy of religion. As these writings persistently emphasized, the likely result of such fundamentalism was either inward retreat or the imposition of millenarian beliefs—in either case the rigid dualism of a "heavenly" and "earthly city." While sharing Kierkegaard's aversion to positive religion (as embodied in established churches), Hegel was unwilling to de-sacralize the public realm or rob it of ethical significance.

Social Praxis: Marx

The most glaring shortcoming of Kierkegaard's approach was his neglect of social and political questions or their subordination to purely private dilemmas. These questions were in the foreground of Marx's concerns and of his intensive critical engagement with Hegel throughout his life. Marx first encountered Hegel's teachings during his student days in Berlin (after the philosopher's death) and immediately was gripped by a mixture of fascination and aversion. This ambivalent attraction was shared by a number of intellectuals (known as Left, or Young, Hegelians) with whom he associated during these years and who, like him, sought to both inherit and subvert the Hegelian legacy. What enticed Marx in that legacy was its thoroughness and its comprehensive dialectical sweep; what repelled him was chiefly its presumed speculative abstractness and its aloofness from concrete social-political struggles of the period. In contradistinction to Kierkegaard, however, the complaint about abstractness did not prompt a flight into inwardness but rather a plunge into the thick of objective reality, with special attention to the social and economic parameters of human action. In Sartre's words, Marx together with Kierkegaard "asserts the specificity of human existence and, along with Hegel, takes the concrete man in his objective reality."

While experienced with particular intensity in his early years, Marx's ambivalent engagement with Hegel remained a persistent ingredient in his evolving opus. Late in his life, in an "afterword" to the second edition of his *Capital,* Marx still affirmed that it had been his lifelong objective to overcome the "mystifying side of the Hegelian dialectic," but without abandoning its basic insights. As he stated:

> The mystification which dialectics suffers in Hegel's hands by no means prevents him from being the first to present its general form of working in a comprehensive and conscious manner. With him it is standing on its head; it must be turned right side up again, if you would discover the rational kernel within the mystified shell.[8]

The notion of turning Hegel "right side up" (repeated by both Marx and Engels on several occasions) has often been taken to herald a simple reversal, in the sense of a substitution of *matter* for *idea* or of empiricism for rational reflection—a construal that largely misses the point. What is turned around in Marx's approach is not so much metaphysics itself as rather the role of "man" in the historical-dialectical process. Following the method of "transformative criticism" (first inaugurated by Feuerbach), Marx relocates or redefines the central motor of historical development and self-actualization. Instead of denoting the steady unfolding of idea, or spirit, *actualization* now means the progressive display of human productive capabilities, capabilities that previously were mystified and alienated under the garb of spirit (as a synonym for the divine). Applied to the social and political domain, transformative criticism of this kind implied a shift of attention from the idealized structures of the state—viewed as the embodiment of reason—to concrete human conditions prevalent in civil society. A corollary of this shift was the need to concretize conflicts or contradictions operative on the level of thought through a closer focus on real-life social and economic conflicts, as manifest particularly in class division and class struggle.

The sense or direction of his transformative move was outlined by Marx eloquently in several of his early writings, dating from the time of his exile in Paris. Prominent among these writings is a long manuscript specifically devoted to the confrontation with Hegel's political thought, the "Critique of Hegel's *Philosophy of Right*" (of 1843-1844). As the manuscript made clear, the critique of politics and political thought was part and parcel of a larger criticism seeking to unhinge the mystifications of idealist speculation and religion. The basic tenet of the latter criticism, Marx wrote, was this: "man makes religion; religion does not make man." Religious belief could provide content to human self-awareness only so long "as man has not found himself or has lost himself again." The truth, however, was that "man is not an abstract being squatting outside the world"; rather, he is a concrete agent in "the human world, the state, society." At present, this human context was disfigured by contradiction and alienation, which was projected onto heaven in a mystified way: "This state, this society, produce religion which is an inverted world consciousness, because they are an inverted world."[9]

Critique of mystification, in Marx's account, was not a recipe for despair or pessimism, but rather a signal for human emancipation and self-government. Religion, he wrote, is "the sigh of the oppressed creature, the sentiment of a heartless world, and the soul of soulless conditions"; abolition of religion as source of the "illusory happiness of men" entailed a demand for their "real happiness." Once man had lost his illusions and regained his "reason," he was finally enabled to "revolve about himself as his own true sun." Once the critique of otherworldly transcendence had been completed, it was the task of social-political thought to direct its attention to worldly or social matters, in an effort to "unmask human self-alienation in its secular form," just as it had been unmasked in its "sacred form." In this manner, the "criticism of heaven" could be transformed "into the criticism of earth" and "the criticism of theology into the criticism of politics."

Hegel's political thought occupied an instructive and important place in this transformative process. According to the manuscript, Hegel's work was pivotal for understanding modern political life—and this despite the general backwardness of Germany in comparison with other Western countries. In the midst of German backwardness or underdevelopment, Hegel had been able philosophically to pinpoint the essential features of the modern bourgeois state and thereby also the shortcomings and defects of this apparatus. By pitching his argument on the level of idealized state structures, his analysis also exposed the mystifying quality of modern politics. In Marx's words:

The criticism of the German philosophy of right and of the state, which was given its most rigorous, profound and complete expression by Hegel, is at once the critical analysis of the modern state and of the reality connected with it, and the definitive negation of all past forms of consciousness in German jurisprudence and politics. . . . If it was only Germany which could produce the speculative philosophy of right—this abstract and extravagant thought about the modern state whose reality remains in another world (even though this is just across the Rhine)—the German conception of the modern state, on the other hand, which abstracts from actual man, was possible only because and insofar as the modern state itself abstracts from actual man or satisfies the whole man only in an illusory way. In politics, the Germans have *thought* what other nations have *done;* Germany was their theoretical conscience.

The abstract or one-sided character of Hegel's thought thus had a parallel in the partial or stunted quality of modern political developments. If, by perpetuating the *ancien régime,* German backwardness constituted the "thorn in the flesh" of the modern state, the level attained in its political reflection captured the "imperfection of the modern state itself," the "degeneracy of its flesh."[10]

In Marx's view, the imperfection of modern politics could no longer be remedied by philosophical thought alone, but required a resolute move from abstract theorizing to political practice—in fact, to radical, revolutionary practice. It is clear, the manuscript continued, that "the arm of criticism cannot replace the criticism of arms" and that "material force can only be overthrown by material force." Proceeding initially from the debunking or abolition of religion, transformative criticism necessarily leads to the insight that "man is the supreme being for man." This insight, in turn, entails a radical postulate, namely, the "categorical imperative to overthrow all those conditions in which man is a debased, enslaved, abandoned, contemptible being." Implementation of this imperative required a social carrier or agent capable of revolutionizing existing conditions.

Relying on a modified Hegelian dialectic—centered now in social practice or *praxis*—Marx argued that modern industrial society by its inner momentum engenders its own "determinate negation" or "grave digger" in the form of the working class or proletariat. According to the argument of the "Critique," the proletariat is "a class in civil society" that is yet not "a class of civil society" but rather the harbinger of "the dissolution of all classes." The latter effect was the result of the proletariat's own disinherited and expropriated status. Thus, in announcing the dissolution of the existing order, the proletariat "only declares the secret of its own existence." Although a particular group in society, the proletariat (evocative again of Hegelian teachings) also had a universal mission or was destined to function as a "universal class," because "its sufferings are universal" and the wrong done to it

is "not a particular wrong but wrong in general." As carrier of the
historical dialectic, the proletariat thus was the agent both of self-
emancipation and of the emancipation of "all other spheres of society."
While initially mired in deprivation and a "total loss of humanity," it
could only save itself through "the total redemption of humanity." Prospects for such a total reversal in Germany were at least encouraging. In a
country that "likes to get to the bottom of things," revolution was likely to
upset "the whole order of things." At this point, philosophy was liable to
be "the head of this emancipation" and the proletariat "its heart."[11]

The critique of idealist political thought was echoed also in another
manuscript composed roughly at the same time, titled "For a Ruthless
Criticism of Everything Existing." Turning attention to the progressive
dismantling of feudal traditions by modern political revolutions, the
essay recognized in modern state structures a clear advance in rationality or rational organization, an advance marred by neglect of social and
economic underpinnings. So far as "real life" is concerned, Marx
observed, the "political state" in all its modern forms—even when not
"consciously imbued with socialist goals"—reflects indeed the "demands of reason." Nor does the state "stop at that," but rather presupposes everywhere "that reason has in fact been realized." With this
latter presupposition, however, the state gets embroiled in contradiction
"between its ideal mission and its real preconditions." It was the task
of "ruthless," or transformative, criticism to garner "social truth" out
of this inherent "conflict of the political state with itself."

The same topic was pursued a few months later in the essay "On the
Jewish Question" (published in 1844). Focusing on the issue of individual rights, particularly the right of religious freedom, Marx distinguished sharply between "political emancipation" involving a reform
of public institutions, on the one hand, and "human emancipation"
ushering in a radical social transformation, on the other. While political
emancipation represented certainly "a great progress," it was not "the
final form of human emancipation" but only the final emancipatory
stage "within the framework of the existing social order." A telling
gauge of the halfheartedness of political emancipation was the status of
religion, which at that stage was not so much abolished as preserved as a
private belief. In Marx's words, "the members of the political state are
religious because of the dualism between individual life and species-life,

between the life of civil society and political life." Religious belief here matches the mystifying quality of state structures, in the sense that "man treats political life, which is remote from his individual existence, as if it were his true life." While attacking traditional modes of public authority, modern political revolutions had left society itself unreformed or unreconstructed; hence a new impulse was needed to liberate the genuine human potential buried in present social conditions. "Political emancipation," we read,

> is a reduction of man, on the one hand, to a member of civil society, an independent and egoistic individual, and on the other hand, to a citizen, to a moral person. Human emancipation will only be complete when the actual individual man has absorbed into himself the abstract citizen; when as an individual being—in his everyday life, in his work and his relationships—he has become a species-being; and when he has recognized and organized his own capabilities as social powers and hence no longer separates this social power from himself as political agent.[12]

The engagement with Hegel reached a high point of intensity during that period in the "Economic and Philosophical Manuscripts," also known as the "Paris Manuscripts" (of 1844). Although directed at Hegel's system as a whole, the work concentrated particularly on his *Phenomenology of Spirit,* termed "the true point of origin and the secret of Hegelian philosophy." As on previous occasions, Marx's analysis reflected again the ambivalent mixture of praise and critical rejection. According to the manuscripts, the "outstanding thing" in the *Phenomenology* was that Hegel conceived "the self-genesis of man as a process" involving objectification seen "as loss of the object, as alienation and as transcendence of this alienation." Differently put, Hegel grasped "the essence of labor" and construed "objective man" as "the outcome of man's own labor." The drawback of this dialectical approach was again its abstractness, that is, its "abstract, logical, speculative" formulation of human self-genesis and labor. In Marx's words, human self-genesis was presented as a "merely formal" act, for the simple reason that "human essence" itself was taken to be only an "abstract, thinking essence, conceived merely as self-consciousness." As a corollary, the dialectic of alienation and its transcendence was restricted to an internal thought process—with the result that alienation was never really overcome but only reconstituted on the higher level of "absolute spirit" (treated as synonym for the divine and hence for religion): "This movement in its abstract form as dialectic" is here regarded "as a divine process, but as the divine process of man, traversed by man's abstract, pure, absolute essence that is distinct from him."

As a counterpoise to Hegel's spiritual idealism, Marx at this point proposed the perspective of a "naturalist humanism" (or humanist naturalism) where "man" is regarded basically as a "*natural* being" endowed with "natural powers of life," but also as a "*human* natural being" who constantly has to invent or constructively produce its means of survival. In the course of concrete human self-genesis, the products of labor are in some contexts, especially the capitalist context, taken away or sundered from the producing agent, a sundering that is the cause of alienated or "estranged labor" involving the estrangement of the worker from his products, from himself and his fellow-workers. Overcoming this estrangement requires a new form of social organization built on the "positive transcendence of private property" and hence on the "real appropriation of the human essence by and for man." Compared with this goal, Hegel's *Phenomenology,* although forward looking, was still an "occult critique," that is, a critique of alienation "still obscure to itself" and thus a "mystifying criticism."[13]

Although impressive in its social-political élan, Marx's critique of Hegelian thought is itself not free of obscurity and certainly remains criticizable in its cogency and overall effectiveness. As in the case of Kierkegaard, one can appreciate the realist impulse motivating the critique, the effort to transgress abstract thought in the direction of concrete life experience. As in the Danish thinker, however, the attack misfires at least in part by ignoring the concreteness of Hegel's conceptualism and the ontological moorings of his categories. Even if abstractness were granted, moreover, the critique remains ambiguous given the strong persistence of Hegelian themes. This persistence is evident on the level of historical dialectics, in the portrayal of social development as a movement from immediacy through determinate negation to a new synthesis. The linkage prevails even in the primacy of subjectivity (and its progressive maturation)—although the accent is shifted from individual to collective identity, from rational-spiritual agency to concretized productive agency or labor. On the social-political plane, Hegel's universalizing or totalizing bent is preserved as well, although the embodiment of universalism is shifted from public officials or the civil service to the industrial proletariat.

While indebted in these and other respects to Hegel's teachings, Marx's critique also strikes out in new directions, directions that are intrinsically problematical and dubious from a Hegelian vantage. Prominent among those innovations is the downgrading of individual ownership—the "positive transcendence of private property"—in favor of communist or collective ownership, a proposal that flies in the face of Hegel's serious reservations regarding communist blueprints. As will be recalled, property for Hegel was an integral feature of modern inwardness and individuality and a necessary ingredient of the maturation of humanity through "diremption" (*Entzweiung*), a diremption that had to run its course in civil society (although not in the form of an extreme disproportion of wealth and indigence). Communism, from this vantage, was liable to short-circuit human and social maturation and hence to obstruct the momentum of modernity.[14]

Even more dubious, from Hegel's view, is the proposed avenue for reaching the communist goal, that is, the method of class struggle and revolution, which accords ill with the integrative cast of Hegel's work and his continuous effort to balance different social estates. The shortcoming of the method is underscored and aggravated by the intrinsic incongruence of means and ends. As an outgrowth of industrial capitalism, the working class is necessarily a contingent part of modern society, a characteristic that threatens to particularize the universal aim of classlessness. More important, the stress on collective agency and productive labor tends to transform universalism (or universal reconciliation) itself into an outcome of human production or productive design. The dismissal of Hegelian *spirit* (in its objective and absolute modes) here carries a price: The radical humanization of agency has as a corollary the "instrumentalization" of public and intellectual life or its reduction to a target of social engineering. The instrumentalist implications of Marx's critique have been perceptively recognized by Taylor in his exegesis of Hegel's work. In Taylor's presentation, Marx's innovation consisted basically in a "transposition of Hegel's synthesis from *Geist* onto man," not in the sense of a simple linkage of the two (already accomplished by Hegel) but in that of a radical substitution of human labor power and productive capabilities for the transhuman workings of spirit. Placing the accent on labor power also meant a shift in the effective locus of power, a shift expanding instrumental human control over the world. In Taylor's words:

> Man is one with nature, because and to the extent to which he has made it over as his expression. The transformation of human society is not aimed at an eventual recognition of a larger order, but ultimately at the subjugation of nature to a design freely created by man.[15]

Will to Power: Nietzsche

The theme of power was intensified in the writings of Nietzsche, with a sharp edge against Hegel and the entire tradition of Western metaphysics. Marx's attempt to turn Hegel "right side up"—still pursued largely within Hegelian confines—took in these writings the more radical form of an assault on the legacy of "Platonism," that is, on the differentiation between the sensible and the supersensible worlds or between the realms of essences and appearances (a legacy still permeating strongly Hegel's work). An inkling of this radical turn can be found in the "Critique of Hegel's *Philosophy of Right*" when Marx writes that Hegel's "chief mistake" resided in the fact that he conceived "the contradiction in appearance as being a unity in essence" (or idea), whereas it certainly had "something more profound in its essence, namely, an essential contradiction."[16]

Pushing beyond this formulation, Nietzsche's thought inaugurated a break with traditional "essentialism" or "foundationalism," with the search for ultimate grounds or moorings (like reason or idea)—although the thoroughness or success of his break remain controversial. Together with Kierkegaard, Nietzsche relocated the philosophical accent from universalism to particularity and individuality, but individuality was now multiple (or decentered) and its link with subjectivity at best fragile. Like the Danish thinker, he sundered the nexus between general reason and will, thus foregrounding the risks of existential self-constitution but without the backdrop of divine grace. Together with Marx, Nietzsche accentuated concrete human self-genesis and productive power. Yet, instead of relying on collective agency or focusing narrowly on industrial "forces of production," he saw human and social life basically as the result of a dispersed "will to power," that is, of the nondialectical (and not reconcilable) play of forces and energies that inevitably lead to interhuman asymmetries (rather than to classlessness). Although including importantly the element of self-control, pursuit of will to power also was bound to lead to modes of external control, thus corroborating (albeit unwittingly) the modern trademarks of divisiveness and diremption.[17]

Given these orientations, Nietzsche's thought from the beginning was set on a collision course with Hegel's teachings, an antagonism that partially was bequeathed to him by Schopenhauer. Largely under the latter's influence, his early writings were sharply dismissive of Hegel's work, castigating it primarily for its (supposed) "historical optimism" and its shallow support of prevailing historical tendencies and developments. By linking the rational and the real or reason and actual life-experience, Hegel was said to encourage an uncritical acceptance of external "necessity" and the oblivion of the agonies of concrete human decision. As Nietzsche stated in one of his early notes (of 1873), Hegel's message was basically this:

> That at the bottom of history, and particularly of world history, there is a final aim, that this aim has actually been realized and is being realized in it (the plan of providence), thus that there is *reason* in history.

From this Hegel derived the conclusion that world history and every story "must have an aim" and that "we demand stories only with aims." But, Nietzsche countered,

> we do not at all demand stories about the world process, for we consider it a swindle to talk about it. That my life has no aim is evident even from the accidental nature of its origin; that I can *posit* an aim for myself is another matter.

With the waning of Schopenhauer's intellectual influence, Nietzsche began progressively to reevaluate Hegel's work, or at least to dissociate himself from (what he called) Schopenhauer's "unintelligent rage against

Hegel." Beginning with *The Dawn* (1881), Nietzsche's comments displayed a greater appreciation of Hegelian insights, although appreciation was still deeply tinged with reservations. Thus juxtaposing German *Geist* and French *esprit,* a passage in *The Dawn* stated that "of the famous Germans, perhaps none had more *esprit* than Hegel; but for all that, he too feared it with a great German fear—which created his peculiar bad style." What Nietzsche came to appreciate was Hegel's concern with historical change and development, as a possible antidote to static essentialism, and particularly his emphasis on historical and social contradictions as a possible gateway to insight into the contradictory or agonistic character of all things and of being itself. As it happens, this insight was barred by Hegel's continued attachment to "sublation" (*Aufhebung*) and synthesis. On balance, Hegel's thought for Nietzsche in the end lapsed into quietism and religious-moral conservatism—a lapse particularly evident in Hegel's failure to explore the implications of the "death of God." In presenting history and the world as manifestations of the divine, his work was said to undermine skepticism and to delay the ascent of atheism. In the words of the *Gay Science* (1882): "Hegel in particular was its [atheism's] delayer par excellence, with his grandiose attempt to persuade us of the divinity of existence, appealing as a last resort to our sixth sense, the 'historical sense.' "[18]

Opposition to Hegelian teleology and quasi-theology also prompted a strong divergence with respect to politics and political thought. In criticizing the actualization of reason in history, Nietzsche's early notes also attacked Hegel's political idealism, that is, his conception of the state as embodiment of historical reason. Just as "my life" is aimless in the absence of deliberate construction, the notes argued, so "a state has no aim—we alone give it this aim or that." Abstracting from deliberate decisions, moreover, Hegel's conception tended to privilege the state over individual particularity and unity over agonistic strife. In terms of the notes, the gist of Hegelian politics was "What happens to a people has essential significance in its relation to the state," while "the mere particularities of individuals are most remote" from political concerns. For Nietzsche, however, the state was at best a means for the preservation of sundry individuals, thus "how could it be the aim?" Basically, the only justification for the state was that "with the preservation of so many blanks one may also protect a few in whom humanity culminates"; otherwise it made no sense "to preserve so many wretched human beings."

The history of the state, from this vantage, was the story of the general struggle for survival and existence, a struggle that sometimes leads to the emergence of exceptional beings: "Individual and collective egoism struggling against each other—an atomic whirl of egoisms—who would look for aims here?" The debunking of the rational state—or of the state as embodiment of universal reason—was nowhere more zestfully articulated than in *Thus Spoke Zarathustra* where Nietzsche announced this political "twilight of idols":

> State? What is that? Well then, open your ears to me, for now I shall speak to you about the death of peoples. State is the name of the coldest of all cold monsters. Coldly it tells lies too; and this lie crawls out of its mouth: 'I, the state, am the people.' That is a lie! It was [individual] creators who created peoples and hung a faith and a love over them: thus they served life. . . . All-too-many are born: for the superfluous the state was invented. Behold, how it lures them, the all-too-many—and how it devours them, chews them, and ruminates! . . . Only where the state ends, there begins the human being who is not superfluous: there begins the song of necessity, the unique and inimitable tune. Where the state *ends*—look there, my brothers! Do you not see it, the rainbow and the bridges of the overman?

In Nietzsche's later notes and aphorisms, Hegel appears mainly as proponent of political quietism, or a "dialectical fatalism," although "in honor of the spirit." In the course of a historical overview, a late note (of 1887) finds in Hegel (and Goethe) a "will to deify the universe and life in order to find repose and happiness in contemplation"; Hegel in particular "seeks reason everywhere—before reason one may submit and acquiesce."[19]

As an antidote to Hegelian rationalism, Nietzsche (as indicated) celebrated individual particularity, agonistic struggle, and especially the role of exceptional agents and creative artists. These themes were steadily accentuated in his late notes—collected under the title *The Will to Power*—in an overall effort to overturn traditional metaphysics in favor of a creative revaluation or reconstruction of all prevailing modes of thought and life. As we read in the section on the will to power as art: "Our religion, morality, and philosophy are decadent forms of man," leaving as the only possible remedy or "countermovement: art," that is, creative agency rooted in the will to power. From a radically antimetaphysical vantage, the same section adds, "metaphysics, morality, religion, science" are nothing but "various forms of lies," although lies that may be conducive to having "faith in life"; all of them, in any case, are only products of the "will to art, to lie, to flight from 'truth,' " hence of the will to power. Overturning of metaphysics means canceling the privileging of truth over lie, of essence over appearance, with the result that "the will to appearance, to illusion, to deception, to becoming and change here counts as more profound, primeval, 'metaphysical' than the will to truth, to reality, to 'mere' appearance."

Regarding the agents of creative reconstruction, the notes leave no doubt about their exceptional character. "In an age of *suffrage universel,* when everyone may sit in judgment of everyone and everything," Nietzsche wrote, "I feel compelled to reestablish order of rank." Such a new ranking in his view was to be predicated on will to power or on "quanta of power, and nothing else," with rank order thus denoting order of power." On behalf of the new ranking, "a declaration of war on the masses by *higher men*" seemed justified. Although forcefully stated, passages of this kind do not necessarily or unequivocally support the proposed exit from metaphysics. Given the focus on particular singularity and will power, Nietzsche's remarks often tend to reduce *overturning* to a simple reversal of priorities, which remain safely lodged in metaphysical thought and its categorical distinctions (of reason and will, universalism and particularism). To the extent that this is correct, Hegel's philosophy is prone to survive Nietzsche's polemics more or less unscathed. The charge of an abstract quietism or fatalism, above all, seems ill-directed or aimed at a strawman, while bypassing the complex subtlety of Hegel's work (including his mediation of reason and praxis). In the words of a recent text on the topic, Nietzsche may indeed have been right in claiming "that Hegel 'delayed the triumph of atheism' by preserving faith in the 'idea,' " but he was surely wrong in grasping idea as something "pre-existing, transcending or riding roughshod over the actions of men."[20]

Politics and Bureaucracy: Weber

Nietzsche's life span coincided with the upsurge of scientific empiricism or positivism, a development that left its distinct imprint on facets of his work. The upsurge reached an initial high point during the subsequent generation, that is, during the era of *fin-de-siècle* and *la belle epoque,* leading up to the first world war and its aftermath. A prominent figure during this era was Weber who, in his own work, combined a quasi-Nietzschean taste for political and intellectual agonistics with a sober dedication to scientific procedure and value neutrality.

Philosophically, Weber was always close to the Kantian tradition with its bifurcation of "pure" and "practical" reason, of "phenomenal" science and "noumenal" morality. However, largely under the impact of Nietzsche's iconoclasm, ethical norms came to be transformed from universally shared "categorical imperatives" into subjectively held value preferences, preferences that inevitably were lodged in tensions and agonistic struggles for moral primacy devoid of standards of adjudication. Through his studies of social groups, economic relations, and administrative structures, Weber became a leading pioneer of empirical or scientific sociological research. But in his attention to motivating ideas and the inner sources of political action and legitimation, he preserved the dramatic intellectual impulses deriving largely from Nietzsche's writings. To this extent, Bendix and Roth seem to be quite correct in asserting that Weber's scholarly endeavors were the most thoroughgoing attempt to implement Nietzschean initiatives within the confines of a strictly empirical science. To be sure, his extensive sociological and economic inquiries were far removed from Nietzsche's literary-philosophical preoccupations. In a sense, this research agenda tended to connect Weberian analysis with Marx's social-economic frame of reference—whose universal-dialectical accents, however, were checked or replaced by a more subjective-individualist and Nietzschean style of argument.[21]

The juxtaposition of scientific method and subjective value preferences is a recurrent feature throughout Weber's far-flung opus. In a particularly instructive way, the combination surfaced in two public addresses delivered at the end of the war: "Politics as a Vocation" and "Science as a Vocation." The first lecture focused right away on the dominant political organization in modern times, namely, the state.

Breaking sharply with the Hegelian legacy, Weber construed the state not as the embodiment of idea or a rational *telos* but strictly as an instrument of domination. "What is a 'state'?" he asked, and responded:

> Sociologically, the state cannot be defined in terms of its ends. . . . Ultimately, one can define the modern state sociologically only in terms of the specific *means* peculiar to it, as to every political association, namely, the use of force.

Elaborating on the definition and fleshing out further its descriptive substance, the lecture added that the state is "a human community that (successfully) claims the *monopoly of the legitimate use of physical force* within a given territory," in the sense that the state alone possesses the "right to use violence." In line with this formula, "politics" broadly speaking meant a struggle for power or an agonistic striving to influence or participate in the exercise of supreme power, either within or between states.

As one should note, state and politics were presented here sociologically, that is, in social-scientific or value-neutral terms, but in terms that Nietzsche would hardly have found objectionable. Empirical description, however, was only one side of the coin: buried in the definition was also a reference to "legitimate" force and to the "right" to use violence and thus to the dimension of moral rightness. In Weber's account, legitimacy and legitimation did not point to universal yardsticks or a substantive *Sittlichkeit* but only to the subjective value preferences, or "inner justifications," with which people approach the state and which accordingly vary with time and place. On an ideal-typical level, three such subjective approaches could be distinguished as the *traditional, charismatic,* and *legal* modes of justification. While the first of these modes was backward looking and the last restricted to formal rules, the second type was singled out by Weber as particularly relevant to politics viewed as a "vocation":

> Here we are interested above all in the second of these types: domination by virtue of the devotion of those who obey the purely personal 'charisma' of the 'leader.' For this is the root of the idea of a *calling* in its highest expression. Devotion to the charisma of the prophet, or the leader in war, or to the great demagogue in the *ecclesia* or in parliament, means that the leader is personally recognized as the innerly 'called' leader of men.[22]

According to Weber, it was important to differentiate between politics seen as a genuine calling or vocation, on the one hand, and politics performed as a pastime or in the subordinate role of civil servant, on the other. As he observed, it was possible to remain an "occasional politician" and hence to pursue politics as a sideline, or avocation. In fact, the activity of most people or citizens tended to be restricted to this level of involvement. The situation was radically different in the case of individuals with a political calling. Someone who lives *for* politics, Weber observed, "makes politics his life, in an internal sense." Compelled by his vocation, "he either enjoys the naked possession of the power he exerts, or he nourishes his inner balance and self-feeling by the consciousness that his life has meaning in the service of a 'cause.' "

In his passionate engagement for a cause, the politician was also sharply distinguished from the class of civil servants or public administrators—whom Hegel had still treated as a "universal class" dedicated to the state as embodiment of reason. Diverging from the Hegelian legacy, Weber insisted that the civil servant "will not engage in politics" properly speaking, rather "he should engage in impartial administration." This abstinence held true even for so-called political administrators, at least insofar as the *raison d'état* or the "vital interests of the ruling order" are not in question. The basic motto for the civil servant's life was value-neutral governance: *"Sine ira et studio,* 'without scorn and bias,' he shall administer his office"; to this extent, he was enjoined *not* to do "precisely what the politician, the leader as well as his following, must always and necessarily do: namely, *fight.*" Accentuating further the divorce between reason and will, or between objective rule-performance and subjective-political agonistics, the lecture went on to contrast the two roles in terms of modes of responsibility:

> To take a stand, to be passionate—*ira et studium*—is the politician's element, and above all the element of the political *leader.* His conduct is subject to quite a different, indeed, exactly the opposite, principle of responsibility from that of the civil servant. The honor of the civil servant is vested in his ability to execute consciously the order of the superior authorities, exactly as if the order agreed with his own conviction. . . . Without this moral discipline and self-denial, in the highest sense, the whole apparatus would fall to pieces. The honor of the political leader, of the leading statesman, however, lies precisely in an exclusive *personal*

responsibility for what he does, a responsibility he cannot and must not reject or transfer.[23]

The remainder of Weber's lecture focused on different modes of political calling, and particularly on different ethical convictions motivating genuine politicians. The main distinction here was between an "ethics of ultimate ends" and an "ethics of responsibility," a contrast that cannot be further pursued in this context (except to note that devotion to ultimate ends was particularly congenial to radically charismatic leaders). The central point for Weber was the built-in tension between ethical goals and prevailing political reality, that is, the set of constraints imposed on subjective convictions by modern political structures and especially by the instruments of power or violence endemic to the modern state. These constraints, in his view, were growing steadily more pronounced in our century, in a manner that rendered prospects of a just and equitable politics increasingly dim or remote. As the conclusion of his lecture observed somberly: "No summer's bloom lies ahead of us, but rather a polar night of icy darkness and hardness, no matter which group may triumph externally now."

In the face of this darkening of the horizon, politics was bound to be a frustrating and arduous task—a "strong and slow boring of hard boards." Only someone who was "sure that he shall not crumble" under the weight of this task could still claim politics as a vocation: "Only he who in the face of all this can say 'In spite of all!' has the calling for politics." The somber picture was elaborated and fleshed out further in the second lecture, "Science as a Vocation." Deviating again from the Hegelian legacy, Weber advanced a sharp separation between knowledge and faith, that is, between the objectivity and neutrality of modern science and the subjective status of all kinds of beliefs, varying from theology through metaphysics to ethics (and political worldviews). The progress of science, in his account, entailed the retreat of all beliefs and values into a sphere of private inwardness, a sphere endowed with its own integrity but in danger of being smothered by scientific realism. "The fate of our time," we read, "is characterized by rationalization and intellectualization and, above all, by the 'disenchantment of the world.' " In this situation, precisely the "ultimate and most sublime values" have retired from the public arena "either into the transcendental realm of mystic life or into the brotherliness of direct and personal human relations."[24]

The tension-rife linkage of objective reality and inner beliefs was also prominently developed in Weber's *magnum opus* titled *Economy and Society* (first published posthumously in 1921). There we encounter again the definition of the state as an institution monopolizing the use of force. In Weber's language, the state is a "compulsory political organization with continuous administrative operations (*politischer Anstaltsbetrieb*)" whose officers successfully uphold the claim "to have the monopoly of the legitimate use of physical force in the enforcement of its order." In the same context, the state is defined as a "dominating organization" (*Herrschaftsverband*), where *domination* means "the probability that a command with a given content will be obeyed by a given group of people."

As before, domination on the part of the state is closely connected with legitimacy or legitimation, terms that again refer to subjective beliefs or inner justifications prompting obedience to the state. The chief types of "legitimating belief" (*Legitimitätsglaube*) are *traditional, charismatic,* and *rational-legal* modes of justification. While the first type rests on "everyday belief in the sanctity of immemorial traditions" and whereas the last type reflects "belief in the legality of enacted rules," charismatic support depends on "the exceptional sanctity, heroism, or exemplary character of a person and of the normative order revealed or ordained by him." The chief tension that arises in the study is between routinized rule-governance and political leadership. In Weber's portrayal, legal order or legitimacy is closely tied to the role of the bureaucracy, a linkage explained by the fact that bureaucratic rule is able to attain the "highest degree of efficiency" and hence represents the rationally most advanced form of control. In fact, rationalization and modernization are said to coincide with "the development and continual spread of bureaucratic administration," a process that is "at the root of the modern Western state." Far from simply extolling this development, however, *Economy and Society* also noted the inevitable conflict between bureaucratic rule and political beliefs or between technical expert and politician. In language reminiscent of the "cold monster" evoked by Zarathustra, the study at one point depicted the modern state as a congealed or "frozen spirit" or as a "living machine":

Together with the dead machine [in the factories], this machine is in the process of erecting the scaffolding of that future subjection or enslavement (*Hörigkeit*) to which someday perhaps human beings, like the fellachs of ancient Egypt, have to surrender helplessly—if, that is, they assign the final and highest value in the conduct of their affairs to a technically well-functioning and that means: rational-bureaucratic administration and management.[25]

Liberal Positivism: Popper

Some of Weber's worst fears or nightmares came to pass in our century, although not precisely in the form he envisaged. In the decade after his death, totalitarian regimes began to flourish in Western Europe and in Russia. Diverging from Weber's expectations, these regimes showed a peculiar combination of charismatic leadership and efficient-bureaucratic control of all facets of society. In response to the totalitarian danger, Western social and philosophical thought tended to reaffirm and (in part) reformulate inherited and proven pathways or intellectual orientations. Foremost among these pathways was positivism or empiricism with its privileging of the role of modern science, a perspective that now was rendered more subtle or nuanced by attention to the logical and linguistic requisites of empirical research. In its refurbished or restated form, positivism continued to cling to the sharp division between facts and values, between objective knowledge and subjective (moral or metaphysical) preferences, although the division was on the whole purged of the dramatic intensity of Weberian agonism or Nietzschean pathos. In political terms, the division conformed fairly closely to the pattern of postclassical 19th-century liberalism with its differentiation between a neutral legal-constitutional framework and partisan policy preferences.

A leading spokesman of the liberal-positivist outlook was Popper, renowned chiefly as a philosopher of science but also for some of his political writings. Initially a member of the so-called Vienna circle (the chief organ of the logical-positivist movement), Popper subsequently developed his own distinctive epistemology, although without departing radically from the empiricist legacy. Apart from certain epistemological refinements, what distinguishes his work from that of earlier empiricists is mainly a greater intellectual militancy. Faced with the political turmoil of our age, Popper saw the need to vindicate his approach resolutely against alternative, nonempiricist positions, particularly those deriving from German idealism and the older metaphysical tradition. Thus, while Weber's departure from Hegel was still largely implicit, Popper frontally attacked the idealist thinker as an enemy of the "open society" and as an advocate of a closed, near-totalitarian regime.

In *The Open Society and Its Enemies*, Hegel shares the limelight with other suspect thinkers of the past, particularly with Plato and Marx. Bracketing the pronounced differences between these authors—differences underscored by Hegel and later by Marx—the study proceeds to attack all three for their presumed enmity to democratic openness, which in turn derives from their attachment to a speculative *historicism* (belief in the predictability of history) and their dismissal of individual freedom in favor of holistic-totalitarian structures. In the present context, only brief glimpses of the anti-Hegelian argument can and need be given. Basically, these glimpses are provided because of the pervasive impact and reverberations of the study and not because of the intrinsic merit of its presentation, which is long on invectives and somewhat short on scholarship or intellectual fair mindedness.

In Popper's portrayal, Hegel—the "source of all contemporary historicism"—was the direct heir and follower of a long line of metaphysical speculation deriving from Heraclitus, Plato, and Aristotle. Together with these predecessors Hegel was ignorant of empirical science and scientific method. Instead of engaging in empirical research, the German thinker relied entirely on speculative insight and dialectical logic—with "miraculous" results: "A master logician, it was child's play for his powerful dialectical methods to draw real physical rabbits out of purely metaphysical silk-hats." One reason why Hegelian philosophy was at all taken seriously in his time was the general "backwardness of German natural science in those days." On the whole, Hegel's following—then and later—was made up of people who preferred "a quick initiation into the deeper secrets of this world to the laborious technicalities of a science which, after all, may only disappoint them by its lack of power to unveil all mysteries." Concentrating on Hegel's philosophy of nature (admittedly a weak link in his overall system), Popper found the Hegelian opus guilty of mystification and in fact of deliberate deception: "The question arises whether Hegel deceived himself, hypnotized by his own inspiring jargon, or whether he boldly set out to deceive and bewitch others. I am satisfied that the latter was the case."[26]

In the political arena, a similar mystification prevailed, namely, the denigration of individual judgment in favor of overarching authoritarian structures. In Popper's account, Hegel's philosophy was basically a handmaiden of the reactionary, anticonstitutional policies of the Prussian state. After the prelude of the Enlightenment, we read,

> the fight for the open society began again only with the ideas of 1789; and the feudal monarchies soon experienced the seriousness of this danger. When in 1815 the reactionary party began to resume its power in Prussia, it found itself in dire need of an ideology. Hegel was appointed to meet this demand, and he did so by reviving the ideas of the first great enemies of the open society, Heraclitus, Plato, and Aristotle. Just as the French Revolution rediscovered the perennial ideas of the great generation and of Christianity—freedom, equality, and the brotherhood of all men—so Hegel rediscovered the Platonic ideas which lie behind the perennial revolt against freedom and reason. Hegelianism is the renaissance of tribalism.

In supporting the Prussian state with its militaristic bent, Popper claimed, Hegel's thought promoted the upsurge not only of tribalism but of a chauvinistic nationalism or collectivism, which, in turn, was the pacemaker of contemporary totalitarian regimes. Discounting or bypassing Hegel's persistent critique of Plato's *substantialism* (his treatment of being as ideal substance), Popper saw a tight chain of intellectual filiation linking classical teachings with recent modes of political repression. In fact, Hegel's historical significance resided for Popper precisely in "that he represents the 'missing link,' as it were, between Plato and the modern form of totalitarianism." Together with Plato, Hegel (we are told) completely rejected or despised individual rights and constitutional safeguards, indulging instead in a "Platonizing worship of the state." Inspired by classical ideals of public unity and homogeneity, Hegelians—both direct disciples and latter-day followers—have all been taught "to worship the state, history, and the nation." Summed up in a nutshell, the political doctrine of Hegelianism was that "the state is everything and the individual nothing," in the sense that the individual "owes everything to the state, his physical as well as his spiritual existence."[27]

As in the case of Plato (and later of Marx), Hegel's totalitarian proclivities were buttressed by his historicism, that is, the assumption of a linear historical evolution. For Plato, the realm of ideas or essences existed before or outside the world of phenomena, and the trend of development was a "movement away from the perfection of the ideas" and hence a movement of decay. While maintaining the distinction between essences and appearances, Hegel reversed the *telos* of evolution by postulating a general trend "towards the idea" and thus an evolutionary scheme of progress. "In Hegel's world," we read, "as in that of Heraclitus, everything is in flux; and the essences, originally introduced by Plato in order to obtain something stable, are not exempted." For Hegel, however, this flux is "not decay" and his historicism is basically "optimistic" by pointing to the steady self-realization or actualization of spirit. Although perhaps innocuous on an abstract level, this actualization showed its pernicious implications in the linkage of spirit with nationalist collectivism and the modern state. In Hegel's political philosophy, it was crucially the "spirit of the nation" that determines its "hidden historical destiny," and in order to actualize this spirit a nation had to assert its individuality by "fighting other nations" in a near-permanent condition of warfare. The dangers of this teleology were clearly evident in the concluding section "World History" in the *Philosophy of Right* where Hegel depicted the evolution of Western civilization in the direction of a "Germanic realm," which Popper quickly identifies with the Prussian monarchy and its still more militant and ethnocentric successors. In the 19th century, chauvinistic nationalism was aggravated by the rise of materialism—"especially Darwinism in the somewhat crude form given to it by Haeckel"—a blending that in due course spawned the ascent of racism, or racialism, and finally the racial-fascist mode of 20th-century totalitarianism. In light of these explicit or implicit forms of intellectual complicity, the verdict on Hegelianism was bound to be severe. In Popper's words:

> I ask whether I was not justified when I said that Hegel presents us with
> an apology for God and for Prussia at the same time, and whether it is not
> clear that the state which Hegel commands us to worship as the divine

idea on earth is not simply Frederick Williams's Prussia. . . . [Ultimately]
conscience must be replaced by blind obedience and by a romantic
Heraclitean ethics of fame and fate, and the brotherhood of man by a
totalitarian nationalism.[28]

German and French Existentialism

Needless to say, Popper's study did not go unanswered. In every one
of its details or facets, his indictment of Hegel in particular has been
challenged and refuted (I believe) by a string of able scholars, from
Marcuse to Avineri.[29] Above and beyond the specific case of Popper's
work, the 20th century has witnessed a sustained challenge, launched
on a broad scale, against positivism in its various forms, that is, against
the primacy or privileged status of scientific epistemology in philosophy
(as well as in social-political thought). Among early modes of insurgency
one might mention neo-Kantianism (especially in its normative and interpretive dimensions), critical social theory, and Wittgensteinian language
theory with its focus on concrete life-forms. By all accounts, one of the
most prominent countermovements (if not *the* most prominent) has been
existentialism or existential phenomenology as it developed on the
Continent during the first half of the 20th century. As one should note,
opposition to positivism in this case did not normally denote opposition
to science as such, but only to the exclusive preeminence accorded to
empiricist methods. This nuanced attitude toward science was already
clearly spelled out by Husserl, the intellectual founder of the "phenomenological movement" and its diverse offshoots.[30]

In challenging positivism, existentialists and existential phenome-
nologists were also more hospitable again to older metaphysical or
nonempiricist traditions, including the legacy of Hegel. Curiously,
attention to Hegelian thought was combined in many instances with a
renewed preoccupation with the works of Kierkegaard and Nietzsche
(with Kierkegaardian teachings initially overshadowing the latter's
influence). As a result of these diverse concerns, existentialism and
existential phenomenology exhibit a complex tapestry of intellectual

strands, although the central strand tends to be the emphasis on individ-ual human existence and action as the focal point of philosophical explorations. Given this central focus (one should further note), spokes-men of these perspectives in their great majority were also firm critics of totalitarianism or repressively closed societies, although without endorsing the intellectual filiation stipulated in Popper's study.

Existentialism broadly conceived emerged first in Germany during the interbellum period, before reaching its high point as a popular vogue in France after the second world war. A leading figure in the German context was Jaspers who for many years taught philosophy and psychol-ogy in Heidelberg (where he still felt Weber's impact). In an instructive manner, Jaspers's work illustrates the multiplicity of intellectual cur-rents that converged or coalesced in early existentialism. As a philoso-pher trained in medical psychiatry, Jaspers was by no means averse to science—provided it remained in its proper bounds. Partly under the influence of Kantian epistemology, he reserved a place in his frame-work for empirical research purviewed from the vantage of *consciousness-in-general* (where the individual encounters the world as an anonymous-universal spectator). While thus paying tribute to Kantian motifs, his work also made room for the Hegelian legacy of objective spirit, namely, on the level of cultural communities and shared traditions of meaning.

What marked Jaspers as a genuine existentialist, however, was his conception of a "transmundane" and intangible individuality or individ-ual uniqueness—a conception that was deeply indebted to the writings of Kierkegaard and (to a lesser extent) of Nietzsche. In Jaspers's thought, the chief accent was squarely on subjective inwardness and singularity, although other perspectives were acknowledged as relevant on more mundane or contingent levels of human experience. As he noted in a series of lectures delivered in the mid-1930s: "The great history of Western philosophy from Parmenides and Heraclitus through Hegel can be seen as a thorough-going and completed unity" whose major expressions continue to be "preserved in the tradition" and even to be hailed as the "true salvation from the destruction of philosophy." Yet, despite this continuity, a subtle subterranean dislocation had oc-curred in recent times that shifted attention from past teachings to new modes of existential or inward experience:

> Quietly, something enormous has happened in the reality of Western man:
> a destruction of all authority, a radical disillusionment in an overconfident
> reason, and a dissolution of conventional bonds have made anything,
> absolutely anything, seem possible. . . . Philosophizing to be authentic
> must grow out of our new reality and there take its stand.[31]

In Jaspers's account, the intellectual dislocation of our age was due chiefly to Kierkegaard and Nietzsche, two philosophers who "did not count in their times," but who meanwhile have "continually grown in significance" until today they stand "unquestioned as the authentically great thinkers" of the epoch. Despite evident differences of accent, the two philosophers were linked—for Jaspers—through their shared and cumulative effectiveness, through the "shock" that both exerted on Western philosophizing. The chief commonality was their attack on all established beliefs or doctrines and their turn toward a radical inwardness seen either as a paradoxical abyss or as a source of spontaneous self-genesis. In their writings, everything stable or permanent was "as if consumed in a dizzying paroxysm": in the case of Kierkegaard, by "an otherworldly Christianity which is like nothingness and shows itself only in negation (the absurd, martyrdom)"; in the case of Nietzsche, by "a vacuum out of which, with despairing violence, a new reality was to be born."

In both cases, philosophical reflection proceeded not from academic debates but "from the depths of *Existenz*"—where *Existenz* means an "unprecedented intensity of self-consciousness." According to Jaspers, the two thinkers, far from being antipodes, were connected mainly through their shared humanism or subjectivism, although the latter was never a safe refuge but only the locus of constant unrest. In his words, both authors pushed "toward that basis which would be being itself in man." In opposition to the philosophical tradition which from Parmenides to Hegel maintained that "thought is being," Kierkegaard asserted the proposition "as you believe, so are you: faith is being," while Nietzsche accentuated the "will to power." But both faith and will to power are "mere *signa*," that is, cues for the process of continual self-interpretation. Thus, although Kierkegaard turned to Christianity and Nietzsche to atheism or nontheism, both thinkers aimed all their attention "toward the substance of being, toward the nobility and value of man." In pursuing this thrust, Kierkegaard and Nietzsche pushed to the limit the "modern" era whose contours Hegel had pinpointed:

They are modernity itself in a somersaulting form. They ran it to the ground and overcame it by living it through to the end. We can see how both experienced the distress of the epoch, not passively, but suicidally by totally doing what most only half did: first of all, in their endless reflection; and then, in opposition to this, in their drive toward the basic; and finally, in the way in which, as they sank into the abyss, they grasped hold of the transcendent.[32]

At the time of Jaspers's lectures, existentialism was beginning to emerge in France—again chiefly as a countermove to positivism or positivist materialism (as well as to an abstract Cartesianism). As in the case of Jaspers, opposition to positivism entailed a turn to (certain forms of) humanism and inner self-genesis, but the mentors animating the turn in France were more varied and not restricted to proponents of individual *Existenz*. The difference was due, at least in part, to concrete social and political circumstances, specifically to the strong tradition of working-class Marxism in France, and also to the imminent threat of fascist totalitarianism (which placed a premium on political concerns). Without shunning Kierkegaard or Nietzsche, French authors at the time were led to search for additional sources of humanist inspiration. One such source of inspiration—not too far removed from the existentialist pioneers—was recent German philosophy, particularly the perspective of phenomenology as it had been inaugurated by Husserl and subsequently reformulated in Heidegger's fundamental ontology.

While this form of outreach was relatively unsurprising, another venture was more unexpected given the course of intellectual history, namely, the reclamation or reabsorption of both Hegel and Marx. Although Kierkegaard and Nietzsche had seen themselves mostly as anti-Hegelian rebels, French existentialism managed to integrate Hegel's philosophy into a broadly humanist and praxis-oriented perspective. And while Marx had remonstrated strongly against the abstractness of Hegelian thought (evident in the *Phenomenology of Spirit* and elsewhere), close focus on the "Paris Manuscripts" now seemed to corroborate not so much the distance as rather the affinity between the "young" Marx and Hegel's early writings (particularly his *Phenomenology of Spirit*). As it happened, the assimilation of Hegel and Marx—and their joint reception by existentialism—was greatly assisted by several French Hegel-experts of the period, most notably Kojève and Hyppolite. Roughly at the time of Jaspers's lectures, Kojève presented in Paris an extensive lecture series—later translated as *Introduction to the Reading of Hegel*—in which he sought to demonstrate the relevance of Hegel's *Phenomenology* for a humanist mode of social praxis. A few years later, Hyppolite published his *Genesis and Structure of Hegel's Phenomenology of Spirit,* to be followed subsequently by his *Studies on Marx and Hegel* (stressing their shared concern with alienation).[33]

The impact of these initiatives on French existentialism was profound. Both Sartre and Merleau-Ponty were schoolmates of Hyppolite, and Merleau-Ponty is reported to have been in Kojève's audience. To be sure, Hegelian themes were quickly blended with phenomenological and broadly existentialist teachings, which required a construal of Hegel's thought along subjective-humanist lines. The combination of strands was clearly evident in Sartre's *Being and Nothingness,* which was written and published during the second world war. The guiding mentors of the study were Husserl, Heidegger, and Hegel (with Marx emerging only later on Sartre's intellectual horizon). While Husserl provided the bedrock of a "constitutive" consciousness and an intentional relation to objects, and while Heidegger concretized the Husserlian approach by focusing on human "being-in-the-world," Hegel's work was invoked chiefly for its dialectical quality, that is, for its attempt to correlate subject and object or ego and alter ego through a process of reciprocal mediation (thematized as a "struggle for recognition").

As Sartre noted in his study, Hegel's *Phenomenology of Spirit* presented intersubjectivity or the existence of others as "indispensable not only to the constitution of the world and of my empirical 'ego,' but to the very existence of my consciousness as self-consciousness." To gain self-awareness, human consciousness or subjectivity in Hegel's view had to manifest or actualize itself outwardly, a process that inevitably involves intersubjective mediation, triggered initially by reciprocal exclusion or negation. In Sartre's words: "The mediator is the Other," someone who "appears along with myself since self-consciousness is identical with itself by means of the exclusion of the Other." Because the other is one "who excludes me by being himself" and "whom I exclude by being myself," there was from the start a "plurality of consciousnesses" all supported by one another "in a reciprocal imbrication of their being." Thus Hegel's "brilliant intuition" consisted in making me "depend on the other in my *being*." Elaborating on the master-slave or lordship-bondage relation, Sartre distinguished Hegel's *Phenomenology* sharply from the unilateral approach of Husserlian or transcendental phenomenology. Instead of taking the *cogito* as a point of departure, Hegel treated self-consciousness as conditioned by "the recognition of the Other," a recognition predicated on reciprocal struggle:

> In order to make myself recognized by the Other, I must risk my own life. To risk one's life, in fact, is to reveal oneself as not bound to the objective form or any determinate existence—as not bound to life. . . . On the other hand, the Other prefers life and freedom even while showing that he has not been able to posit himself as not bound to the objective form. Therefore he remains bound to external things in general.[34]

While thus appreciating important facets of Hegel's analysis, *Being and Nothingness* stopped short of endorsing the broader aims of his work. Resuming reproaches articulated by earlier existentialists, Sartre found Hegel's thought marred by speculative abstractness and by the assumption of a possible synthesis or sublation (*Aufhebung*) of intersubjective antagonisms. Following his abstract-metaphysical bent, Hegel failed to perceive the difference between existing and knowing, between the "very *being* of consciousness" and rational knowledge, that is, the fact that "consciousness was there before it was known." In this respect "as everywhere," Sartre affirmed, "we ought to oppose to Hegel Kierkegaard, who represents the claims of the individual as such"—of an individual who asserts his singularity by demanding the "recognition of his concrete being." According to Sartre's study, Hegel's blending of knowing and being (or of reason and will) seduced him into embracing a twofold "optimism" on both an epistemological and an ontological plane. Epistemologically, his treatment of mediation barred him from grasping the necessary conflict between subjective existence and its external manifestation, that is, between the transcendental self-genesis of consciousness (its being "for itself") and its appearance as an object of knowledge for others. For Sartre, the other is "not a for-itself as he appears to me" just as I "do not appear to myself as I am for the Other." As a consequence, Hegel's rational optimism results in failure: between the Other-as-object and me-as-subject there is no common measure, no more than between self-consciousness and consciousness *of* the Other. I cannot know myself *in* the Other if the Other is first an object for me; neither can I apprehend the Other in his true being—that is, in his subjectivity. No universal knowledge can be derived from the relation of consciousnesses. This is what we shall call their ontological separation.

Neglect of individual separateness was compounded by a still more basic ontological optimism, manifest in Hegel's conception of "objective" and "absolute spirit." In discussing individual human experience, Hegel ascended from the beginning to a higher plane, namely, the vantage point of "truth" or of "the whole." From the angle of absoluteness, individual existences were at best "moments in the whole," moments that "by themselves are *unselbständig*" (not independent); in his relentless pursuit of mediation, plurality for Hegel was constantly "surpassed toward the totality," a surpassing that could happen only because he had "already given it to himself from the outset." In canceling this surpassing move, *Being and Nothingness* stopped dialectics basically at the point of diremption or "unhappy consciousness," thus resonating again with Kierkegaardian motifs.[35]

In a less conflictual manner, Merleau-Ponty invoked Hegel's philosophical legacy—for the sake of invigorating a humanist social praxis. In an essay of the early postwar years, Merleau-Ponty explicitly profiled a "Hegelian existentialism," which needed to be retrieved from a welter of lopsided interpretations. According to the essay, all the great philosophical ideas of the 19th century, including the works of Marx and Nietzsche, had their beginnings in Hegel. Yet, Hegel's successors tended to place more emphasis on points of disagreement than elements of continuing affinity. An important philosophical task of the time was to reverse this imbalance:

> If we do not despair of a *truth* above and beyond divergent points of view, if we remain dedicated to a new classicism, an organic civilization, while maintaining the sharpest sense of subjectivity, then no task in the cultural order is more urgent than re-establishing the connection between, on the one hand, the thankless doctrines which try to forget their Hegelian origin and, on the other, that origin itself. That is where their common language can be found and a decisive confrontation can take place.

One of the first to reject Hegel in the interest of concrete individual existence had been Kierkegaard. While significant and valuable, however, Kierkegaard's objections had been addressed to the "late Hegel" who enshrined himself in a "palace of ideas" and who subordinated individual life experience to the correlation of logical concepts. As Merleau-Ponty conceded, this Hegel of the Berlin days had indeed understood and taken into account everything "except his own historical situation" and "his own existence." To this extent, Kierkegaard's remonstration—which was "in profound agreement with that of Marx"—was right on target, by reminding the philosopher of "his own inherence in history" and his social-historical context. Both Kierkegaard and Marx had sought to lure Hegel away from abstract conceptualism and to redirect his attention to the agonies and dilemmas encountered by human existence as it attempts to design its future through concrete praxis; hence, their efforts to remind the philosopher of his own "existence and subjectivity" merged with "the recall to history."[36]

What was appropriately criticized in the late Hegel, however, was by no means relevant to his philosophy as a whole, and especially not to his early writings. Focusing on the *Phenomenology of Spirit*—as illuminated by Kojève and Hyppolite—Merleau-Ponty saw the early Hegel preoccupied not just with abstract concepts but with "all the areas which reveal the mind at work": with customs, economic structures, and legal institutions as well as philosophical texts. Even the notion of absolute spirit, as delineated in the *Phenomenology,* could be viewed not as a speculative idea but as a way of life, a stage in the evolution of spirit where consciousness at last "becomes equal to its spontaneous life and regains its self-possession." In light of this orientation of the *Phenomenology,* it was possible to speak of an Hegelian existentialism, or an existentialist Hegel—a thinker who "does not propose to connect concepts but to reveal the immanent logic of human experience in all its sectors." At this point, the term *experience* denotes no longer a passive sense perception, but instead reveals its "tragic resonance" by pointing to the trials and errors human existence undergoes or has "lived through." Hegel's thought, from this vantage, is existentialist in that it starts not from a self-transparent consciousness but from an obscure sense of life that clarifies itself progressively in its attempt to gain its bearings in an ongoing historical movement.

Turning specifically to the master-slave encounter and the ensuing struggle for mutual recognition, Merleau-Ponty agreed with Hegel regarding the life-and-death quality of the struggle, an agonism intelligible under existentialist auspices: for "each consciousness seeks the death of the other which it feels dispossesses it of its constitutive nothingness." Yet, contrary to Sartre's reading, the essay did not terminate the encounter on the level of conflict, but granted the point of Hegelian mediation and sublation, a mediation implicit in reciprocity itself:

> We cannot be aware of the conflict unless we are aware of our reciprocal relationship and our common humanity. We do not deny each other except by mutual recognition of our consciousness. . . . And just as my consciousness of myself as death and nothingness is deceitful and contains an affirmation of my being and my life, so my consciousness of another as an enemy comprises an affirmation of him as an equal. If I am negation, then by following the implication of this universal negation to its ultimate conclusion, I will witness the self-denial of that very negation and its transformation into coexistence.[37]

Merleau-Ponty's celebration of the existentialist Hegel was not his last word on the philosopher. As one can readily see, the celebration foregrounded subjective-humanist features while truncating Hegel's broader ontological or metaphysical concerns, especially his accent on the actuality of reason or spirit as differentiated from inwardness. As it happens, Merleau-Ponty's subsequent writings were marked by a steady endeavor to overcome his early existentialism and to develop a viable ontology of his own. This endeavor reached its culmination in *The Visible and the Invisible* (a work published after his untimely death in 1960).

Pursuing the bent toward concreteness, but without subjectivist accents, this study confronted the central point of Hegel's metaphysics—the identification of actualized being with conceptual idea, or subjectivity—and sought to subvert this conception through a turn to "brute" or "situational being," that is, to a dimension in which idea is always already embedded (and which hence cannot be subsumed under concepts). This turn was particularly relevant to the status of dialectics. Opposing the thesis-antithesis-synthesis formula (as well as Sartre's being-nothingness antinomy), Merleau-Ponty criticized the purely dichotomous view of affirmation and negation (and its transcendence through double negation), insisting instead on the complex intertwining of being and nonbeing, presence and absence on the level of pre-conceptual experience. As he pointed out, the kind of being that his study intimated was in fact "not susceptible of positive designation" or of conceptual negation. From the vantage of "situational thought, a thought in contact with being," the task of dialectical reflection was thus "to shake off the false evidences, to denounce the significations cut off from the experience of being," and "to criticize itself in the measure that it itself becomes one of them." In lieu of the contrast of thesis and antithesis, of "in-itself" and "for-itself," there was a need to envisage the possibility of a nonpositive affirmation and a nondichotomous difference. Merleau-Ponty at this point introduced the notion of a *hyperdialectic* set off against a "bad dialectic" buried in conceptual formulas or propositional assertions:

> What we call hyperdialectic is a thought that on the contrary is capable of reaching truth because it envisages without restriction the plurality of relationships and what has been called ambiguity. The bad dialectic is one which thinks its recompenses being by a thetic [positive] thought, by an assemblage of statements, by thesis, antithesis, and synthesis; the good dialectic is that which is conscious of the fact that every *thesis* is an idealization, that being is not made up of idealizations or of things said, as the old logic believed, but of bound wholes where signification never is except in tendency, where the inertia of the content never permits the defining of one term as positive, another term as negative, and still less a third term as absolute suppression of the negative by itself.[38]

Postmetaphysics: Heidegger

As is readily apparent, Merleau-Ponty's last work introduced a new element into the discussion of Hegelian thought, an element that touched at its metaphysical core or its underlying ontology. Bypassing customary criticisms relying on inwardness-outwardness, singularity-universality contrasts (readily encompassed by Hegel's system), the notion of a hyperdialectic implied a new view of the nexus of thought and being as well as a reinterpretation of being, nonbeing, and their correlation. In fairness, Merleau-Ponty was not the first to venture into this terrain. Several decades earlier, Heidegger (whose name surfaces repeatedly in Merleau-Ponty's *The Visible and the Invisible*) had begun to renew vigorously the "question of being," although in explicit differentiation from the long tradition of Western metaphysics. A close student or associate of Husserl, Heidegger during the interbellum years had started to extricate himself from "transcendental" (subject-centered) phenomenology, shifting the focus instead to the "being-status" of both the phenomenologist and targeted phenomena. In pursuing this line of inquiry, he inevitably encountered the formidable edifice of Hegel's *Science of Logic*.

As will be recalled, Hegel in that work had treated being and nonbeing as equally vacuous—as identical in their nullity—prior to the intervention of discriminating reflection proceeding by means of determinate negation. In thus foregrounding reflective-conceptual labor (anchored in subjectivity), the *Logic* in the end absorbed being into idea or a universal-conceptual category, while erasing every trace of precognitive experience. For Heidegger, renewing the "question of being" meant first of all to counter this cognitive privilege. The opening paragraph of *Being and Time* (1927) immediately confronted this issue: the traditional streamlining of being for conceptual purposes, a tradition inaugurated by Plato and Aristotle, continued in revised form by medieval scholasticism, and culminating in Hegel's *Logic*. As Heidegger noted, traditional (Western) metaphysics construes being simply as the "most general and most vacuous concept"; and when Hegel finally defines being as "indeterminate immediacy" and erects all his further arguments in the *Logic* on this basis, then he simply "follows the same orientation which governed classical ontology." In more explicit terms, this confrontation surfaced in Heidegger's inaugural lecture in Freiburg (1929), titled "What Is Metaphysics?" Opposing the treatment of being as a category and of nonbeing as conceptual negation, the lecture presented the former as a concrete experience antedating all conceptualization, and included nonbeing as one mode of experiential disclosure. Hegel's proposition in the *Logic* (regarding the identity of pure being and nothing), Heidegger observed, is correct. Being and nothingness hang together, but not because the two—from the vantage of the Hegelian concept of thought—are one in their indefiniteness and immediacy, but because being itself is finite in essence and is only revealed in the transcending move of *Dasein* as projected into nothingness.[39]

The reference to "finiteness" or finitude requires elaboration. In criticizing the conceptual treatment of being, Heidegger also challenged Hegel's quasi-Platonic metaphysics, particularly the notion of the timeless permanence of the idea as distinguished from the temporal flux of the phenomenal world. As *Being and Time* tried to show, this metaphysics was predicated on an inadequate or "vulgar" conception of time and temporality that had to be revised in light of the reinvigorated "question of being." According to Heidegger, the traditional or vulgar conception construed time basically as a linear sequence of moments or "now-points," moments that were strung together in analogy with spatial points. This view was still evident in Hegel's philosophy, which treated time as a "perceived (or intuited) becoming," where *becoming* means the sequential connection of now-points in which every point negates the preceding point (in a manner constituting time itself as negation of negation). In Heidegger's words, "the being of time is the 'now'; but since every now is also either no-longer or not-yet, it can also be taken as non-being."

The connection of Hegelian spirit with time or history, from this vantage, was merely external (or else predicated on the formal definition of spirit as negation of the negation). Given the notion of time as a string of observable points, spirit for Hegel was not intrinsically temporal but had somehow to "fall into time," where the character of this falling, or temporal actualization, remained largely obscure. Renewal of the question of being entailed for Heidegger a different approach, one in which time is seen as constitutive for human existence (or *Dasein*) and in which being reveals itself as essentially temporal (thereby transforming the traditional meanings of finitude and infinity). As Heidegger stated:

Our existential analytic of *Dasein,* on the contrary, started from the concrete facticity of 'thrown' existence itself in an effort to unveil temporality as its

primordial condition of possibility. Spirit does not fall into time, but exists
as the primordial temporalizing of temporality.[40]

As one should note, emphasis on time and temporality does not mean
the enclosure of existence in a mundane context, but rather its embeddedness in an open-ended horizon, in a "clearing," which allows all phenomena to appear but which can never be exhaustively grasped by idea (or
universal concepts). This aspect was strongly underscored in a lecture
course presented a few years after *Being and Time* and devoted to an
interpretation of Hegel's *Phenomenology of Spirit*. Far from being
animated by a polemical impulse, the lecture course was in fact a
sustained tribute to Hegel's thought, although a tribute paid through an
intensive scrutiny of his metaphysical premises. As Heidegger observed
at the time, there has been much talk of the "collapse" or breakdown of
Hegel's philosophy after his death, but the situation was the reverse:
"It is not that Hegel's philosophy has broken down; rather, his contem-
poraries and successors have not even managed to rise up to measure
themselves against his height."

In the terms of the lecture course, the central theme of Hegel's
Phenomenology was the progressive appearance or "parousia" of absolute spirit—a movement that presupposed already as its starting point
the anticipation of absoluteness (though in nonactualized form). In line
with the long tradition of Western metaphysics, the aim of Hegel's
entire philosophical endeavor was "to overcome finite knowledge
through the attainment of infinite knowledge," effected in the manifestation of absolute spirit. Heidegger's own endeavor, as he made clear,
was by no means averse to this direction of thought and was in fact
guided by the search for absoluteness and its appearance. At issue,
however, was the precise construal of the finite-infinite, contingent-
absolute correlation. "It is in the *problematic of finitude*," Heidegger
observed, "where we try to meet and join Hegel in the commitment to
the inherent demands of philosophizing," which means that "on the
basis of our own inquiry into finitude and in confrontation with his
problematic of infinity, we try to foreground *that* kinship which is
needed to uncover the spirit of Hegel's thought." Renewing the question
of being here signified reassessing the finitude-infinity nexus. The
question remains, we read,

whether the finitude which was prevalent in philosophy up to Hegel, was the original and effective finitude operative in philosophy, or whether it was only an incidental finitude that was carried along nilly-willy. What needs to be asked is whether Hegel's conception of infinity did not itself arise from that incidental finitude, in order then to reach back and absorb it.[41]

The status of finitude in its relation to absoluteness is the pervasive theme in the interpretation of Hegel's *Phenomenology*. The crucial issue for Heidegger was the relevance of finitude to the being-time nexus, that is, the question "whether being is in its essence finite" and whether and how this finitude "can be brought to bear on the problematic of philosophy." Conversely, in Hegelian terms, the issue was whether the infinity of absolute knowledge "determines the truth of being in such a manner as to sublate everything finite into itself"—with the result that philosophizing moves "only *in* and *as* such a sublation, that is, as dialectics." The confrontation with Hegel was hence placed at the crossroads or intersection of finitude and infinity in their metaphysical or postmetaphysical understanding. Following the tradition of metaphysics, Hegel equated infinite being with *idea* or *logos,* terms that, in the aftermath of Descartes and Kant, were more specifically identified with reason, spirit, and subjectivity. In the unfolding of that tradition, Heidegger noted, it "fell to Hegel" to "inscribe the essence of true, logically conceived infinity into, or else let it derive from, the nature of subjectivity or ego-hood"—that is, to "conceive the subject as absolute spirit." Because the absoluteness of spirit was treated here as a synonym for the divine, Hegel's philosophy could be broadly described as an "onto-theo-logy" where both "being" (*on*) and the "divine" (*theos*) are seen from a logical-subjective vantage. Deviating from the Hegelian focus, Heidegger's lectures shifted the accent from idea or *logos* to time and temporality, thus transforming *onto-theology* into something like *ontochrony,* meaning the temporalizing quality of being. Construed as idea or *logos,* being for Hegel was infinity or infinite being, with time figuring as a mode of appearance of that being on the level of spatial nature—and hence as an antipode to spirit's pure absoluteness. By injecting temporality into the essence of being, Heidegger's interpretation intimated the notion of an open-ended finitude, of finite being as "horizon of ek-static time." Without damage to the status of absoluteness, the question was whether the latter should be seen as idea "absolved" from time, or else as a temporalizing transcendence permeating finitude.[42]

The question of the possibility of a nonmetaphysical or postmetaphysical absoluteness was pursued in an essay composed about a decade later and devoted again to the *Phenomenology of Spirit,* this time to Hegel's famous "Introduction" to that work. As will be recalled, Hegel in his introduction challenged the notion of human reason as a mere "instrument" of cognition, and hence the status of critical epistemology as the gateway to knowledge (which always remains limited). In lieu of this instrumentalism, the introduction portrayed cognition as the progressive self-transformation of consciousness, as the movement leading from "natural" or "appearing" consciousness to "real" or true knowledge—though a movement undertaken from the beginning under the auspices of absoluteness. In the course of this transformation, natural consciousness suffers shipwreck by undergoing the wrenching "experience" of its dislocation under the impact of the *parousia* of (absolute) spirit. In the words of the essay:

> The path of [Hegel's] presentation does not simply lead from natural to real consciousness; rather, consciousness itself—which as this distinction between natural and real exists in every form of consciousness—proceeds from one shape to the next. The progression is a course whose movement is determined by the goal, that is, by the power of the will of the absolute. . . . At this point, the natural view of absolute knowledge—that it is a means—has vanished.

In elaborating on this path, Heidegger's exegesis did not adopt an anti-Hegelian stance—despite important shifts of accents. While translating the distinction between natural and real consciousness into that between "ontic" and "ontological" thought, the essay fully endorsed the view of experience as a movement of disclosure or as the *parousia* of being. Honoring the thrust of Hegel's argument, the comments also supported the need of radical "inversion" or *metanoia (Umkehrung),* a notion obviously akin to Heidegger's much-discussed "turning" *(Kehre).* The point of divergence centered again on Hegel's foregrounding of conceptual idea or subjectivity, that is, on his privileging of "conscious being" *(Bewusstsein)* over mere or vacuous being. In contrast to this metaphysical view (negligent of time), Heidegger observed, "we do not interpret being" from Hegel's vantage "as the objectivity of an immediately representing subjectivity which has not yet found itself," rather "we view it on the basis of the Greek *aletheia* as the arrival from and in unconcealedness." The latter view involved a rethinking of metaphysics, that is, a departure from the dualism of essence and appearance (or conscious being and mere being) in the direction of an intertwining of being and beings in the context of "worldliness" seen as the "clearing" of truth.[43]

Philosophical Hermeneutics: Gadamer

A similarly nuanced engagement with Hegel marks the writings of Heidegger's foremost student, Gadamer. In developing the perspective of philosophical hermeneutics, Gadamer's *Truth and Method* (1960) portrayed the encounter with historical texts as patterned broadly on Hegelian dialectics. The notion of "effective history" (*Wirkungsgeschichte*), in particular, was closely modeled on the concept of "experience" as outlined in Hegel's *Phenomenology,* although with significant reservations (pointing beyond metaphysical idealism). In an instructive fashion, the chapter on effective history in *Truth and Method* reveals the linkage as well as the divergence of philosophical perspectives.

In an initial move, Gadamer strongly defended Hegel's philosophy against objections or counterpositions that, in his view, missed their target. One such counterposition was Kantian critical epistemology with its sharp separation of internal reason and external "thing-in-itself." Relying on the "Introduction" to the *Phenomenology,* Gadamer was able to expose the pitfalls of this approach with arguments akin to those advanced in Heidegger's essay. For in separating itself from absolute reality, reason was in effect "proving this distinction to be its very own," thereby showing that it had already "gone beyond that limit." Generally speaking, what makes a limit a limit "always includes knowledge of what is on both sides of it," hence it belongs to the dialectic of the limit "to exist only by being overcome." Other prominent objections have to do with the presumed abstractness of Hegel's thought, that is, his neglect of the concrete immediacy either of individual singularity or of

social-economic conditions. Pointing to the reflective quality of all philosophizing, *Truth and Method* underscored the mediated character of the
claimed immediacy and its dependence on interpretive understanding:

> The appeal to immediacy—whether of bodily nature, or of a 'Thou'
> making claims on us, or of the impenetrable factualness of historical flux
> or of the reality of relations of production—has always been self-refuting,
> in that it is not itself an immediate attitude, but a reflective activity. The
> Left-Hegelian critique of a mere intellectual reconciliation which does not
> really change the world, the whole doctrine of the reversal of philosophy
> into politics, implies inevitably the self-abolition of philosophy.

From this vantage, it was evident that the line of rejoinders—from
Kierkegaard to Feuerbach and Marx—was already prefigured and contained in Hegel's own discussion of modes of consciousness.[44]

Appropriating Hegel's teachings for the tasks of hermeneutics, Gadamer stressed particularly the dialectical character of his notion of
experience, a notion that refers not only to a series of external events
but to the self-transformation of consciousness. A similar process
occurs in the interpretive encounter with historical texts, which accounts for the hermeneutical relevance of Hegel's work, especially his
Phenomenology. As Gadamer observed, in his *Phenomenology* Hegel
had shown what happens to consciousness in its struggle to gain self-
knowledge. The target for consciousness is initially an "in-itself," but
the latter can be known only "as it presents itself to experiencing
consciousness"; thus consciousness makes or undergoes this experience
"that the in-itself of the object is in-itself 'for us.' " In undergoing this
process, consciousness experiences, an inversion (*Umkehrung*) or self-
transformation whereby the initial outlook of natural consciousness found-
ers to make room for the emergence for a new awareness. In Hegelian
terms, experience is the movement and "completion of skepticism," though
a movement that does not end in disillusionment and despair, but instead
leads on to new vistas and the discovery of new horizons.

According to *Truth and Method,* in encountering unfamiliar or unexpected events or phenomena "the experiencing consciousness reverses
its direction, that is, it turns back on itself"; by becoming conscious of
this process, the individual may be said to be experienced, in the sense
that "he has acquired a new horizon within which something else can

become an experience for him." The relevance for hermeneutics relies in the experiential encounter with texts and historical traditions. In approaching a text, the interpreter must recognize not only its distant otherness but also its ability "to say something to me." Rising above positivist description, hermeneutical, or effective-historical consciousness allows tradition to be experienced or undergone. In this manner, hermeneutical consciousness betrays "the same readiness for experience that distinguishes the experienced man from one captivated by dogma."[45]

While thus acknowledging Hegel's importance, *Truth and Method* was by no means a Hegelian treatise. Like Heidegger, Gadamer sought to transgress the "spell" (*Zauberkreis*) of Hegelian reflection, without lapsing either into irrationalism or a celebration of particular immediacy. The precise task was to construe hermeneutics in such a manner as not to dissolve the fabric of texts into conceptual ideas or transparent knowledge. For Gadamer, the pitfall of Hegelian thought was its endeavor to reach cognitive transparency, that is, a type of "self-knowledge purged entirely of otherness or of anything alien beyond itself." In centerstaging this kind of knowledge, Hegelian dialectics culminated inevitably in the overcoming or "transcendence of all experience," in the complete or absolute "identity of consciousness and object." From this vantage, the labor and concrete texture of experience were sidestepped or devalued; instead, the nature of experience was conceived from the beginning "in terms of something surpassing experience."

In opposition to this triumph of reason or idea, Gadamer pleaded in favor of the continuity and open-ended character of experience, its embeddedness in an ever-receding horizon. Together with Heidegger, he construed absoluteness not in terms of a thought "absolved" from time, but of an experience finding truth in and through temporality—that is, in the mode of human "finitude." Experience, we read, "is experience of human finitude; the truly experienced man is one who has taken this to heart, who knows that he is master neither of time nor of the future." Experience, for Gadamer, is not an exit route from time and worldly contexts or a gateway to absolute ideas. Contrary to Hegel's assumption, the notion of a complete or perfect experience does not signify "that experience has ceased in favor of a higher form of knowledge," but rather "that for the first time experience fully and truly *is*" (in an ontological sense). Without negating truth or absoluteness, this perspective puts a damper on all attempts to streamline or entirely "rationalize" the world or else to instrumentalize the absolute for partisan purposes. In Gadamer's words, "genuine experience is one whereby man becomes aware of his finitude. Such awareness places a limit on fabrication and on the self-knowledge of instrumental reason."[46]

While *Truth and Method,* in discussing Hegel, centerstages the notion of experience, Gadamer's subsequent writings shifted attention to language as the precondition of interpretive understanding and especially to the inexhaustibility of ordinary language or its excess over conceptual categories. The decade following the publication of his major study witnessed a steady preoccupation with Hegelian themes, manifest in a series of essays collected under the title *Hegel's Dialectic* (1971). The accent on language emerges particularly in the essay on "The Idea of Hegel's Logic" (of which only glimpses can be offered here). As Gadamer observed, Hegel's conception of logic was thoroughly predicated on the traditional metaphysics of *logos* with its assumption that language naturally harbors within itself clear and univocal concepts which reflection only needs to profile or sharpen. In light of recent philosophical developments, however, it was questionable whether language is indeed only "an instinctive logic waiting to be penetrated and conceptualized by thought." As both hermeneutics and contemporary language theory have shown, the "natural logic" embedded in ordinary language is by no means exhausted in the function of being "a prefiguration of philosophical logic." On the contrary, the variety of existing languages discloses a great diversity of schemata permitting "linguistic access" to the world.

No matter how reflectively sharpened, concepts rely for their functioning on the texture of ordinary language; their usage thus is bound to resonate with the complex shadings of the word "with all of its many meanings playing a role." This aspect reveals again the pervasive impact of finitude, seen not as a prison house but as condition of possible understanding. From the angle of finitude, language is not an external accessory or "temporary medium" of reason that could be discarded when thought becomes "completely transparent to itself." Rather, language is the matrix that allows reflection to develop its concepts and to clarify itself—in a process of clarification that is constantly transgressed and eroded by the evolving fabric of language.

Relying on arguments of the later Heidegger, Gadamer perceived in language a dual movement or a pull in two directions: one leading toward the objectivity of thought and reason, the other signaling a return of meaning "in the reabsorption of all objectification into the concealing and sheltering power of the word." As the essay conceded, this duality or intertwining had been anticipated in the Heideggerian notions of *clearing* and *Ereignis:*

> What makes it possible for language to speak is not 'being' as the abstract immediacy of the self-determining concept. Instead, it is much better described in terms of the being which Heidegger refers to as 'clearing'—which implies both disclosure and enclosure or concealment. . . . There is a hint here of that conception of 'truth' which Heidegger seeks to formulate as *'Ereignis'* (appropriating event) and which initially opens up the space for knowledge and the entire movement of reflection.[47]

Poststructuralism and Deconstruction

In the meantime, Hegel's effective history has taken a new turn—toward its radical negation. In lieu of the nuanced engagement with Hegel characterizing the writings of Heidegger and Gadamer, contemporary philosophy—especially its Continental variant—tends to favor polemical rejection or dismissal. This tendency is particularly pronounced in recent poststructuralism and deconstruction, movements that have assumed centerstage following the eclipse of French existentialism and existential phenomenology. In place of the complex effort to overcome traditional metaphysics by shifting its accents, proponents of those movements on the whole prefer a frontal assault on the entire tradition, especially its key metaphysical categories of *logos, idea,* and *subjectivity.* Shunning the Hegelian notion of sublation, or transformative preservation, the approach tends to privilege rupture over continuity, in a manner inverting or reversing traditional metaphysical priorities from universality to particularism, from holism to diversity, and from reason to decision.

A crucial role in this philosophical realignment is played by the pervasive upsurge of Nietzsche in recent times. Under the impact of a radicalized Nietzscheanism, philosophers are prone to downplay connections or linkages in favor of separateness and particularity—the latter seen not in terms of (Kierkegaardian) inwardness but simply as an instance of dispersal. As a corollary, emphasis is placed on agonism or agonistic struggle, a struggle not necessarily yielding mutual recognition but a continual interplay of forces anchored in the will to power. In the political arena, the Nietzschean upsurge stands opposed to all kinds of universal or "totalizing" institutions, especially the structures of the modern state, as well as to comprehensive modes of integration or mediation (epitomized in the notion of a universal class). In language sometimes reminiscent of Popperian invectives, Hegel in this context is often accused of harboring total, if not totalitarian, political designs, to the detriment of individual, local, or ethical freedom and diversity.

Proponents of poststructuralism and deconstruction differ from each other in many details; what tends to unite them, however, is their attachment to Nietzsche combined with a vehement anti-Hegelianism. The combination is clearly evident in one leading contemporary French philosopher, Deleuze. In his *Nietzsche and Philosophy* and other writings, Deleuze presented Nietzsche as the great iconoclast of the Western metaphysical tradition, as a thinker bent on decodifying the universal categories or premises of traditional thought. In terms of these studies, *decodification* meant the effort to dislodge or shatter the codes of all overarching patterns of thought and conduct—patterns enshrined in the "fundamental bureaucracies" of the state and the family as well as in legal institutions and conventional rules of behavior. In opposition to general codes, Nietzsche was said to espouse radical disjuncture and disproportion, especially the disproportion evident in differential human capabilities rooted in the will to power. Nietzsche's will to power, in Deleuze's account, is basically an interplay of "active" and "reactive" forces that produces a differential or hierarchical arrangement of power.

As Deleuze observed in *Nietzsche and Philosophy,* "there are nothing but quantities of force in 'relations of tension' between one another; every force is related to other forces, and it either obeys or commands." In analogy with bodily energies, the superior or dominating forces were called *active* and the inferior or dominated forces, *reactive;* the entire difference of forces, "qualified as active and reactive in accordance with their quantity," is then termed their "hierarchy." In human relations, active force was the central emblem of affirmation of life, of a vigorous sense of self-worth, the latter term denoting "some fundamental certainty which a noble soul possesses in regard to itself." Deleuze's chief objection to Hegel was that, in relying on mediation through negation, the Hegelian dialectic was vitiated by its complicity with purely reactive or life-sapping forces. In fact, all human distinctions and power differentials were allegedly absorbed and dissolved in a uniform rationality purged of the will to power. Against this background, Nietzsche's philosophy emerged as the life-affirming antipode of dialectics, while Hegel was denounced for sponsoring a nihilistic speculation "weary of willing" (*las de vouloir*):

> There is no possible compromise between Hegel and Nietzsche. Nietzsche's philosophy has a great polemical range; it forms an absolute anti-dialectics and sets out to expose all the mystifications that find a final refuge in the dialectic. . . . The dialectic expresses every combination of reactive forces and nihilism, the history or evolution of their relations.[48]

A similar attitude toward Nietzsche and Hegel can be found in the work of Foucault. Like Deleuze (whom he admired), Foucault opposed dialectics seen as the steady unfolding of meaning culminating in the actualization of reason. Close historical study, he wrote in an essay devoted to Nietzschean genealogy, yields "not a timeless and essential secret" but only the secret that events "have no essence or that their essence was fabricated in a piecemeal fashion from alien forms." Examining in particular the history of reason or rationality, the genealogist learns merely that reason was "born in an altogether 'reasonable' fashion—from chance"; instead of disclosing a continuous pattern, genealogical analysis uncovers the basic "dissension" among events and periods, that is, their discontinuity, disparity, and difference.

Disparity here does not just mean differentiation (amenable to mediation), but rather conflict, struggle, or contestation. Interpreting Nietzsche through Deleuzian lenses, Foucault portrayed history as an ongoing struggle of forces rooted in the will to power. As he wrote, the analysis of development must "delineate this interaction, the struggle these forces wage against each other or against adverse circumstances" and also the constant attempt "to avoid degeneration and regain strength by dividing these forces against themselves." Akin to the interplay of active and reactive forces, the will to power "reacts against its own growing lassitude" and thereby reaffirms itself; on occasion, it masks this affirmation as a "higher morality," a stratagem that allows it to "regain its strength." Viewed against this background, historical contests are not struggles for mutual recognition but clashes between separate and incommensurable forces; while constituting a place of confrontation, history is not a "closed field offering the spectacle of a struggle among equals." Far from revealing an ascent of spirit, development simply involves the "endlessly repeated play of dominations," a play that cannot be successfully tempered by legal rules or reciprocal acknowledgment. "On the contrary," we read,

> the law is a calculated and relentless pleasure, delight in the promised blood, which permits the perpetual instigation of new dominations and the staging of meticulously repeated scenes of violence. . . . Humanity does not gradually progress from combat to combat until it arrives at universal reciprocity, where the rule of law finally replaces warfare; humanity installs each of its violences in a system of rules and thus proceeds from domination to domination.[49]

Historical combat and struggle for dominion are not merely observable occurrences but infiltrate human understanding itself. In fact, reason and truth are themselves implicated in the will to power: "Nothing in man—not even his body—is sufficiently stable to serve as the basis for self-recognition or for understanding other men." Unable to yield universal insight or genuine synthesis, reason is a partisan accessory of power: "Knowledge is not made for understanding; it is made for cutting." Contrary to idealist teachings, knowledge does not slowly arise from initial needs to turn into "pure speculation"; its genesis is not tied to "the constitution and affirmation of a free subject" but rather involves a "progressive enslavement to its instinctive violence." In Foucault's essay, Nietzschean themes of this kind were not just implicitly but expressly linked with anti-Hegelian accents. As he observed, it was time to replace the "two great problems of nineteenth-century philosophy, passed on by Fichte and Hegel (the reciprocal basis of truth and liberty and the possibility of absolute knowledge)," in favor of Nietzschean life-affirmation.

More subtly, the critique of Hegel was fleshed out in Foucault's inaugural lecture at the Collège de France, titled "The Discourse on Language"—curiously in the course of a tribute paid to Jean Hyppolite. As the lecture noted, Hyppolite was associated in the public mind chiefly with the exegesis of Hegel's work. Thus he seemed ill-suited as a mentor for one of the deepest aspirations of our age: the attempt "to flee Hegel." This assessment, however, was superficial, for

> truly to escape Hegel involves an exact appreciation of the price we have to pay to detach ourselves from him. It assumes that we are aware of the extent to which Hegel, insidiously perhaps, is close to us; it implies a knowledge, in that which permits us to think against Hegel, of that which remains Hegelian. . . . If, then, more than one of us is indebted to Jean Hyppolite, it is because he tirelessly explored, for us, and ahead of us, the path along which we may escape Hegel, keep our distance.

In his interpretation of Hegel, Hyppolite was not merely a disciple content with offering a loyal description. Rather, he endeavored to turn Hegel into "a schema for the experience of modernity" and, conversely, to make modernity "a test of Hegelianism and of philosophy itself." The basic question raised in his exegesis was: If philosophy really implies absolute knowledge, "then what of history, and what of that beginning which starts out with a singular individual, within society and a social class, and in the midst of struggle?"[50]

Escaping Hegel is a less urgent motive in Derrida's writings, but it is present nonetheless. Together with Foucault, Derrida tends to foreground discontinuity over dialectics, dispersal over unity, and difference over sameness; a closer proximity to Heidegger, however, usually guards him against metaphysical reversals. Still, in its more Nietzschean moods, "deconstructive" thought courts a stark exodus from tradition and a preference for radical (even violent) rupture.[51] The safeguards operative in Derrida's case are completely set aside in Lyotard's postmodernist bent.

According to Lyotard's *The Postmodern Condition,* our age is marked by the crisis and disintegration of the great "metanarratives" or unifying schemes of the past, including the Hegelian scheme of dialectics with its focus on the self-actualization of spirit. To vindicate this conception, German idealism, in Lyotard's view, had to have recourse to an abstract metaprinciple, "called 'divine life' by Fichte and 'life of the spirit' by Hegel," a principle legitimating universal knowledge, thus entitling the latter to say "what the State and what Society" are. In light of recent linguistics and language pragmatics, however, this recourse was entirely spurious and untenable. What contemporary developments accentuate and bring to the fore is the experience of fragmentation, disjuncture, and agonal contestation—and hence the dispersal of traditional philosophical systems into "clouds of narrative language elements." In reorienting philosophical thought, the same developments are also bound to reshape profoundly social and political practices, namely, by patterning social and political relations increasingly on a "pragmatics of language particles" with the accent on the "heterogeneity of elements" and "local determinism." To understand society in this manner, Lyotard comments, what is needed is not so much a theory of communication but "a theory of games which accepts agonistics as a founding principle." The emphasis on agonistics is underscored further in a subsequent study titled *The Differend,* in which agonal "contest" (*differend*)—as distinguished from simple litigation—is portrayed as a conflict between parties that "cannot properly be resolved" due to the absence of a superior principle applicable to different language games or modes of discourse. Depicting the resort to universal ideas as a form of totalitarism, the study promptly denounces Hegel's philosophy as both theoretically flawed and politically pernicious: given the incommensurability of discourses and life-forms, the notion of "an absolute triumph of one discourse over others is senseless."[52]

Notes

1. Jacques Derrida, *Margins of Philosophy,* trans. Alan Bass (Chicago: University of Chicago Press, 1982), 119.

2. See Walter Kaufmann, *Hegel: Reinterpretation Texts and Commentary* (Garden City, NY: Doubleday, 1965), 144; Rudolf Haym, *Hegel und seine Zeit* (Berlin: Gaertner, 1857), 243, 364; Arthur Schopenhauer, *Sämtliche Werke,* 2nd ed., Vol. 2, ed. Julius Frauenstadt (Leipzig: Brockhaus: 1888), xvii. Cf. also V. R. Mehta, *Hegel and the Modern State* (New Delhi : Associated Publishing House, 1968), 107. In the following I also bypass for the most part attempts at political labeling (Hegel as liberal, conservative, reactionary, militarist, and the like), attempts that reduce his philosophy to partisan ideology.

3. Søren Kierkegaard, *Fear and Trembling and the Sickness unto Death,* trans. Walter Lowrie (Garden City, NY: Doubleday, 1955), 146, 148-149, 162. Cf. also the concluding statement: " 'By relating itself to its own self and by willing to be itself, the self is grounded transparently in the Power which constituted it.' And this formula again, as has often been noted, is the definition of faith" (*Fear and Trembling,* 262).

4. Søren Kierkegaard, *Concluding Unscientific Postscript,* trans. David F. Swenson, compl. Walter Lowrie (Princeton, NJ: Princeton University Press, 1944), 109, 270-271, 273, 302-303. In the above, I follow to some extent the insightful account offered by Bernstein; Richard J. Bernstein, *Praxis and Action: Contemporary Philosophies of Human Activity* (Philadelphia: University of Pennsylvania Press, 1971), 100-118.

5. Bernstein, *Praxis and Action,* 114, 117, 123.

6. Jean-Paul Sartre, *Search for a Method,* trans. Hazel E. Barnes (New York: Knopf, 1963), 11; Bernstein, *Praxis and Action,* 88. Noting also the affinity on the level of unhappy consciousness, Sartre adds,

> [For Kierkegaard] the surpassing of the unhappy consciousness remains purely verbal. The *existing* man cannot be assimilated by a system of ideas. . . . Thus Kierkegaard is led to champion the cause of pure, unique subjectivity against the objective universality of essence, the narrow, passionate intransigence of the immediate life against the tranquil mediation of all reality, faith, which stubbornly asserts itself, against scientific evidence—*despite* the scandal. . . . This inwardness, which in its narrowness and its infinite depth claims to affirm itself against all philosophy, this subjectivity rediscovered beyond language as the personal adventure of each man in the face of others and of God—this is what Kierkegaard called *existence. (Search for a Method,* 10-11)

7. Sartre, *Search for a Method,* 12.

8. Karl Marx, "Afterword to the Second German Edition" (1873), in *The Marx-Engels Reader,* ed. Robert C. Tucker (New York: Norton, 1972), 197-198; Sartre, *Search for a Method,* 14.

9. Karl Marx, *Critique of Hegel's* Philosophy of Right, trans. and ed. Joseph O'Malley (Cambridge, UK: Cambridge University Press, 1970), 131. The above passages are actually taken from Karl Marx, "Introduction" in *A Contribution to the Critique of Hegel's* Philosophy of Right, which was first published in 1844 (while the rest of the manuscript remained unpublished until 1927). Avineri deserves major credit for having alerted Marx scholars to the importance of the manuscript; cf. Shlomo Avineri, *The Social and Political Thought of Karl Marx* (Cambridge, UK: Cambridge University Press, 1968); Shlomo Avineri, "The Hegelian Origins of Marx's Political Thought," *The Review of Metaphysics* 21 (1967): 33-56.

10. Marx, *Critique,* 136-137.

11. Marx, *Critique,* 137, 141-142. The bulk of Marx's manuscript offers a detailed commentary not on the *Philosophy of Right* as a whole but only on the sections dealing with the internal constitutional structure of the state (par. 261-313). In this commentary—too extensive to be reviewed here—Marx criticizes chiefly the separation of state and civil society, the privileging of constitutional monarchy over democracy, and the organic mode of representation through estates rather than through universal suffrage (one man one vote).

12. Karl Marx, "For a Ruthless Criticism of Everything Existing," "On the Jewish Question," in *The Marx-Engels Reader,* ed. Robert C. Tucker (New York: Norton, 1972),

9, 33, 37, 44. The term *species-being* here denotes the essential character of "man" as a freely producing agent relating to other producers in the mode of mutual recognition.

13. Karl Marx, "Economic and Philosophic Manuscripts," in *The Marx-Engels Reader,* ed. Robert C. Tucker (New York: Norton, 1972), 60-64, 70, 86, 89-90, 93-94, 99. Limiting itself to "occult critique," Marx adds, Hegelian transcendence of alienation does not lead to the transcendence of religion, which conflicts with the demands of transformational criticism:

> If I know religion as alienated human self-consciousness, then what I know in it as religion is not my self-consciousness, but my alienated self-consciousness confirmed in it. . . . In Hegel, therefore, the negation of the negation is not the confirmation of the true essence, effected precisely through the negation of the [religious] pseudo-essence. With him the negation of the negation is the confirmation of the pseudo-essence or of the self-estranged essence in its denial. ("Economic and Philosophic Manuscripts," 96)

14. The downgrading of property is particularly emphatic in Karl Marx, "Communist Manifesto" in *The Marx-Engels Reader,* ed. Robert C. Tucker (New York: Norton, 1972), which proclaims that "the theory of the communists may be summed up in a single sentence: abolition of private property." The "Manifesto" is eloquent in describing the diremption marking modern society:

> The bourgeoisie cannot exist without constantly revolutionizing the instruments of production, and thereby the relations of production and with them the whole relations of society. . . . Constant revolutionizing of production, uninterrupted disturbance of all social conditions, everlasting uncertainty and agitation distinguish the bourgeois epoch from all earlier ones. All fixed, frozen relations, with their train of ancient and venerable prejudices and opinions, are swept away; all new-formed ones become antiquated before they can ossify. All that is solid melts into air, all that is holy is profaned, and man is at last compelled to face with sober senses his real conditions of life and his relations with his kind. (*The Marx-Engels Reader,* 338, 346)

15. Charles Taylor, *Hegel and Modern Society* (Cambridge, UK: Cambridge University Press, 1979), 143, 145. Taylor also counters Marx's complaint about abstractness: "The Hegelian synthesis is denounced as one achieved in thought only, masking the effective diremption of the real. In the polemic Marx inevitably distorted Hegel, speaking at times as though he was somehow concerned with 'abstract thought' alone, and was not also the protagonist of another kind of praxis" (*Hegel and Modern Society,* 145).

16. Marx, *Critique,* 91.

17. In the words of Schacht:

> Marx differs from Hegel in that, first of all, he regards nature as ontologically independent of consciousness and, secondly, he does not regard the emergence of the world of nature as itself constituting a part of the actualization of the ultimate end he envisages. For him the world of nature has significance primarily as material to be used in the realization of that end. . . . Marx also differs from both Kierkegaard and Hegel in that, for him, the ultimate

significance of the individual is *not* to be found in a condition which radically transcends the realm of sensuous and practical life—neither in faith nor in absolute knowledge.

See Richard Schacht, *Hegel and After: Studies in Continental Philosophy between Kant and Sartre* (Pittsburgh, PA: University of Pittsburgh Press, 1975), 9.

18. Walter Kaufmann, ed., *The Portable Nietzsche* (New York: Viking Press, 1968), 39-40, 83; Friedrich Nietzsche, *Werke*, Vol. 2, ed. K. Schlechta (Munich: Hanser, 1956), 227-228, 664. In the opinion of Loewith, Nietzsche's atheist leanings connected him with the young Hegelians and with Marx; contrary to Nietzsche's own view, however, he detects the seeds of this atheism already in Hegel's rationalism:

> Nietzsche is related to the revolutionary criticism of the left-wing Hegelians not only through Wagner's relationship to Feuerbach, but also by his own literary attack upon D. F. Strauss, which reaches a logical conclusion with the *Antichrist*. In his criticism of Christianity, he concurs with Bruno Bauer, whose criticism of religion developed out of Hegel's philosophy of religion. . . . Nietzsche seems never to have concerned himself with Marx. A comparison of the two is nevertheless justified, because Nietzsche is the only man, after Marx and Kierkegaard, who made the decline of the bourgeois-Christian world the theme of such a fundamental analysis. . . . Whatever abyss separates Nietzsche's anti-Christian philosophy from Hegel's philosophical theology and his 'hammer' from Hegel's 'speculation' is bridged by Hegel's pupils through a consequent series of revolts against the Christian tradition and bourgeois culture.

See Karl Loewith, *From Hegel to Nietzsche: The Revolution in Nineteenth Century Thought,* trans. David E. Green (Garden City, NY: Anchor Books, 1967), 173-174.

19. Kaufmann, *The Portable Nietzsche*, 40-41, 160-163; Friedrich Nietzsche, *The Will to Power*, ed. Walter Kaufmann, trans. Walter Kaufmann and R. J. Hollingdale (New York: Vintage Books, 1968), p. 60, par. 95; p. 227, par. 422.

20. Stephen Houlgate, *Hegel, Nietzsche and the Criticism of Metaphysics* (Cambridge, UK: Cambridge University Press, 1986), 37. As Houlgate points out, the aim of his book is to show that "*pace* Nietzsche, a return to Hegel is defensible," mainly for the reason that "Hegel is more far-reaching and more profound than Nietzsche in precisely the area in which Nietzsche's philosophy has been held to be so revolutionary: the critique of the conceptual distinctions and oppositions (*Gegensätze*) of metaphysical thought, and in particular the distinction between the subject and the predicate" (*Hegel, Nietzsche,* ix). Regarding the ambivalent character of Nietzsche's departure from metaphysics cf. also Fred R. Dallmayr, "Farewell from Metaphysics: Nietzsche" in *Critical Encounters* (Notre Dame, IN: University of Notre Dame Press, 1987), 13-38. For Nietzsche's passages see *The Will to Power*, p. 419, par. 794; pp. 451-453, par. 853; p. 457, par. 854-856; p. 458, par. 861.

21. See Reinhard Bendix and Guenther Roth, *Scholarship and Partisanship: Essays on Max Weber* (Berkeley: University of California Press, 1971), 22-25. According to Gerth and Mills, Weber attempted

> to incorporate the points of view both of Marx and Nietzsche in his discussion. With Marx, he shares the sociological approach to ideas: they are powerless

in history unless they are fused with material interests; and with Nietzsche, he is deeply concerned with the importance of ideas for psychic reactions. Yet in contrast to both Nietzsche and Marx, Weber refuses to conceive of ideas as being "mere" reflections of psychic or social interests.

See H. H. Gerth and C. Wright Mills, trans. and eds., *From Max Weber: Essays in Sociology* (New York: Galaxy Books, 1958), 62. For Weber's early fascination with Nietzsche, a fascination that later gave way to more sober appreciation, cf. Robert Eden, *Political Leadership and Nihilism: A Study of Weber and Nietzsche* (Tampa: University Presses of Florida, 1983), 36-71.

22. Max Weber, "Politics as a Vocation," in *From Max Weber: Essays in Sociology,* ed. and trans. H. H. Gerth and C. Wright Mills (New York: Galaxy Books), 77-79.

23. Weber, "Politics as a Vocation," 83-84, 95.

24. Weber, "Politics as a Vocation," 120, 128; Max Weber, "Science as a Vocation," in *From Max Weber: Essays in Sociology,* ed. and trans. H. H. Gerth and C. Wright Mills (New York: Galaxy Books), 154-155.

25. Max Weber, *Economy and Society, An Outline of Interpretive Sociology,* Vol. 1, ed. Guenther Roth and Claus Wittich (Berkeley: University of California Press, 1978), 52-54, 212-219, 223-226; Max Weber, *Wirtschaft und Gesellschaft Grundriss der verstehenden Soziologie,* Vol. 2, ed. Johannes Winkelmann (Cologne: Kiepenhauer and Witsch, 1964), 1043, 1060-1062.

26. Karl R. Popper, *The Open Society and Its Enemies* (New York: Harper Torchbooks, 1963), 27-28. A star witness in Popper's indictment is Schopenhauer, whose diatribes have been mentioned before.

27. Popper, *The Open Society,* 30-31.

28. Popper, *The Open Society,* 36-37, 48-49, 61. Another passage was even more severe: "The transubstantiation of Hegelianism into racialism or of spirit into blood does not greatly alter the main tendency of Hegelianism. It only gives it a tinge of biology and of modern evolutionism" (*The Open Society,* 62).

29. The linkage of Hegel with totalitarianism and a reactionary militarism was strongly contested by Marcuse in Herbert Marcuse, *Reason and Revolution: Hegel and the Rise of Social Theory,* 2nd ed. (Boston: Beacon Press, 1960). See also Shlomo Avineri, *Hegel's Theory of the Modern State* (Cambridge, UK: Cambridge University Press, 1972), 115-117, 194-195. For the entire debate surrounding Hegel and Prussian nationalism cf. Walter Kaufmann, ed., *Hegel's Political Philosophy* (New York: Atherton Press, 1970).

30. See esp. Edmund Husserl, *The Crisis of European Sciences and Transcendental Phenomenology,* trans. David Carr (Evanston, IL: Northwestern University Press, 1970).

31. Karl Jaspers, *Reason and Existenz,* trans. William Earle (New York: Noonday Press, 1955), 22-23. The lectures were presented in Groningen, Holland, in 1935. The combination of continuity and rupture was stated even more clearly in Jaspers's "On My Philosophy" (1941) where he observed:

> Even in the history of philosophy we can witness the tremendous incisiveness of our age. Hegel is a consummation of two and a half millennia of thought. True, in his basic philosophical attitude, although not in his concrete positions, Plato is as alive today as ever, perhaps more than ever. Even now we can philosophize from Kant. In actuality, however, we cannot forget for one moment what has been brought about since by Kierkegaard and Nietzsche. . . .

At the present moment, the security of coherent philosophy, which existed from Parmenides to Hegel, is lost. This does not prevent us from philosophizing from the single foundation of man's being on which was based the thinking of those millennia in the Occident which are now, in some sense, concluded.

Quoted in Walter Kaufmann, ed., *Existentialism from Dostoevsky to Sartre* (New York: Meridian Books, 1975), 164-165.

32. Jaspers, *Reason and Existenz,* 23-25, 27, 30-31, 40.

33. See Alexandre Kojève, *Introduction to the Reading of Hegel,* ed. Allan Bloom, trans. James H. Nichols, Jr. (New York: Basic Books, 1969); Jean Hyppolite, *Studies on Marx and Hegel,* ed. and trans. John O'Neill (New York: Basic Books, 1969); Jean Hyppolite, *Genesis and Structure of Hegel's Phenomenology of Spirit,* trans. Samuel Cherniak and John Heckman (Evanston, IL: Northwestern University Press, 1974). Kojève's lectures were held at the *École des Hautes Études* from 1933 to 1939. About a decade earlier, Lukács had defended a close linkage of Hegel and Marx; see Georg Lukács, *History and Class Consciousness: Studies in Marxist Dialectics,* trans. Rodney Livingston (Cambridge: MIT Press, 1971).

34. Jean-Paul Sartre, *Being and Nothingness: An Essay on Phenomenological Ontology,* trans. Hazel E. Barnes (New York: Philosophical Library, 1965), 235-237.

35. Sartre, *Being and Nothingness,* 239-243. In Bernstein's words,

With Sartre's ambitious phenomenological ontology, we find a systematic attempt to expose the principle of ideality and its promise of an escape from unhappy consciousness. . . . The realization that at the heart of being there is consciousness or being-for-itself is what Hegel means by the principle of ideality. Where Hegel argues that the distinction between being-in-itself and being-for-itself is progressively mediated, Sartre claims that there is an ontological chasm that cannot be mediated. (*Praxis and Action,* 130-131)

Cf. also Klaus Hartmann, *Sartre's Ontology: A Study of "Being and Nothingness" in the Light of Hegel's Logic* (Evanston, IL: Northwestern University Press, 1966).

36. Maurice Merleau-Ponty, "Hegel's Existentialism" in *Sense and Non-Sense,* trans. Hubert L. Dreyfus and Patricia A. Dreyfus (Evanston, IL: Northwestern University Press, 1964), 63-64.

37. Merleau-Ponty, "Hegel's Existentialism," 64-65, 68. As Merleau-Ponty added: "Learning the truth about death and struggle is the long maturation process by which history overcomes its contradictions and fulfills the promise of humanity—present in the consciousness of death and in the struggle with the other—in the living relationship among men" ("Hegel's Existentialism," 69).

38. Maurice Merleau-Ponty, *The Visible and the Invisible,* ed. Claude Lefort, trans. Alphonso Lingis (Evanston, IL: Northwestern University Press, 1968), 92-94. As one of the attached "Working Notes" added:

Position, negation, negation of negation: this side, the other, the other than the other. What do I bring to the problem of the same and the other? This: that the same be the other than the other, and identity difference of difference— this (1) does not realize a surpassing, a dialectic in the Hegelian sense; (2) is

HEGEL

realized on the spot, by encroachment, thickness, spatiality. (*Visible and the Invisible*, 264)

39. Martin Heidegger, *Being and Time*, trans. John Macquarrie and Edward Robinson (London: SCM Press, 1962), pp. 21-22, par. 1; Martin Heidegger, "What Is Metaphysics?" in *Existentialism from Dostoevsky to Sartre*, ed. Walter Kaufmann (New York, Meridian Books, 1975), 255. In the above and the following citations the translation has been slightly altered. The complex difference between Heidegger and Hegel is completely ignored by Popper who treats both as speculative metaphysicians cut from the same cloth (*Open Society and Its Enemies*, 76-78). By contrast, the two thinkers are sharply opposed to each other by Kaufmann, but in an equally unenlightening way; see Kaufmann, *Hegel*, 213-214. The genuine significance of Heidegger for Hegelian philosophy has been noted, however, by Taylor, who writes that Heidegger "accords a pivotal position to Hegel," although his outlook is "systematically different from Hegel's. For he rejects the Hegelian cumulation [of metaphysics] in the total self-clarity of subjectivity. He sees in this rather an extreme, indeed unsurpassable expression of the metaphysical stance of objectification"; see Charles Taylor, *Hegel* (Cambridge, UK: Cambridge University Press, 1975), p. 570, n. 1.

40. Heidegger, *Being and Time*,, pp. 474-475, 482-483, 486, par. 81-82. For a perceptive study of the relation between Heidegger and Hegel from the vantage of finitude, see Dennis J. Schmidt, *The Ubiquity of the Finite: Hegel, Heidegger and the Entitlements of Philosophy* (Cambridge: MIT Press, 1988). Cf. also Jacques Taminiaux, "Finitude and the Absolute: Remarks on Hegel and Heidegger," in Thomas Sheehan, ed., *Heidegger: The Man and the Thinker* (Chicago: Precedent Publishers, 1981), 187-208.

41. Martin Heidegger, *Hegel's Phenomenology of Spirit*, trans. Parvis Emad and Kenneth Maly (Bloomington: Indiana University Press, 1988), 11, 38, 40. The lecture course was presented in winter of 1930-1931.

42. Heidegger, *Hegel's Phenomenology of Spirit*, 65, 75, 77, 98-100, 145. Pointing to the equation of idea and subjectivity, Heidegger noted the dubious character of Kierkegaard's stress on inwardness in his critique of Hegel (*Hegel's Phenomenology of Spirit*, 137). Like Merleau-Ponty, Heidegger also warned against a schematic application of Hegelian dialectics—the temptation to treat dialectics as a "clever gimmick," a gimmick which would "open all doors," but only to let us "fall from one vacuity into another" (*Hegel's Phenomenology of Spirit*, 74). As one should note, absoluteness in Heidegger's case refers no longer to an absolute transparency of spirit but only to the escape of being from manipulative-instrumental designs (an escape achieved precisely through withdrawal or self-concealment).

43. Martin Heidegger, *Hegel's Concept of Experience*, trans. J. Glenn Gray and Fred I. Wieck (New York: Harper & Row, 1970), 69, 84, 107-108. The translation has been slightly altered. The text was prepared for seminars and some lectures in 1942-1943. Cf. also Heidegger's comment:

Experience is the being of beings. Beings have meanwhile been profiled from the vantage of consciousness and exist in representation as phenomena. However, if presentation belongs to the nature of experience; if presentation is grounded in inversion (*Umkehrung*); and if inversion as our contribution is the fulfillment of our essential relation to the absoluteness of the absolute—then *our nature belongs itself into the parousia of the absolute.* (*Hegel's Concept of Experience,* 130)

44. Hans-Georg Gadamer, *Truth and Method,* 2nd rev. ed., trans. Joel Weinsheimer and Donald G. Marshall (New York: Crossroad, 1989), 342-344. Regarding charges of a neglect of otherness by Hegel, the study added:

> That the other must be experienced not as the other of myself grasped by pure self-consciousness, but as a Thou—this prototype of all objections to the infiniteness of Hegel's dialectic—does not seriously challenge him. The dialectical process of the *Phenomenology of Spirit* is perhaps determined by nothing so much as by the problem of the recognition of the Thou. (Gadamer, *Truth and Method, 343*)

45. Gadamer, *Truth and Method,* 354-355, 361-362.
46. Gadamer, *Truth and Method,* 342, 355, 357.
47. Gadamer, *Hegel's Dialectic: Five Hermeneutical Studies,* trans. P. Christopher Smith (New Haven, CT: Yale University Press, 1976), 92-96. The translation has been slightly altered. Cf. also Gadamer's comments:

> Heidegger's thought reflects specifically upon the nature of language. Thus, in opposition to the Greek *logos*-philosophy, to which Hegel's method of self-consciousness is pledged, he advances a counter-thought. . . . For Heidegger, who is not oriented toward speaking in the form of (propositional) statements but rather toward the temporality of the presence itself which speaks to us, saying is always more a holding or keeping to the whole-of-what-is-to-be-said and a holding back before the unsaid.

See Hans-Georg Gadamer, "Hegel and Heidegger," in *Hegel's Dialectic: Five Hermeneutical Studies,* trans. P. Christopher Smith (New Haven, CT: Yale University Press, 1976), 115.
48. Gilles Deleuze, *Nietzsche and Philosophy,* trans. Hugh Tomlinson (New York: Columbia University Press, 1983), 40, 120, 174, 195-196; cf. also Gilles Deleuze, "Nomad Thought," in David B. Allison, ed., *The New Nietzsche: Contemporary Styles of Interpretation* (Cambridge: MIT Press, 1985), 142-149. For an able critique of Deleuze's position (esp. his misconstrual of dialectics) see Houlgate, *Hegel, Nietzsche,* 6-8.
49. Michel Foucault, "Nietzsche, Genealogy, History," in *Language, Counter-Memory, Practice,* ed. Donald F. Bouchard, trans. Bouchard and Sherry Simon (Oxford, UK: Blackwell, 1977), 142, 149-151.
50. Foucault, "Nietzsche, Genealogy, History," 153-154, 163; Michel Foucault, "The Discourse on Language," in *The Archaeology of Knowledge,* trans. A. M. Sheridan Smith (New York: Pantheon Books, 1972), 235-236. According to the same lecture, "the theme of universal mediation is, I believe, yet another manner of eliding the reality of discourse" (p. 228). The essay on Nietzsche appeared first in Michel Foucault, *Hommage à Jean Hyppolite* (Paris: Presses Universitaires de France, 1971), 145-172. For a critique of

Hegel's political philosophy, strongly influenced by Nietzsche and Foucault, see William E. Connolly, *Political Theory and Modernity* (Oxford, UK: Blackwell, 1988), 86-115.

51. See esp. Jacques Derrida, *Of Grammatology,* trans. G. C. Spivak (Baltimore, MD: Johns Hopkins University Press, 1976); Jacques Derrida, *Spurs: Nietzsche's Styles,* trans. Barbara Harlow (Chicago: University of Chicago Press, 1979); Jacques Derrida, *Glas,* trans. John P. Leavy, Jr., and Richard Rand (Lincoln: University of Nebraska Press, 1986); Jacques Derrida, "Force of Law," *Cardozo Law Review,* 11 (1990): 919-1045. For a more balanced statement see Jacques Derrida, "Violence and Metaphysics," in *Writing and Difference,* trans. Alan Bass (Chicago: University of Chicago Press, 1978), 79-153.

52. Jean-François Lyotard, *The Postmodern Condition: A Report on Knowledge,* trans. Geoff Bennington and Brian Massumi (Minneapolis: University of Minnesota Press, 1984), xxiii-xxv, 15-17, 33-35; Jean-François Lyotard, *The Differend: Phrases in Dispute,* trans. Georges Van Den Abbeele (Minneapolis: University of Minnesota Press, 1988), xi, 92, 138. For a fuller discussion of these writings see Fred R. Dallmayr, "Rethinking the Hegelian State," in *Margins of Political Discourse* (Albany, NY: SUNY Press, 1989), 149-152.

5

Minerva at Dawn:
Hegel's Political Thought Today

H istorical accounts do not offer a reprieve from judgment; in the
end, interpretation is our own task today (*abeunt studia in*
mores). The story of Hegel's critical reception was not recounted
for its own sake. His effective history deeply affects our understanding of
his work as well as our self-understanding. Approached from the distance
of nearly two centuries, Hegel's philosophical opus still exudes the vi-
brancy and allure of a classical artwork, but one covered over by the patina
of later intellectual accretions and prejudgments. On his own terms, these
prejudgments—although corrigible—are not simply mistaken or dispens-
able, because they reflect the intrinsic experiences of successive generations, that is, the march of spirit through time. Attentive to ongoing
historical lessons, these generations are entitled to sort out what is living
and what is dead in a past work, without thereby confining it to a shallow
relevance or trendiness.

What prevents or counteracts such confinement is the open-ended character of time or temporality itself. Hegel may have been quite correct in stating that philosophy ultimately is "its time grasped in thought." But time here is not merely clock time or a succession of now points (where every now would be the negation of preceding moments). In trying to capture its historical time, reflective thought necessarily ponders also sedimentations of previous ages as well as latent possibilities and anticipations. Precisely in its effort to understand the present, philosophy thus is not only the custodian of past teachings but also the herald of future hopes, visions, and dreams, which does not make it into a blueprint for social engineering. Seen against this background, philosophy—although recollective—is not merely the owl of Minerva at dusk, recording accomplished shapes of spirit. It also signals the flight of Minerva's owl at dawn, scanning the horizon for emergent figures and life-forms.

The contours of our own time are still hazy and elusive, but they gain profile through comparison with the past. By contrast to the Age of Reason, marked by a confident belief in progress, our time has witnessed the rise of various postmetaphysical or postmodern modes of thought that (without discarding reason) are profoundly wary of this belief. In comparison with the traditional European state system wedded to dynastic regimes, our century has experienced the tumultuous birth pangs of a nascent global order inspired largely by democratic commitments. To the extent that Hegel is a representative both of the Age of Reason and the European state system, how can he still serve as interlocutor in contemporary philosophical and political discussions? To the extent that his thought embodies the culmination of Western modernity, how can he address us in the voice of an early-rising Minerva, responding to the queries and agonies of our dawning age?

In tackling these questions, an important point to be noted here again is the confluence of temporalities: Our dawn is not separated by a rigid hiatus from his dusk. Differently phrased, whatever the term *postmodernity* may mean, it cannot signify a complete dismissal or reversal of modernity—whose lessons and accomplishments still profoundly shape and guide our lives. In this respect—even disregarding long-range anticipations—Hegel retains for us a permanent significance. As teacher of modernity, Hegel provides a key to the welter of ideas and social-political practices that remain our inheritance today. As such a teacher or mentor, Hegel leads us onto the high road of modernity rather than its shadows or abysses; still loyal to classical teachings, he perceives the modern age as a station in the education and possible perfection of humanity, an education nurtured by the ascent of reason and absolute spirit. Although marked by growing individuation, modernity for Hegel heralds not simply the upsurge of private self-centeredness or else of anthropocentric self-enclosure. Although an agent of differentiation and determinate negation, reason in his work does not simply serve as an instrument of domination or technological mastery. Private-individual autonomy remains embedded in the framework of the *polis,* just as reason exceeds partisan designs through its universally mediating capacity.

Mediation, to be sure, is not easily accomplished and the road of modernity far from smooth. One of the most important and distinctive contributions of Hegel's philosophy is the emphasis on divisiveness or diremption (*Entzweiung*) as an unavoidable stage in individual and social maturation. In embarking on the path of reflection and self-knowledge, reason or spirit necessarily distances itself from familiar surroundings and customary habits, thereby undergoing the travail of alienation or estrangement, an alienation dividing individual consciousness both from others and from itself. Similarly, in the process of modernization or rationalization, society is wrenched away from traditional moorings and quasi-natural conventions, and thus is set adrift in the turbulent sea of competition and agonistic struggle (for recognition).

As shown above, a crucial feature of Hegel's political philosophy is his discussion of civil society seen as ethical life in its mode of diremption or alienation, a dimension that was absent in classical politics but enshrines both the glory and the agony of modern freedom. Contrary to the accusations of a shallow holism, Hegel's work is relentless in underscoring the role of diremption in individual and social development—to the point of denouncing and rejecting facile or utopian remedies (like the abolition of private property). In this respect, his thought exudes a dramatic and even tragic quality, a quality manifest in the clash of affirmation and negation, of natural life and death. In poignant language, the maturation of consciousness is portrayed as the "highway of despair," leading finally to a "speculative Good Friday." Yet, as has also been shown, despair is not Hegel's last word; in the midst of divisiveness, his work holds out the promise of reconciliation. As we read in the preface to the *Philosophy of Right,* reason is the "rose in the cross of the present," a flower reconciling us with reality through understanding. Thus, while honoring the tragic quality of human life and the significance of the Christian symbol, Hegel gently places a rose in the middle of the cross, in a gesture subtly differentiating him both from radical agonistics and from a fundamentalist faith placing hope only in transcendent intervention.[1]

In the context of political philosophy, the bent toward reconciliation and sublation surfaces in numerous ways, particularly in the celebration of public life or the *polis* as the arena of shared *Sittlichkeit.* As indicated, the modern state for Hegel was the actualization and embodiment of objective spirit, that is, an institution geared not merely to the satisfaction of private needs or to the advancement of partisan schemes but to the promotion of the common good, or of the good life (where justice and happiness blend). To buttress and safeguard the common good, his *Philosophy of Right* provided for a series of devices designed to counteract social atomization and excessive divisiveness. An important device was the establishment of a rational civil service seen as a universal class able to mediate and sublate the conflicting interests of individuals and social groups. Closely linked with this device was the provision for a welter of intermediary institutions and associations, and particularly for the complex fabric of social estates—the latter viewed not as closed or ascriptive bodies but as freely chosen organs representing concrete occupational or professional concerns.

Still on the public level, divisiness was also checked by the system of interlocking (though separate) governmental powers, by the harmonious juxtaposition of church and state, and by the scrupulous observance of the rule of law and the protection of civil rights (including equality before the law). Beyond the range of legal and governmental safeguards, Hegel's writings also made room for social and economic antidotes to diremption, especially for programs of social welfare and public assistance which, without hamstringing individual initiative, were intended to curb class division and the growth of an impoverished underclass (or rabble)—those glaring byproducts of industrialization. Counterweights to divisiness extended from the domestic arena to international conflicts. Although not strongly critical of modern warfare, the *Philosophy of Right* stressed various breaks on enmity, especially cross-cultural learning and the need to conduct hostilities with a view to peace—brakes that still deserve careful attention in our age of "total" wars.

In large measure, the present study means to remind contemporary readers of the high road of modernity and of Hegel as a teacher of this road. In our own time, when the shadows and drawbacks of modernity are in plain view and expose (in a famous phrase) the inner tension or "dialectic of enlightenment," it is important to remember the deeper point of that road.[2] Contrary to claims of historical randomness, Hegel saw modernity not as a contingent or accidental occurrence but as a crucial phase in human development, although a phase that eventually we may have to pass *through*. Far from serving partisan (bourgeois) class interests, the modern era for him was the harbinger of general or universal freedom, a freedom permeating cognitive inquiry, ethical *Sittlichkeit,* as well as social and political institutions (in the form of constitutional government).

This is a legacy that cannot readily be brushed aside by his heirs—especially in an age when freedom seems in short supply, a period populated by totalitarian or quasi-totalitarian regimes, military caudillos, and petty despots. As one should note, modernity in Hegel's account was limited neither to select groups nor to restricted geographical areas; transgressing its European (or Western) place of origin, the upsurge of freedom was bound to have global effects or repercussions, effects bound to undermine native traditions everywhere and thus to inaugurate a broad-scale sense of estrangement (as gateway to a freer engagement of spirit). This aspect was dramatically underscored by Marx when he spoke of the "constant revolutionizing of production" and "uninterrupted disturbance of all social conditions" brought about by modern modes of industry, modes that give a "cosmopolitan character" to economic relations and that draw "all, even the most barbarian, nations into civilization." While Marx ascribed these changes chiefly to bourgeois or capitalist class interests, Hegel perceived in them the inner motivation of Western expansion or cosmopolitanism, specifically, the emancipation of spirit as part of a global education of humankind. As he observed in the *Philosophy of Right,* modern developments bring "distant countries into commercial relations based on contractual rights, relations which are the preeminent means of education (*Bildung*) and through which trade gains its world-historical significance."[3]

To be sure, developments of this kind can no longer be viewed totally as unmitigated progress; social-political as well as philosophical transformations since Hegel's time have eroded confidence in dialectics construed as the steady unfolding of reason. In their combined effect, these changes jeopardize some of Hegel's key metaphysical premises—without necessarily silencing his voice at Minerva's dawn. As the review of Hegel's effective history has shown, his work has spawned a long series of criticisms and rejoinders. The pervasive tenor of these criticisms, however, was the demand for greater concreteness or experiential concretization, although this demand was often phrased in ambiguous and potentially misleading terms (which failed to unsettle Hegelian metaphysics).

In the case of Kierkegaard and early existentialism, the demand was raised in the name of unique singularity and individual-existential action (a plea congruent with modernity's stress on subjective inwardness). In the case of left-Hegelians and Marx, the demand was issued on behalf of social-economic infrastructures and the collective aspirations of the proletarian underclass (a move transposing Hegel's universalism into a new register). In Nietzsche's writings, anti-Hegelian critique surfaced both in the celebration of singularity and in the attempt to invert or overturn traditional metaphysics, that is, in the shift from universals to particulars and from reason to nonreason. In a less dramatic manner, metaphysics was shunned by Weber and the later positivist movement, but only to make room for scientific empiricism coupled with ethical or normative subjectivism. Bypassing reversal and simple rejection, postmetaphysical thought began to probe the underpinnings of metaphysics or the matrix undergirding modern reason. Starting with Heidegger's ontology and continued by Gadamer and Merleau-Ponty, philosophical attention turned to an "analytics of finitude" permeated by a worldly reason. What started on the level of oblique objections thus gathered into a critical engagement appropriate to the level of Hegel's work. Cumulatively, the initiatives sketched here point toward a reassessment of the status of reason, that is, toward a rethinking (not reversal) of modern metaphysics—away from the primacy of *logos* and subjectivity in the direction of the linguistic and experiential contexts "always already" operative in reflective thought.

As it happened, philosophical trends toward concretization were matched by a parallel development in the social-political sphere, namely, the steady democratization of institutions and life-forms—a process that, starting in Western countries, has by now reached global or cosmopolitan proportions. The combination of theoretical and practical-political mutations has profound repercussions for Hegel's entire work, but especially for his political philosophy. One crucial implication pertains to the character of constitutional government. As has been pointed out, modern constitutionalism for Hegel found its ideal expression in constitutional monarchy with its overarching institution of royal power. This argument, as has also been indicated, was predicated not on personal political preferences but on the basic structure of Hegelian metaphysics. A philosophy premised on the actualization of spirit and subjectivity was bound to find the apex of the constitutional edifice in an actual human subject, that is, the king.

The process of democratization spreading since Hegel's time has the effect of challenging both his metaphysical premises and their manifestation on the political plane: as a governmental regime, democracy can no longer be construed under the rubric of subjectivity. Contrary to traditional contractual or organicist approaches, democracy is neither an assortment of subjects nor a collective subject, for the simple reason that the *demos* or "people" cannot be identified either with singular individuals or with a general collectivity. To this extent, democracy and democratization stand ajar to a central ingredient of traditional metaphysics: the division of universals and particulars or of essence and appearances. By elevating the ruled at least incipiently to the position of rulers, democracy above all undermines the privilege or supremacy bestowed on essence and the subordination of everyday phenomena under the governance of the idea.[4]

The spreading of democracy, one should note, does not by itself invalidate Hegel's comments on constitutionalism or his view of the *polis* as an arena of *Sittlichkeit*. What troubled Hegel about democracy was chiefly the prospect of an amorphous or atomized mass of people lacking a well-balanced constitutional structure. As historical experience has shown, however, this danger is not necessarily endemic to democratic societies. Despite deficiencies—even glaring shortcomings—in particular instances, democracy makes room for a richly layered fabric of institutions and offices and even for a welter of intermediary powers (like parties and associations) mediating between center and periphery and between people and their elected representatives. Most important, democracy does not by itself militate against ethical relations or bonds of *Sittlichkeit* on various levels of society. To this extent, poststructuralist reversals of metaphysics (in their extreme forms) seem to miss the point. Although crisscrossed by multiple conflicts between individuals and groups, democracy remains a public regime, that is, a constitutional order not simply reducible to power contests or "an-archistic" agonisms of particularist impulses.

In a similar vein, Hegel's fears regarding social atomization can find antidotes in democracy itself, although these antidotes remain often latent or untapped. One of the main complaints leveled against (Western) democracy in its current operation concerns precisely the downgrading of public bonds, that is, the rampant colonization of public life by private economic interests. In a spirited attack on this state of affairs, a contemporary author, Barber, has denounced the prevalence of "thin democracy," a regime entirely subservient to individual rights and privileges and held together only by a minimal set of abstractly formal rules. As a counterpoint to this condition, Barber proposed a strengthening of democratic engagement through a welter of local and regional institutions (like neighborhood assemblies, town meetings, civic cooperatives, and the like)—without abandoning the protection of individual rights. "My argument," he stated, "is that strong democracy is the only fully legitimate form of politics; as such, it constitutes the condition for the survival of all that is most dear to us in the Western liberal tradition."[5]

In its correlation of individual rights and shared public institutions, Barber's proposal clearly resonates with a central motif of Hegel's political philosophy: the balancing of individual freedom and public responsibility, of civil society and the state. The point at which contemporary democracy demands a revision of Hegel's formula concerns chiefly his conception of the state. Once the traditional metaphysics (of subjectivity) is set aside, the state can no longer be viewed as the actualization of reason or spirit superimposed—as a higher essence—on the multiplicity of social life. Quite apart from metaphysical considerations, the untenability of this conception has been shown by practical-political developments during the last 100 years, developments that have transformed the state increasingly into an instrument of political programs and partisan designs. In a dramatic vein, this transformation was captured by Weber in his political sociology, particularly in his definition of the state as an agency of domination wielded through an efficiently organized bureaucratic apparatus.

Weber's analysis of bureaucracy also jeopardizes or renders implausible Hegel's notion of the civil service as a universal class devoted purely to the promotion of the public good. And, in turn, this implausibility affects the Hegelian conception of hierarchically structured estates as well as their representation in legislative assemblies. In a democratic setting, universalism or commonality can no longer be embodied in a specially trained class (of higher civil servants) but must be dispersed or disseminated in the social fabric itself, in a manner allowing all members to be active also as public citizens. This was an insight that was keenly grasped by Marx (in his critique of the *Philosophy of Right*), although he proceeded to ascribe absolute qualities to the working class. Honoring the intent of Marx's correction without embracing his solution, contemporary democracy militates in favor of a closer blending of *polis* and society and thus of a tighter intertwining of public universalism or *Sittlichkeit* and everyday social life. This means that public bonds must be forged right in the bosom of civil society—that is, apart from and often even in opposition to formal state structures. Without damage to the realm of private economic initiatives, democracy tends to replace the society-state dichotomy by a less categorically structured political society.[6]

The retreat of the state into social relations is only one of the implications of the upsurge of democracy (construed in a postmetaphysical vein). Another repercussion has to do with the character of *Sittlichkeit* in the private realm, that is, in family life. As has been shown, Hegel—as a product of his time—assigned to the husband and father a clearly dominant or controlling position, while relegating the wife and mother to a subordinate role closely tied to household functions. Whereas the husband transcended the family circle by participating in society and the state, the wife's task was confined mainly to the nurturing of children. Again, this outlook should be attributed not simply to personal (patriarchal) leanings of the philosopher, but rather to deep-seated metaphysical premises. In line with a long tradition of Western thought, Hegel associated the husband-father with the realm of reason or rationality, and the wife-mother with the domain of feeling or sensation. Differently put, the masculine partner represented the level of reflective subjectivity, the female the stage of natural immediacy. Because, in Hegel's account, human maturation involved the ascendance of reason over nature, of reflective mediation over simple immediacy, the husband-father emerged as the more highly developed individual—and hence as the partner destined to govern family life.

Recent postmetaphysics has challenged the traditional reason-nature correlation and, accordingly, has impugned the supremacy of (masculine) reason in favor of more democratic interpersonal arrangements—and this without relinquishing the role of reason itself. Even if it is granted that maturation involves the ascent of reflection over immediacy, this process is neither unilinear nor does it yield a higher stage that would "sublate" immediacy without a trace. Precisely in transgressing immediate sensation, reason can also ponder the losses entailed in progressive rationalization—and hence remain mindful of its indebtedness to precognitive (immediate) experience. Approached from this angle, Hegelian dialectics is profoundly transformed, namely, from a formula for the linear advance of spirit or reason (over nature) into a trope suggestive of reciprocal entwining or recollective interdependence. In the context of family life, this transformation argues for more open-ended relationships where the nature-reason syndrome is more equally distributed among both partners and where both share evenly in reflection and nurturing and in the tasks of public and private life.[7]

Beyond the level of family relations, the entwinement of reason and nature affects or jeopardizes many additional facets of Hegel's political-philosophical edifice. As in the case of individual maturation, social development in his work is ascribed to the steady overcoming of primitive or natural modes of social life, a process epitomized by the rise of modern industry. Throughout his writings but particularly in the *Philosophy of Right,* industrialization and rational-scientific modernization are hailed as the harbingers of universal enlightenment and social emancipation. In this respect, experiences in our century have impelled a serious reconsideration of the parameters of social progress. Environmental pollution and rampant spoliation of natural resources have spawned a widespread concern with ecological needs, concerns that accord ill with conceptions of unmitigated rationalization (or the linear actualization of spirit).

As it happens, concerns of this kind are buttressed and corroborated today by a social-political occurrence of unprecedented historical significance, namely, the emergence onto the world stage of a multitude of non-Western or third world countries previously subjected to colonial (or quasi-colonial) tutelage. Frequently labeled *developing* or *underdeveloped,* these countries inject a new dimension into global politics, by raising development itself into an intensely contested issue and a topic of widespread political debate. Seen against this background, our era witnesses a broad-scale confrontation between West and non-West (and also between North and South)—a confrontation that is likely to demand sustained attention for a long time to come. Unless radically reformulated, Hegel's philosophy is particularly vulnerable on this score. As sketched in the concluding pages of the *Philosophy of Right* (and fleshed out in the *Philosophy of History*), social evolution proceeds from primitive substantialism over modes of diremption toward higher and higher stages of rational order, seemingly without any need for reciprocal learning. Culminating in Germanic or modern Western civilization, history seems to supersede completely earlier stages, especially Asian and Indian modes of life—a view reflecting deep-seated Western (or Orientalist) prejudgments. Under postmetaphysical and democratic auspices, these prejudgments must be revised: Shunning global mastery, Western civilization must be ready to undergo the lessons of non-Western countries, which, in turn, cannot remain immune from modernity and Western forms of democracy.[8]

On a deeper level, to be sure, global learning of this kind still resonates with Hegelian dialectics, especially his notion of mediation or reconciliation. By experiencing each other's influence, representatives of different cultures, or worlds, are not separated by a radical gulf, although encounter is liable to subvert their customary self-understanding. Moreover, as Hegel might have conceded, mediation between past and future, tradition and modernity, may take different forms transgressing the pattern of Western development. Concern with historical concreteness (and aversion to abstract formalism) would seem to support the possibility of diverse avenues of social transformation. Exceeding the confines of

current Western practices, some of these avenues may emulate the high
road envisaged by Hegel in his epoch—a road refusing to collapse
modernity into private acquisitiveness and human mastery (over nature). Even in the Western context, efforts are presently afoot to recap-
ture this road—as is evident in contemporary debates over liberalism
and communitarianism. Steering a course between radical individualism and unified holism, Barber's notion of strong democracy pays equal
tribute to individual freedom and public engagement or *Sittlichkeit*—in
a manner reminiscent of Hegel's political thought. As he points out,
strong democracy adumbrates

> a community that does not oppress individuals, a consensus that respects
> dissent, a politics that recognizes conflict without enthroning permanent
> factions, and a democracy that is strong without being unitary, rich
> without being fragmented, and consensual without being monolithic.

As presented by Barber, a democratic politics judiciously entwining public
and private life eschews traditional metaphysics with its foundational or
essentialist pillars (of subjectivity or spirit). Mindful of the blind spots of
human reason, such a politics in his view also is bound to "institutionalize
regret": that is, to build into reforms "limits on the will to change" and into
mechanisms of public power "limits on all political will."[9]

Still, democratic politics (of a post-Hegelian sort) remains fraught
with intrinsic hazards. Even along its high road, historical development
is a wrenching or uprooting experience—as Hegel has amply shown.
No matter how cautiously or judiciously pursued, modernization and
democratization are bound to be marked by diremption, that is, a
process of dislocation, alienation, and expatriation. In Hegel's account,
such alienation is the inevitable lot of spirit venturing into the terrain
of otherness and thus entering the highway of despair. Yet, dislocation
is not necessarily—or should not be reduced to—a synonym for defeat.
Once uprooted from traditional moorings, individuals and groups also gain
a new kind of creative freedom, the freedom to recuperate imaginatively
ethnic or cultural legacies in a nonoppressive fashion. Abandoning claims
to mastery or exclusivity, world cultures on this level become able to
acknowledge each other without succumbing to uniformity.

Bypassing both assimilation and chauvinism, this interplay of cultures may well be the most genuine promise of modernity on a global-democratic scale. Instead of denoting stark deracination, modern freedom at this point acquires a new texture or worldly context: the texture of a recollected way of life creatively competing for global recognition. In Hegelian terms, the march of the world spirit here turns into the path of a worldly spirit freely embracing finitude in its complex temporal dimensions. To the extent that his political philosophy captured the rise and perfection of modern freedom, Hegel's legacy is liable to reverberate in the dawn of our more contextualized, cross-national freedom. By recollecting Minerva at the falling of the dusk we are better able to glimpse the owl's wings against our hazy morning sky.

Notes

1. G. W. F. Hegel, *Hegel's Philosophy of Right,* trans. T. M. Knox (London: Oxford University Press, 1967), 12. The image of the rose in the cross is borrowed, of course, from Rosicrucian teachings. For a discussion of Hegel's use of the image (and its critique from a more orthodox religious vantage) see Karl Loewith, *From Hegel to Nietzsche: The Revolution in Nineteenth Century Thought,* trans. David E. Green (Garden City, NY: Anchor Books, 1967), 13-28.

2. The reference here is to Max Horkheimer and Theodor W. Adorno, *Dialectic of Enlightenment,* trans. John Cumming (New York: Herder and Herder, 1972).

3. *Hegel's Philosophy of Right,* par. 247, p. 151. The translation has been slightly altered. See also Karl Marx, "Communist Manifesto," in Robert C. Tucker, ed., *The Marx-Engels Reader* (New York: Norton, 1972), 338-339. In his "Manifesto," Marx was an unabashed defender of Western supremacy over the globe:

> The need of a constantly expanding market for its products chases the bourgeoisie over the whole surface of the globe. . . . Just as it has made the country dependent on the towns, so it has made barbarian and semi-barbarian countries dependent on the civilized ones, nations of peasants on nations of bourgeois, the East on the West. ("Manifesto," 338-339)

4. See Claude Lefort, *Democracy and Political Theory,* trans. David Macey (Minneapolis: University of Minnesota Press, 1988); also Fred R. Dallmayr, "Post-Metaphysics and Democracy," in *Political Theory,* Vol. 21 (1993). As one may recall, in substituting for Hegel, his student Eduard Gans promptly interpreted the *Philosophy of Right* in a democratic direction. Occasionally, Hegel himself subordinated the question of regime type to the broader concern with constitutionalism as such.

5. Benjamin Barber, *Strong Democracy: Participatory Politics for a New Age* (Berkeley: University of California Press, 1984), xvi. Regarding the decline and colonization of the public sphere cf. also Hannah Arendt, *The Human Condition* (Chicago: University of Chicago Press, 1958); Richard Sennett, *The Fall of Public Man* (New York: Random House, 1978); Jürgen Habermas, *The Structural Transformation of the Public Sphere,* trans. Thomas Burger and Frederick Lawrence (Cambridge: MIT Press, 1989), and Jürgen Habermas, *The Theory of Communicative Action,* Vol. 2, trans. Thomas McCarthy (Boston: Beacon Press, 1987), 332-373.

6. For recent transformations of the state-society relationship cf. Charles Mayer, ed., *Changing Boundaries of the Political: Essays on the Evolving Balance between the State and Society Public and Private in Europe* (Cambridge, UK: Cambridge University Press, 1987); and John Keane, *Civil Society and the State: New European Perspectives* (London: Verso, 1988). Compare also Jean L. Cohen and Andrew Arato, *Civil Society and Political Theory* (Cambridge, MA: MIT Press, 1992). I have suggested possible ways of strengthening public *Sittlichkeit* on the level of social life in Fred R. Dallmayr, "Rethinking the Hegelian State," in *Margins of Political Discourse* (Albany, NY: SUNY Press, 1989), 137-157.

7. For insightful comments on this issue see, e.g., Judith P. Butler, *Subjects of Desire: Hegelian Reflections in Twentieth-Century France* (New York: Columbia University Press, 1987); also Jean Bethke Elshtain, *Public Man, Private Woman: Women in Social and Political Thought* (Princeton, NJ: Princeton University Press, 1981).

8. Cf. in this context Edward W. Said, *Orientalism* (New York: Vintage Books, 1979); Wilhelm Halbfass, *Europe and India: An Essay in Understanding* (Albany, NY: SUNY Press, 1988); and Ashis Nandy, *Traditions, Tyranny and Utopias* (Delhi: Oxford University Press, 1987); also Fred R. Dallmayr, "Polis and Cosmopolis," in *Margins of Political Discourse,* (Albany, NY: SUNY Press, 1989), 1-21.

9. Barber, *Strong Democracy,* 114, 308. Cf. also his comment that

> the theory of strong democracy is both dialectical and pragmatic. The democratic politics it envisions is autonomous of independently grounded metaphysics, achieving its legitimacy through self-generating, self-sustaining, and self-transforming modes of reasoning and from the kinds of political interaction that incarnate that reasoning. (*Strong Democracy,* 44)

For arguments pointing in a similar direction see Ernesto Laclau and Chantal Mouffe, *Hegemony and Socialist Strategy: Towards a Radical Democratic Politics,* trans. Winston Moore and Paul Cammack (London: Verso, 1985).

Index

About the Author

Fred R. Dallmayr is Packey Dee Professor of Political Theory at the University of Notre Dame. A native of Germany, he holds a Doctor of Law degree from the University of Munich and a Ph.D. degree in Political Science from Duke University. Before joining the University of Notre Dame in 1978, he taught at the University of Wisconsin-Milwaukee, the University of Georgia, and at Purdue University where he also served as department chair for five years. He has also served as a visiting professor at Hamburg University in Germany and at the New School for Social Research in New York; and he has been a research fellow in Oxford, England, and a senior Fulbright scholar in India. Among his publication are: *Beyond Dogma and Despair* (1981); *Twilight of Subjectivity* (1981); *Polis and Praxis* (1984); *Language and Politics* (1984); *Critical Encounters: Between Philosophy and Politics* (1987); *Margins of Political Discourse* (1989); and *Life-World, Modernity, and Critique* (1991; American edition published as *Between Freiburg and Frankfurt: Toward a Critical Ontology*).

K+   Smith
32-3   19
        55, 58
        124f